PRAISE FOR

Choosing to Lead Against the Current

To navigate today's complex social change landscape, leaders must have grit, creativity, and courage. For those who also contend with racism, sexism, homophobia, and other forms of oppression, the challenges become even more monumental.

Choosing to Lead Against the Current guides us through the critical components of leadership necessary to effectively engage with the significant organizational and societal challenges we face in pursuit of social change. Eveline inspires us to break free from conventional leadership models and cultivate an environment for success that is anchored in our moral compass and deepest purpose. Her Courageous Operating System details the inner transformation required for effective leadership and offers a clear pathway to achieve meaningful results, even in the face of setbacks.

Perhaps most importantly, this book encourages us to discover and honor the unique gifts we each bring to our leadership, as we make the change we so urgently need in this moment. This book is for any leader working to envision a better world.

HEATHER McGHEE, *New York Times* best-selling author of *The Sum of Us*

This book is a manifesto for every leader fighting to dismantle oppressive systems and build something bold, just, and liberatory. Eveline Shen's Courageous Operating System is more than a framework—it's a call to action for those of us who refuse to bow to the forces of greed and brutality. This is the blueprint we need to lead with audacity, transform oppression into power, and ignite a future rooted in collective liberation.

LATEEFAH SIMON, US Congress member and MacArthur "Genius" Fellow

This book is an extraordinary gift to movement workers everywhere. *Choosing to Lead Against the Current* is a must-read for anyone harnessing people power for justice and social change in the twenty-first century. With a masterful blend of history, strategy, and actionable advice, Eveline offers an indispensable guide for change-makers determined to transform our world. Eveline's humble and remarkable guidance has profoundly shaped my life and leadership. I'm thrilled that her invaluable lessons are now accessible to a broader audience through this book.

SHANELLE MATTHEWS, former director of communications for the Movement for Black Lives and distinguished lecturer in anthropology and interdisciplinary studies at City College of New York

I have been fortunate to know Eveline Shen for over two decades. Many of my leadership skills that I apply in my work I have learned from her. I devoured *Choosing to Lead Against the Current* in two sittings. This is an important and accessible resource that new and experienced changemakers can use to strengthen their own leadership and their organizations. While Eveline's purpose is to focus on BIPOC and gender-diverse leaders, the wisdom and practical approaches of the Courageous Operating System could benefit any person confronting a myriad of leadership issues. I can't wait to integrate these practices into my day-to-day and to share these with my leadership team.

LOURDES A. RIVERA, president of Pregnancy Justice

Choosing to Lead Against the Current is an essential guide for changemakers, offering a bold and beautiful blueprint for courageous leadership in these high-stakes times. Shen masterfully weaves wisdom from her decades of experience as a social change leader with inspiring stories and actionable practices, creating a must-read resource for those committed to leading with purpose.

DIMPLE ABICHANDANI, philanthropic advisor and author of *A New Era of Philanthropy*

What a remarkable gift to changemakers! This book's lessons and offerings will deeply resonate with social justice leaders. The Courageous Operating System provides a framework for making meaning of challenging experiences and concrete approaches for overcoming them.

I reflected on my own experiences as a woman of color in every chapter and have immense gratitude for the powerful compilation of tools and approaches that Eveline brings together in her model—insights I have learned and will continue to explore on my leadership path.

I especially appreciate the way Eveline beautifully centers the stories of women and gender-expansive leaders, providing examples of courageous leadership and innovative solutions to structural barriers they face. Knowing the challenges that new and seasoned executive directors face today, this book will be an invaluable resource as we all continue to navigate how to effectively lead against the current.

SARITA GUPTA, vice president of programs at Ford Foundation

If you are ready to elevate your leadership, then read this book! Ev provides us with the powerful framework we need to cultivate our courage, define success according to our values, move through self-doubt, and achieve the impact we seek. Our movement is undeniably stronger because of her visionary leadership and steadfast support for all of us.

WENDY CHUN-HOON, former director of the Women's Bureau at the US Department of Labor

This book takes leaders on a transformative journey to connect with their unique gifts, strengths, and powers. It is an excellent resource for coaches and those who work to empower women and gender-expansive leaders of color. It is inciteful and practical, with stories and case studies that illustrate the Courageous Operating System, which is intended to inspire and elevate leadership and/or coaching practices.

AKAYA WINDWOOD, author of *Leading With Joy*, activist, and coach

Eveline is one of the rare leaders in our movement who has achieved tremendous success in bringing people together to create structural change while embracing the challenges that often hold us back. Her commitment to addressing these difficulties has made our movements stronger and more adaptive.

As a leader in the transformational movement field, Eveline has taught us that liberation cannot be achieved by intellect alone. She emphasizes the importance of integrating mind, body, and spirit into our leadership to effectively tackle the complex challenges facing our communities. Her transformative work within her organization and the powerful coalitions she has built over the years exemplify the principles of the transformative leadership framework she developed and embodied.

Eveline's wisdom is hard-earned, not just from her successes, but from her willingness to help us confront our breakdowns, unconscious habits, and the ways we get in our own way. She has done this work herself, emerging as a trusted coach and guide to some of the most powerful and effective leaders in our movements. It takes real wisdom to help brilliant, strong leaders grow even stronger, and Eveline has consistently done just that.

Choosing to Lead Against the Current is a must-read for anyone who wants to leverage their full selves in a mindful and strategic way as they step fully into their leadership power. I am deeply grateful that her practice and approach are now accessible to so many others through this inspiring and practical guide.

TAJ JAMES, founder of the Movement Strategy Center and Full Spectrum Capital

Choosing to Lead Against the Current is essential reading for women of color in leadership roles. As the number of women of color leaders rises, we find ourselves navigating a landscape marked by political polarization and a backlash against DEI initiatives. This complex environment calls for new rules of engagement and, above all, immense courage.

Having had the privilege of working directly with Eveline and her transformative Courageous Operating System (COS) during the early stages of our co-directorship, we can attest to its profound impact. The COS provided us with a structured framework that encouraged us to ask bold questions of ourselves and each other, allowing us to delve into the intricate dynamics of leadership at the intersection of race, gender, and power.

Embracing a leadership style that moves away from traditional "pale and male" paradigms requires bravery, and the COS empowered us to pursue a more authentic and inclusive approach.

Moreover, the COS fostered an environment of trust that developed surprisingly quickly as we explored our shared vision for leadership within a social justice organization. The time we spent working through the COS laid a solid foundation for our successful partnership, enabling us to explore our similarities and differences with openness and respect.

Eveline's unique insights and innovative approach, as articulated in the Courageous Operating System, offer a valuable framework for problem-solving and fostering iterative conversations. Rather than presenting a prescriptive one-size-fits-all solution, her work encourages leaders to engage in meaningful dialogue and adapt this model to fit their unique contexts.

In a time when courageous leadership is more crucial than ever, *Choosing to Lead Against the Current* is an essential guide for those ready to embrace their power and lay the foundation for their leadership success.

MARIKO MIKI AND DENISE TOMASINI-JOSHI, co-directors of If/When/How

As women of color leaders, we encounter distinct challenges, including leadership models that feel inauthentic and a lack of safe space to stretch ourselves and experiment with our leadership. Working with Ev and using the Courageous Operating System during a critical juncture in my journey enabled me to take a significant leap forward and expand my vision of what was possible. This experience helped me develop the muscle memory to lead with integrity, confidence, generosity, and strength.

I am so excited about Eveline Shen's new book, *Choosing to Lead Against the Current*. I wish I had such a clear and complete guidebook to back me up at the start of my leadership journey. When I transitioned into leadership as the first Black executive director of a historically white-led organization, I was fortunate to have Eveline as an advisor and thought partner after participating in the inaugural Stepping into Power leadership development training in 2016. Since my time in that program, the components of the Courageous Operating System have been touchstones in my growth as a leader. But to see those elements become a book with stories and examples from Eveline's life is incredibly special and a welcome gift to our movement.

This book centers the humanity of those we serve, those we work alongside, and ourselves in decision-making and response to conflict, threats, and obstacles. This book demonstrates that leading with integrity can get us to better outcomes that do not compromise our commitment to liberation. I look forward to sharing this book with other leaders of color who are navigating their leadership while making radical change in an unjust world.

KWAJELYN JACKSON, executive director of Feminist Women's Health Center, Atlanta

I wish I had this book twenty years ago! Eveline offers a practicable path to courage, making tough decisions as a leader, and facing and transforming failure. She lovingly invites us into self-knowing and real self-care, as a ground for vision and collective power.

STACI K. HAINES, founder of generative somatics and author of *The Politics of Trauma*

Until our oppressive societal systems change, we have to focus on what we can change—ourselves. In this book, Ev masterfully distills her brilliance, wisdom, and experience into a practical guide for any changemaker to lead organizations and movements from the inside out. I am confident that by applying the tools outlined in this book, we can cultivate greater balance, precision, and possibility in our leadership. For over a decade I have looked to Ev as a mentor and movement sage, and this book serves as a powerful reminder of the invaluable lessons she has imparted—lessons I am eager to revisit and apply.

> YAMANI YANSÁ HERNANDEZ, CEO of Groundswell Fund/Groundswell Action Fund and former executive director of the National Network of Abortion Funds

Eveline Shen provides the inspiration we need to step up and lead in this moment. *Choosing to Lead Against the Current* is a breath of fresh air, a much-needed reminder to keep pushing forward. This book is both a motivation and a powerful reminder that the answers we've been seeking have always been within us.

> SULMA ARIAS, executive director of People's Action

I am so grateful for Ev's work and for this book. Her leadership experience and the Courageous Operating System grounded and inspired me in times of great organizational transition. Ev's practical insights and wisdom guided my leadership transformation with purpose and love. This book gives us critical examples of moving collectively toward gender, racial, and economic justice while challenging and changing ourselves and our movement-building organizations.

> BIA VIEIRA, CEO of Women's Foundation California

Choosing to Lead
Against the Current

CHOOSING TO LEAD
AGAINST THE CURRENT

THE COURAGEOUS OPERATING SYSTEM FOR CHANGEMAKERS

*Empowering leaders to transform the world
with integrity, impact, and purpose*

EVELINE SHEN

North Atlantic Books
Huichin, unceded Ohlone land
Berkeley, California

North Atlantic Books
Huichin, unceded Ohlone land
2526 Martin Luther King Jr Way
Berkeley, CA 94704 USA
www.northatlanticbooks.com

Cover art © PON-PON via Shutterstock
Cover design by Jess Morphew
Book design by Happenstance Type-O-Rama
Printed in the United States of America

Choosing to Lead Against the Current: The Courageous Operating System for Changemakers is sponsored and published by North Atlantic Books, an educational nonprofit that collaborates with partners to develop cross-cultural perspectives; nurture holistic views of art, science, the humanities, and healing; and seed personal and global transformation by publishing work on the relationship of body, spirit, and nature.

North Atlantic Books's publications are distributed to the US trade and internationally by Penguin Random House Publisher Services. For further information, visit our website at www.northatlanticbooks.com.

The authorized representative in the EU for product safety and compliance is Eucomply OÜ, Pärnu mnt 139b-14, 11317 Tallinn, Estonia, hello@eucompliancepartner.com, +33757690241.

Library of Congress Cataloging-in-Publication Data

Names: Shen, Eveline, 1968- author.
Title: Choosing to lead against the current : the courageous operating
    system for changemakers / Eveline Shen, MPH.
Description: Berkeley, California : North Atlantic Books, [2025] | Includes
    bibliographical references and index. | Summary: "Heart-centered tools
    for social change leaders to foster courage, keep momentum, and manage
    burnout"– Provided by publisher.
Identifiers: LCCN 2024059517 (print) | LCCN 2024059518 (ebook) | ISBN
    9798889842118 (paperback) | ISBN 9798889842125 (epub)
Subjects: LCSH: Leadership. | Social change.
Classification: LCC HD57.7 .S48285 2025 (print) | LCC HD57.7 (ebook) |
    DDC 303.3/4–dc23/eng/20250219
LC record available at https://lccn.loc.gov/2024059517
LC ebook record available at https://lccn.loc.gov/20

1 2 3 4 5 6 7 8 9 Kingery 30 29 28 27 26 25

*For my parents, who taught me
the power of taking a stand.*

*To my daughters, Jessica and Rose—
may you always be able to let
your light shine.*

Contents

List of Illustrations

CHAPTER 1: LEADERSHIP OPERATING SYSTEMS

- Karpman's Drama Triangle
- Systems Map of Courageous Operating System

CHAPTER 2: BUILDING YOUR WELL OF COURAGE

- Everyday Acts of Courage

CHAPTER 3: FINDING THE RIGHT PURPOSE

- The Purpose Picture: Far-Term Time Horizon; Mid-Term Time Horizon, and Near-Term Time Horizon

CHAPTER 6: POWERING UP YOUR LEADERSHIP

- Diagram of Three Components of Powering Up: Set of Internal Resources, Leadership Needs, Superpower of Self-Growth
- Dashboard and Gauges of Leadership Needs

Introduction

IT IS NOT EASY being a leader when the world is coming undone. As leaders committed to making radical social change, we are engaging in something revolutionary. We are leading *against* the current. A current that is carrying us toward a world evermore brutal, disconnected, and unsafe. A world where environmental degradation, state-sanctioned violence, walls to keep people out, walls to keep people in, and authoritarian leaders are on the rise. A world where the gap is widening between those in power who make the decisions and those who bear the brunt of these decisions. In this world, making connections across this chasm seems increasingly impossible.

As a leader who has experienced hardships and victories, including helping to build the Reproductive Justice movement for two decades, I see you. I honor those of you who have honed your leadership as you move against this current while you simultaneously fight against your daily dose of sexism, racism, or transphobia. I get that you are leading the way despite the actions of key stakeholders around you who may not have complete confidence in your leadership. I see all you have accomplished, and I know that your successes are rarely met with the recognition they deserve.

Social change is powered by leaders like you, who are moving against the current. Throughout my career, I have experienced what happens when leaders are constantly pressured to do more with fewer resources as we face tremendous odds. I have witnessed how systemic oppression can severely hinder our leadership potential and effectiveness. Conversely, I know the remarkable outcomes that can arise when we leverage our leadership to create meaningful change for our communities in the face of significant obstacles and oppressive forces.

This book takes you through the Courageous Operating System I developed out of love. Love for the leaders who wake up every day to fight for change; who lead from behind and within to make sure we are bringing everyone along; who resist putting up armor and use their vulnerability to connect and inspire; who are mission-driven, not ego-driven; and who operate with humility and fierceness.

This book is for anyone who is leading against the current or interrogating traditional leadership models. It is also designed to help executive coaches, academics, and other practitioners who support leaders moving upstream.

Creating Fertile Ground in Which Leadership Can Grow

My leadership journey was informed, early on, by supporting the leadership of young people. In graduate school, I accepted an internship opportunity sponsored by a local nonprofit, called APIRH (Asian Pacific Islanders for Reproductive Health).[1] In this internship, I developed a one-time summer training for an incoming group of Southeast Asian high school–aged girls who were part of APEN's (Asian Pacific Environmental Network) leadership program based in Richmond, California.

This experience was profoundly healing to me because it allowed me to create a program that I wished I had growing up as the daughter of Chinese immigrants in Colorado. At the time, I was one of a handful of Asians in my grade, and we were part of a tiny group of students of color in our school. Starting in kindergarten, I was teased with anti-Asian taunts. I remember when a couple of boys in my neighborhood, about five years older than me, encouraged their dog to chase me as I walked from my school bus stop to my house in elementary school. I would run from bush to car, trying to hide from them, with my heart pounding and sweat pouring down my face as I made my way past their house.

Fortunately, most of what I faced from the other kids were microaggressions that did not threaten my physical safety. However, feeling ashamed of what I ate, the clothing my mom sewed for me, or my parents' accents took its toll. Once, I tried talking with my parents. They did their best to understand and laughingly told me to turn around and make fun of "those bullies." Even at six, I knew that this would not work. I had no one to turn to; I internalized a lot of negative messages about my body, my culture, and my identity, and as a result, I tried to distance myself from each of them.

Two decades later, within that summer internship program, I created a curriculum to help these young women understand the impact of race, gender, and class on their experiences. I included sessions on how oppression negatively affected their body image. We worked on developing positive feelings about their bodies, sexuality, and reproductive health. We discussed assets in their culture and families they could draw upon for support and strength.

Oppression often works by creating these divisions within us. To combat this, I invited these girls to use their full senses and selves in various ways, including through daily physical activities, art, writing, and ongoing personal reflection. It was thrilling to see so many of these young people engaging earnestly with each other and hungry for the material I offered. Getting to know them and witnessing their growth was incredibly rewarding.

For example, this was Lio Sandy Saeteurn's first leadership program. At first, she didn't have a lot of interest in activism. She initially joined to hang out with other Laotian girls her age and receive a stipend for participating.

Like any young woman about to enter high school, Sandy was curious and had questions about sexuality and reproductive health that she couldn't discuss at home or at school. Sandy appreciated the safe space we created for the group to learn and discuss these personal issues together. She became more comfortable with her body, and as a result, her self-confidence increased.

Sandy became particularly agitated after one discussion about the gender-role disparities that she and her peers were experiencing in their families. She bravely went home and named this inequity with her mom. Then, she talked to her younger brother about helping out more with the laundry and dishes. She was learning to find her voice and speak up for herself.

When the summer ended, I was sad to leave Sandy and the other young women, but I was happy that APEN's leadership program would continue for them over the next few years. I looked forward to seeing what path each would take once they graduated high school. After the internship, I continued my leadership journey and accepted a position at APIRH to be their first associate director. A little over a year later, I would become the executive director (ED).

To my delight, a few years later, during my tenure as ED, Sandy applied for a youth organizing position at APIRH. Since I last saw her, Sandy had not only graduated from APEN's leadership program but was now running part of it! We hired her immediately. Sandy contributed her skills and experience to help us expand *our* program for young Asian women in high school to fight for reproductive justice in their communities.

After a few years, she left that position to take on even more responsibility and leadership as an APEN organizer against environmental injustice in the neighborhood where she grew up. She organized her community to address the dangerous levels of air pollution, lead, pesticides, and other chemicals they were exposed to from the 350 toxic facilities near them. She, along with other organizers, successfully built grassroots power over time, and she began to receive national recognition for her leadership. In 2009, Sandy received the SEARAC National Award, given to individuals under thirty-five, to highlight their achievements in environmental justice. She would continue to help her community achieve big wins, including the 2024 settlement against Chevron, one of the largest polluters in the state, to pay $550 million to the City of Richmond over the next ten years.

Sandy taught me never to underestimate anybody's leadership potential. When she joined the leadership program, she didn't express much interest in activism, but the seeds of her incredible leadership were planted that summer.

When I started as ED, I was determined to create a vibrant and effective organization, building upon what I had learned from my past experiences as a manager. I led a strategic planning process to get input and feedback from the organization's stakeholders. I facilitated frequent staff retreats to deepen trust and enhance communication among the staff. Then, the organization was focused within a local community, which shortened the distance between decision-makers and community members, making change more feasible.

Like most executive directors, when I became the ED, I received little guidance about how to lead and grow an organization, so I sought additional support. I went to leadership trainings to gain new skills and insights. I brought in organizational consultants to help us create systems as we became a newly established nonprofit organization. I did my best to look for resources, but 90 percent of these were created by and for white leaders, primarily white men. This was the beginning of an effort on my part, spanning many years, of having to adjust leadership tools and resources I received so that they would be appropriate for the BIPOC (Black, Indigenous, People of Color) staff, organization, and communities with whom I worked.

In the first few years, we won two of our campaigns and created significant changes in health and safety for our community members. Our organization grew exponentially. However, despite my best intentions of moving forward, I soon ran into trouble. Along with growth came increased complexity in how we worked together. Miscommunication and misunderstandings happened more frequently among staff. Conflicts erupted over our changing ways of operating, eroding trust. I was unprepared as a leader to deal with these dynamics effectively, and I struggled to keep the organization together.

Outside of the organization, I saw similar dynamics. I witnessed collective alliances, years in the making, collapse from other leaders being unable to resolve tensions with each other that stemmed from them competing for funding and failing to deal effectively with race and power. Other factors were also at play in creating these conditions. Unlike today, it was not part of the culture for grassroots nonprofits and their donors to prioritize administrative and operational infrastructure resources to support programming work. This meant that many of our organizations failed to put in place adequate leadership, systems, and structures to support our larger teams and more extensive efforts. These conditions led to disruptive dynamics like the breakdown of internal communications within staff or teams and a lack of collective investment in decisions made within the organization or coalition. These processes were painful for everyone involved.

In light of these struggles, I started feeling like a failure as a leader. Given what I saw when I looked at the bigger picture, I saw how our change movements were failing our leaders. Some days, I felt utterly defeated. However, I was determined to learn everything I could from what was happening to prevent these ruptures from occurring in the future.

After working with consultants and evaluators, doing deep reflection, and finding practices that addressed conflict and complexity, I emerged from these challenging experiences much more able to navigate these rough waters. I learned how to build a vibrant organizational culture that integrated a mind-body practice to help develop a common language and trust. I created ways to normalize disagreements and gave coalition members tools to deal with conflict without demonizing each other. I fostered a strength-based collaborative approach to help staff and colleagues feel valued for their contributions rather than continue to compete.

I was determined to build a *leader-full* culture, one that valued and supported leadership of all kinds and recognized the importance of different people taking leadership at different times within organizations and movements. A leader-full culture nurtures collaboration, community, and relationship building.

What started as a four-person project when I first came on grew rapidly and became one of the larger multi-issue women-of-color-led organizations in the country by the time I left. During my tenure there, I had the honor of working with talented and dedicated leaders. Together we built grassroots power and passed numerous state-wide policies protecting reproductive justice. We created a vibrant movement by weaving together collaborations with organizations across the country and partnerships with artists and writers to create better conditions in which all families could thrive.

From these experiences, I learned that leadership is a process of discovery. It's a journey that requires us to adapt to shifting currents, wade into new waters, and learn as we go. It is not a fixed destination. At its best, it can be a profoundly fulfilling path of continued growth, nourished by our connections with kindred spirits as we make positive changes for our communities.

The Struggle Is Real

Along the way, I noticed that people who lead *with* the current have the resources they need. They often see others who look and act like them in comparable leadership posts. Their ideas and opinions are not questioned but adopted quickly. These leaders are lucky and privileged.

I wanted to help leaders move *against* the current. In 2014, over a six-month period, I was approached by several executive directors who were looking for informal and formal mentoring and coaching. They were isolated, and each felt overwhelmed or daunted by their challenges in building and growing their leadership and organization. I identified with many of their experiences and wished there was more significant support for them throughout the movement.

I wanted to help leaders like Jeanine, Esperanza, and Misha.

Jeanine, a Korean American executive director who replaced the organization's founder, a charismatic white woman. The staff engaged in what they called idea jostling, where one of them would throw out an idea, and others would play devil's advocate and try to shoot it down. Jeanine, an experienced ED of three prior organizations, was uncomfortable with this communication style and found it intimidating. She was more comfortable with a collaborative approach, enlisting the support of her staff in creating a vision for their future. A few of the staff who had been there the longest dismissed her processes and subtly questioned her credibility in undermining ways. Sadly, Jeanine lasted one year before she resigned.

Esperanza, a Latinx immigrant from El Salvador, had spent her life working for LGBTQ+ immigrants. She was now the executive director of her organization. The board was pressuring her to have a more public presence in the community and the media. But Esperanza's family had experienced trauma from state-sanctioned violence and war in her home country. Every time she spoke to the press, her trauma was triggered. She was terrified of greater visibility since it could lead to such an attack. As her social media presence grew, her fears came true. She began to experience more negative attention and even threats from trolls and right-wing users. Esperanza's anxiety increased exponentially, and she developed debilitating nightmares.

Misha, a nonbinary African American leader, was the head of a racial justice organization for two years. They came to me in tears when their staff filed into their office en masse, upset about the organization's recent firing of a young employee. They accused Misha of abusing their power and demanded they rehire the young employee. Since it was a personnel issue, Misha couldn't tell their staff that they had to let the employee go because the employee was sexually harassing younger staff members. It was dismaying that no one on the board would publicly support Misha's decision because they worried the staff would call them out for being "anti-youth." Misha had to weather that situation in total isolation from the board and staff.

The Creation of the Courageous Operating System

Hearing about these leaders' experiences brought to mind similar dynamics and challenges I faced as a leader making my way upstream. I decided to do whatever I could to help these three remarkable women and other leaders like them. But I didn't just want to give them more tools as a breadth of leadership resources is already available for various leadership tasks. Although I know that finding the right tool for the task at hand is helpful, I wanted to develop a framework that would help these leaders make their way through the complex terrain they invariably face.

So, I got to work and created the Courageous Operating System, drawing on what I've learned from my own experience as a leader and also from supporting the leadership of others. In the years I've been using and teaching this system, I've found that it can be very helpful in supporting leaders grappling with dilemmas and complex dynamics generated by structural oppressive forces and interactions with people from diverse backgrounds. My hope is that leaders will use it to navigate the ever-changing challenges that come from turbulent waters so that they not only survive but can thrive even in the most demanding conditions.

Each component of this system encourages us to do the inner work that is necessary to create conditions for our success. Working through it will help us find the answers to the following questions: How can we summon our courage to keep moving forward? How do we stay connected to our purpose as the challenges we face pull us away from our north star? How will we pivot when things don't go as planned? How can we align our decision-making and behavior with our values? How can we use hurdles to evolve our leadership capacity? The Courageous Operating System recognizes the interconnectedness of critical leadership elements and helps us engage with them to make our impact more dynamic, formidable, and robust.

The components of the Courageous Operating System work together, and each element enhances and reinforces the others, creating a tapestry of support. Only focusing on one or two areas may not get you the desired results. For example, identifying the proper purpose for your endeavor will only be helpful if you have enough courage to accomplish it. Similarly, if you have great courage but ignore fortifying yourself, you may peter out before completing your purpose. And if you are traveling upstream toward your destination without understanding how to work with failure, your efforts could be derailed from losing your balance repeatedly as you navigate those crosscurrents.

As you begin to apply the system to a situation you are facing, especially if you're dealing with a particularly challenging problem or need guidance on how to move forward, I recommend starting with courage and purpose. After establishing that foundation, you can navigate through the rest of the system. Once you're more familiar with the components, you can choose the part that resonates with you the most to start with and then proceed through the system from there, moving on to the next component as needed. By engaging these components as a system, you can move through challenging and complex situations with more ease and impact. The more you use this system, the quicker you will be able to determine which combination of components you need, and the more generative the process will become as you deepen your capacity to lead.

How to Use This Book

This book is designed for you to return to on an ongoing basis. Chapter 1 discusses operating systems and why adopting the right one for your leadership is important. Chapters 2 through 8 take you through each component of the system. Chapter 9 provides two in-depth case studies that demonstrate how you can use the components of the Courageous Operating System together to help your leadership soar.

Throughout the book, I have included stories from my leadership and those of other leaders to provide concrete examples and inspiration as you explore the system for your leadership. Examples identified by a first name only are either thoroughly disguised to protect the person's privacy or presented as composites of coaching sessions.

At the end of each chapter, I have suggested activities to help you immediately start using the system. Before you begin, spend a few minutes calming, grounding, and centering yourself. In addition, because being in a trusted, supportive community helps to facilitate learning and growth, I have designed some of these activities to be done with a partner or in small groups. Chapter 9 provides examples of ways to engage multiple parts of the system to help you, other leaders, and your team move successfully upstream.

To conclude this introduction, I'm sharing three quick stories of leaders who triumphed using the Courageous Operating System. As you read these, I encourage you to imagine what would be possible if you applied the Courageous Operating System to your leadership and life.

Using the Courageous Operating System to Help Them Soar

In her first year of college, as a low-income young mother, Adriann Barboa, now Commissioner of Bernalillo County in New Mexico, faced stigma from every direction. The father of her baby responded in anger to the news of the pregnancy by physically beating her. Even though Adriann was excited to become a mother, no one in her family supported her, and she had to go to all of her medical appointments alone. When she applied to Medicaid to cover the hospital costs, they pressured Adriann to talk with the baby's father, even when she told them he had endangered her and the baby's safety. After seventeen hours of labor, during which she was not given any water or food, she was sent home with no support. The medical staff told her, "You are a mother now. You will have to figure things out alone, so you better start now." As a result of her experiences, Adriann was determined to make changes in her community so that other young parents would be treated with care and dignity. Years later, the Courageous Operating System is helping Adriann leverage the strengths, courage, and lessons she learned from formative experiences, like becoming a young parent, to move policy-level changes at the state level and run for public office.

Wendy Chun-Hoon faced multiple challenges working and parenting. Wendy hid the fact that she was getting fertility treatments because she was concerned she would be fired if her boss knew that she was trying to get pregnant. As a leader fighting for policies like paid sick leave, it dawned on her one day that her family would not benefit from the changes she was seeking since there were no provisions for queer-led families. Wendy credits engaging with the Courageous Operating System in our leadership sessions as "just the support she needed at the right moment to catapult her leadership." In early 2021, President Biden appointed Wendy the Director of the Women's Bureau of the US Department of Labor, where she served for four years.

Angie DeLille, a member of the Lake Manitoba First Nation, grew up in foster care before being adopted and saw the devastating consequences of mental illness in her community. Angie attended my training program and used parts of the Courageous Operating System to communicate the powerful contributions she would bring as an Indigenous leader of health services at the state level. She was recently promoted to Director of the Office of Indian Policy at the Minnesota Department of Human Services.

Adriann, Wendy, and Angie have different life experiences, but they have one thing in common. As leaders, they are among many who are moving against the current. They know that the current is treacherous and unforgiving. They know it is doing its best to pull them further downstream, away from their goals, by throwing giant boulders in their path and creating dangerous rapids that threaten to push them out of the water altogether. Yet, they are determined to move toward their vision of a better world for themselves and their communities.

The title of this book begs the question: Why would anyone choose to lead against the current? You and I know the answer. It's an answer that resides deep in our hearts and drives us to continue moving upstream, even when our muscles ache from pushing against the water, even as we must clammer over the rocks the river has thrown in front of us. We choose to lead this way because we know this is the only path to a future of collective liberation.

I honor you and your heroic journey, and my hope is that this book will offer you a way forward that gives you back much more than what you are giving out.

Come, let's travel upstream together!

1

LEADERSHIP OPERATING SYSTEMS

You don't choose the times you live in, but you do choose who you want to be. And you do choose how you want to think.

—GRACE LEE BOGGS

Self-definition and self-determination is about the many varied decisions that we make to compose and journey toward ourselves, about the audacity and strength to proclaim, create, and evolve into who we know ourselves to be.

—JANET MOCK

Operating Systems Help Us Navigate Our World

My leadership journey brought me face to face with difficult situations and challenges, raising the following questions: How do I want to show up as a leader in this moment? How do I stand firm amid the intense pressure to compromise a core value? How do I find meaning in taking the hard way forward instead of the easy way out? Whether I was tackling a new project, learning a new skill, launching a new strategic initiative, or dealing with a crisis, I inevitably had to wrestle with a constellation of questions like this. And the answers to these questions depended on what was demanded of me and my capacity to respond.

The most important insight I have gained through my work and by supporting other leaders is that when we are going upstream against a formidable current, we need more than a box of leadership tools. We need an internal leadership system or an operating system that we can call on to guide us as we make our way upstream effectively.

The advent of computers popularized the term operating system, but living organisms also have operating systems that guide how they navigate their surroundings. A redwood tree's operating system includes extensive roots that allow it to withstand winds and flooding, chemical compounds that provide it with resistance to pests and disease, and protective bark that acts as a barrier from forest fires. These characteristics allow this tree to grow and live for thousands of years, making it older than most other living beings on Earth.

Similarly, elephants have an extraordinary operating system that has helped them live to an average age of sixty-five in the wild, even when they continue to face many threats from nature and humans. Elephants live in herds of up to one hundred, creating close and enduring cooperative social relationships that are "rare in the animal kingdom."[1] Members of these social networks work collaboratively to defend each other, find food, care for offspring, and make decisions.

Each herd is led by mature matriarchs: The older the leader, the greater the chance of survival for the entire herd. The herd leverages the wisdom gained from an older matriarch as part of their operating system to navigate the various threats in their environment. Science journalist Lesley Evans Ogden describes the survival advantage based on decades of research.[2] Older matriarchs are more adept at identifying which elephants from other herds might be dangerous or antagonistic. They are also better at leading their networks to hard-to-find water sources during droughts as they remember the location of rare water and food resources from different parts of their lifetime. And older matriarchs are more skilled than younger ones at being aware of and fending off predatory lions.[3]

Like plants and animals, humans have operating systems that help us navigate the world. Whether we know it or not, these operating systems also profoundly affect how we lead. They inform the way we communicate with our team members and the way we approach tough decisions. Our leadership operating system influences the kinds of impact we make and how we respond to adversity and conflict. It shapes the examples we set for others by informing how we treat those around us, the values we embed in our actions, and how willing we are to learn from our mistakes.

Thus, our operating system serves as an internal guide to approaching work and the world. It informs the answers many of us come up with to the plethora of challenging questions we face as leaders. For example, a leader with a command-and-control operating system has different answers to questions like "How will I invite and incorporate constructive feedback?" or "How can we create a culture that welcomes creativity and new ideas?" than a leader who uses a collaborative approach.

Often, the most critical questions take work to address. Grappling with complex dilemmas requires time and care. Along the way, we may wrestle with the needs and values of others if they conflict with our own. Although this kind of work may be challenging, it is easier when we have an effective leadership operating system that can guide us.

Operating Systems That Hold Us Back

Many of us developed ways to cope with oppression and significant challenges we've faced in our lives that prevented us from operating in our ideal leadership flow. Here are some examples of operating systems that I have observed pulling leaders, including myself, away from their core assets and power.

The Perfectionism Operating System

The seeds of my perfectionism operating system were fertilized when I was five. I will share my story with you in some depth so you can see how early an operating system can begin, how long it can last, and the kind of damage it can do if it's a negative one.

It was a lovely spring day, and I was skipping from kindergarten to the yellow school bus waiting to take me home. Out of the blue, Billy, a white boy in my class, stopped me in my tracks. He pulled his eyes back to make them smaller and tighter and started singing "ching chong Chinaman."

The effect he had on me was immediate. My whole body shut down as other students walked by me, unphased by what they saw. I lost my breath. My legs froze as I stood there watching him taunt me. Fortunately, his friends called him over, and he left with a smirk. I can hear his laughter ringing in my ears to this day. I remember wanting to shrink into a tiny ball and roll into the crack of the sidewalk so that no one could see me.

Out of the corner of my eye, I saw that my bus was about to leave, and I willed my legs to move forward. Keeping back tears, I got on the bus, sat on a seat by myself, and stared out the window, feeling numb. I don't remember telling anyone about what happened that day—including my parents.

Shame had not been part of my life experience until that moment. But Billy sent me the message loud and clear that something was inherently wrong with me. As these microaggressions from Billy and others continued from grade school to high school, I learned to build a wall around my heart and was determined not to be caught off-guard again. To compensate for what I then regarded as inherent deficiencies, I focused on accomplishing things to prove my value.

In first grade, I found my love for music while learning the piano. I practiced diligently for years and was rewarded with winning state and national piano competitions, which made my parents proud. In junior high, I stayed late at school to hone my jump shots and ball-handling skills so I could be a helpful member of our basketball team. In classes, I found teachers who would take an interest in and appreciate me. When I graduated from high school, one of my favorite teachers, Mr. Schell, gave me a piece of art he had made for me. It was a blank piece of orange construction paper, and near the bottom was a tiny circle with a small pie piece cut out of it. He captioned it, "Almost perfect."

Mr. Schell witnessed my drive for perfection years before I saw it in myself. I had no awareness at the time that my strategy of pushing away the shame from racism had turned into a strong desire to demonstrate my value through my achievements. Now, it is so clear to me that I was playing right into anti-Asian racism and trying my best to be that model minority, but back then, with no one to talk with, I didn't have this awareness. And I didn't see that my strategies of "blending in" and "excelling" were aligned with white supremacy and anti-Black racism. But I knew, even back then, that the racism I experienced was very different from the racism that my African American and Latinx peers faced, the kind that leads to higher rates of suspension or expulsion and being tracked into classes for lower-performing students. I had access to almost any class I wanted and my behavior at school was never policed.

Years later, after graduate school, this drive to prove my value was very much alive within me when I became an executive director for the first time at Asian Pacific Islanders for Reproductive Health (APIRH), which has since been renamed Forward Together. Because it was then a small organization, I was involved with almost every essential function. I was the primary fundraiser. I oversaw the hiring and management of all staff. I created and implemented the organizational programs. I led the strategic planning processes. And even though I entered with experience in organizing and program development, I was new to the other aspects of the work. Yet, I was determined to master these newer skills quickly. I enrolled in training on fundraising, finance, and organizational development. I told myself that I could only call myself a real executive director once I had a great facility with financial tracking and could readily raise the organization's annual budget. I pressured myself to get to a point where I could feel at ease networking and giving speeches in front of large groups of people. I worked hard to make staff meetings enjoyable and engaging for my team. I longed for the day when I would have most if not all of the answers to our organization's problems and could confidently direct my team in the right direction. What I was hiding, perhaps even from myself as I was flying by the seat of my pants, was that I often felt like an imposter.

As I continued in my career, I stuck with this system of punishing perfectionism because I believed it motivated me to be the best leader I could be. I was getting good results. My grueling perfectionism did help me eventually attain the skills I so desperately desired. I was able to read and work with financial reports. I successfully raised the organization's annual budget along with a reserve. I became increasingly comfortable connecting with people in a group setting and doing public speaking. Although I can't say every staff meeting was a blast, I significantly increased my meeting design and facilitation skills to where I now consider them some of my core strengths. Five years after I started, I finally felt comfortable introducing myself as an executive director.

Fast forward another five years, and the organization was growing quickly. Our staff had quadrupled; we had moved from organizing at the local school district level to launching national work. I now had senior staff who could oversee the organization's core functioning. My time was spent planning large national strategic initiatives, diversifying our funding sources in creative ways, and providing thought leadership to the movement. We were making impacts in ways I had never even dreamed of. Our staff passed legislation at the state level that protected reproductive justice, immigrant rights, and economic justice. We launched our first national strategic initiative with leaders from multiple states across the country. We were successful beyond what I had ever imagined.

So why was I still plagued with feelings of self-doubt? Even though I was experiencing the fruits of my labor and accomplishing what I had set out to do initially, the pressure to do more intensified. It would not let me rest. It lashed me with a cruel voice that whispered, "You are still not enough."

The way I was operating had other harmful effects. I set high standards for and was exceedingly hard on myself. When I made a mistake, I would berate myself with harsh messages about how incompetent I was, even when I was trying something for the first time. I judged myself by how others reacted and responded to me.

Perfectionism took me away from myself. It robbed me of my ability to fail. It used relentless pressure to motivate me, completely missing that I already had big doses of self-initiative. It diminished my strengths and kept me from celebrating my victories. It created a harsh internal environment, which made it harder to learn and have self-compassion.

Deep down, I still carried the shame from the racism that I experienced as a child. I believed I was not inherently deserving of love and respect. I felt the need to constantly prove my value to myself and others while at the same time blending in so that I could avoid being targeted. Instead of continually feeling strong and stalwart like a redwood tree or an elder matriarch, I found myself at times wanting to hide or shrink, unable to step fully into my power.

The Self-Sacrificial Operating System

The self-sacrificial operating system is quite common for leaders moving against the current. We come to this work because we are deeply committed to the cause and the vision for change. And the work to make the change happen is never-ending. We face a lot of pressure from society and our colleagues to demonstrate how down we are for the cause by how much of our lives we are willing to sacrifice. Also, many of us are socialized because of our gender to put the welfare of others before our own. Because of this, and perhaps because of the messages we received when we were younger, some of us deprioritize ourselves to the point where it damages our well-being.

If you give yourself some version of these messages, you may be operating within this system:

- I must put others first.
- My needs are not as important as my team's.
- It's my job to carry the burden.
- I have to be the strong one.
- Taking care of myself is selfish.
- I inevitably have to give up time with my family and friends if I'm working for the cause.

This operating system drives us toward burnout. It leads to unbalanced lives, where we focus only on work at the expense of being with our family and friends and experiencing relaxation and joy. It makes our needs invisible, so we neglect our health and well-being. It prevents us from living whole and robust lives.

The People Pleaser Operating System

The primary motivator of this system is the desire for approval from others. This desire for approval is part of our evolutionary history, as our ancestors lived in close-knit groups where social acceptance was critical for survival. From a young age, we are socialized to seek approval from our guardians, peers, and trusted adults. However, this operating system can skew our actions and decisions away from our vision and purpose because we over-prioritize approval from others. For example, we may refrain from making an unpopular decision when we operate this way. We may have difficulty saying no to the requests of others or setting boundaries with teammates because we don't want to risk them getting angry at us. We may go out of our way to ensure that others are satisfied, even if it means compromising our interests or needs.

People pleasing leaders often tell themselves:

- It's my job to make everyone happy.
- I can't say no because people won't like it.
- I can't let anyone down.
- I have to be available to everyone.
- If I have disappointed someone, I have failed.
- It's better to avoid conflict than to speak my truth.
- It's essential that people like me.

This operating system focuses primarily on how others feel about us. It discourages us from acting authentically or making necessary decisions that may be unpopular. It keeps us from developing deep relationships with those around us as we focus primarily on what we believe will curry positive feedback from others.

The Imposter Operating System

This operating system is a common one adopted by leaders with whom I work. Self-doubt and lack of confidence are outcomes of facing oppression on an ongoing basis. When we are barraged with negative messages from our family, community, or society about ourselves or our leadership, it is difficult for us not to internalize some of them and believe them. When we use this operating system, we can be plagued with self-doubt, which undermines our ability to act and make decisions because we often second-guess ourselves. We may constantly fear that we will be exposed and that people will see that we don't belong.

The following are the messages this system gives to us:

- People will find out that I don't know what I'm doing.
- Others are more qualified than I am.
- I didn't earn this and am lucky to be here.
- I am not worthy of praise.

- I am not as capable as others think.
- I shouldn't put out my opinions because they aren't as valuable as others.
- I have to prove my worth.

The imposter operating system can hinder our growth as leaders in terms of professional development or advancement because we feel that we do not deserve recognition. It can also prevent us from connecting with others and building our network because we fear we are not as good as our colleagues. We may also seek excessive approval from others because we don't believe in and trust ourselves.

The Rescuer Operating System

Many leaders have adopted part of the rescuer operating system in their leadership history. For those of us trying to make change and dedicated to serving our communities, it can be seductive to use this system. After all, why wouldn't we want to do everything we can to help those in need around us? And how many of us have told ourselves the following messages:

- I'm the only one who can do this.
- If I don't jump in, everything will fall apart.
- If I don't act, I'm letting everyone down.
- It's my responsibility to help if I can.
- I can't let anyone struggle on their own.

In rescuer mode, we think in polarized terms that obscure the truth. For example, it is not a given that things will crumble if we take a step back. Sometimes, if we don't act, we create more space for others to step in. And if things do fall apart because we are the only ones holding it together, then maybe it's for the best since it wasn't a sustainable effort because not enough people were invested in it.

It can be problematic when we assume that people around us need rescuing. Assuming we have all the answers or can swoop in and fix things for others is unrealistic as we only have control over our actions and responses. Also, we may be perpetuating oppressive dynamics if we try to rescue those who have less privilege than we do.

The operating system creates harmful dynamics for us and those around us. For example, in the early 1970s, psychiatrist Stephen Karpman developed his Drama Triangle to illustrate his theory that when we are playing the role of rescuer/hero, we create a dynamic that involves two other players: the victim who feels helpless and needs someone to rescue them; and the persecutor/villain, who is angry, controlling, and blaming. Karpman believes that while each person in that triangle may have a role they tend to play more often, each member will play all three roles at some point.

KARPMAN'S DRAMA TRIANGLE

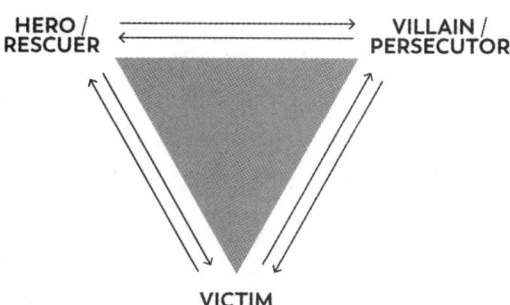

Eveline Shen, Diagram designs: Amy Wu, duende.us

Here's a typical example of how this dynamic can play out at work. Let's say that Nina supervises Lola, who is overseeing a team under great pressure to complete a critical report that the organization will release in the next few months. Lola is getting increasingly frustrated with Bob, one of her team members, who has consistently turned in his work late. Lola starts to push him assertively to meet his deadlines and expresses anger and frustration with his actions during their meetings. Bob is a decent writer, but writing is not his favorite, so his motivation is low. He needs help to keep up with the pace of the rest of the team. Bob feels resentment that Lola put him on this team in the first place and doesn't understand why she is so hard on him. He feels like he is drowning with no way out. Nina is an experienced writer. She sees Bob drowning and wants to rescue him by taking over some of his assignments. So, in this moment, Bob is the victim, Lola is the villain, and Nina is the rescuer.

Flash forward a few weeks when Bob starts handing over more and more of his work to Nina, significantly increasing her workload. Nina, now feels like the victim, with Bob being the villain, as she gets increasingly overwhelmed. Over time, Nina's resentment builds up, and she gets furious at Bob, making her take on the villain role. Bob, Nina, and Lola are stuck in this dynamic where each can cycle through each role. When we use this operating system, it keeps us from seeing things clearly and encourages us to act in ways that are not beneficial to us or those around us.

You are not alone if any of these operating systems feel familiar. Throughout my career, I have experienced aspects of each at different times. We adopt these ways of being to help us cope with the challenges, trauma, socialization, and oppression we have experienced over our lifetimes. We initially adopt these strategies for getting by in the world because we are missing something we need, namely a complete sense of how powerful we can be.

However, you may be starting to see how the operating systems may no longer be serving you or others around you. If you are like me, perhaps you notice that you want more for yourself. What would it be like to embrace your authentic self fully? How would it feel if you could make decisions based on your values and purpose without second-guessing yourself so much? What might change if you could take risks without worrying about failing? What would happen if you surrendered to everything you don't have control over and focused on what you can control? How can you focus on your strengths and assets instead of being concerned that you are insufficient? How much longer can you use these systems that take you away from who you are and prevent you from claiming your full leadership power?

The Courageous Operating System

The Courageous Operating System is designed to bring us back to ourselves in a world constantly pushing us to the sidelines or diminishing our value. It honors the courage we use every day and calls forth the courage within us that is still hidden and not used. It acknowledges the oppressive forces we contend with on an ongoing basis. It connects us with a moral compass to ensure our purpose and actions align with our deeply held values. It shines a light on our strengths and helps us nurture our superpowers. The Courageous Operating System is a developmental system that will help us foster our growth and increase our ever-growing capacity to lead. It helps us step back into our leadership flow.

You can use it to:

Build your well of courage: Create an abundant reserve of courage by turning your encounters with the raging waters that surround you into a constant source of fuel for your leadership.

Find the right purpose: Stay true to your purpose, even when the current pulls you in the opposite direction.

Cultivate success: Identify what success looks like for you and create your own metrics that align with your values.

Transform failure: Turn failures into forward progress.

Power up your leadership: Supercharge your leadership by harnessing your strengths, using your moral compass, and continuing to grow even more robust with each challenge.

Take care of yourself and the world: Embark on a deeper journey of caring for yourself, the people around you, and the world in which you live.

Create momentum: Generate momentum that propels you forward exponentially in a world doing everything possible to hold you back.

This operating system creates conditions that allow us to achieve our mission and to bring others along with more ease. It helps us navigate systemic oppression and complex challenges with exponentially more impact as we move toward our ambitious social change goals. It helps us access our full selves and invites us to use our mind, body, and spirit to help strengthen and expand our leadership.

Some aspects of the Courageous Operating System may come easily to you, while others might challenge your usual ways of responding, encouraging you to act differently. This system is bold and bracing, created to help you resist the societal norms and messages that undermine your leadership. Each element invites you to pause and reflect on how internalized oppression might show up in your actions and emotions. It encourages a shift in mindset and a reset of your perspective, helping you realign with your leadership, power, and values. Ultimately, it's designed to support the growth and flourishing of your leadership, even in the face of external pressures that seek to diminish or sideline you.

This system is inherently generative, and simply engaging with it can spark meaningful shifts and transformations. For instance, the more you practice everyday acts of courage, the deeper your reservoir of courage grows. Each time you learn and evolve from failure, you become stronger and more adaptable, gaining wisdom that you can share with others facing similar challenges. By redefining success according to your own values and on your own terms, you'll build greater confidence as you begin to reach these personal milestones. And when you recognize and consistently apply your strengths, you can leverage them in ways that create even greater, more impactful results.

THE COURAGEOUS OPERATING SYSTEM

Leadership requires us to act out of courage: to stand up to oppositional forces, to move through our fears, to be emboldened to take risks, and to fight for our vision when the odds are against us.

- Big Acts of Courage
- Everyday Acts of Courage
- Growing Your Courage

- Avoiding Purpose Pitfalls
- Developing a Purposeful Mindset
- Putting Yourself in the Purpose Picture

- Defining Success on Your Terms
- Identifying the Multidimensions of Success
- Aligning Success Metrics With Core Values

- Building a Springboard
- Leveraging Strengths and Values
- Harnessing the Wave
- Building Critical Mass

FIND THE RIGHT PURPOSE

CREATE MOMENTUM

CULTIVATE SUCCESS

BUILD YOUR WELL OF COURAGE

TAKE CARE OF YOURSELF, TAKE CARE OF THE WORLD

TRANSFORM FAILURE

POWER UP YOUR LEADERSHIP

- Exploring Difficult Emotions
- Connecting with Community
- Committing to Transformation Over Time
- Contextualizing Experiences

- Assessing Your Dashboard of Needs
- Growing Your Inner Wealth of Assets
- Using Your Superpower of Self-Growth

- Embracing Failure as Part of the Landscape
- Understanding How Oppression Impacts Failure
- Exploring the Benefits of Failure
- Working with Failure

Eveline Shen, Diagram designs: Amy Wu, duende.us

Each component is designed to support you in your work. However, when you begin using them in combination, you'll experience a synergistic effect that amplifies your leadership power and helps you move upstream. As you become more familiar with the system, you'll also be able to apply it not just to yourself but to your team, strengthening your collective efforts to overcome challenges and drive strategic initiatives or projects forward.

From our own experiences, we know that leadership can take many forms and manifest in countless ways. Think about the leaders who have made a significant and meaningful impact on your life, your community, and the broader movements you care about. Notice how some of their leadership qualities and outcomes stand in stark contrast to those typically celebrated by society at large. When we embrace an operating system that helps us bring our best selves forward—aligning our actions and decisions with our values and staying connected to our purpose and courage—the impact of our leadership grows exponentially. My hope is that the Courageous Operating System will provide you with clarity, confidence, and direction so your leadership can thrive as you pursue your mission of social change.

Your Turn

Getting into a State of Readiness

Before you do the Your Turn activities in this and the other chapters, it's important to take a moment to relax into a state of openness, readiness, and expansiveness. There are countless ways to achieve this state, and many of you probably have your favorite methods.

Here is one suggested process that I use regularly:

1. Get into a comfortable position for your body.

2. Take a few deep breaths.

3. Expand your awareness so you are attuned to not only what is directly in front of you but also all around you, on top of you, and underneath you.

4. See if you can expand your awareness out as far as it can go, past the ceiling, past the clouds, past the sky, and into the universe. Once you have expanded your awareness, bring that spaciousness back to your body.

5. Take three deep breaths, exhaling twice as long as you inhale.

6. Scan your body for places of tension you want to dispel. Stretch or use your breath or touch to help that part of your body release.

7. Take another set of three deep breaths, making your exhale longer than your inhale.

8. Let the universe nurture your heart with compassion and love and affirm that you are enough.

Please take your time as you proceed with the next activity. A number of questions may require focused and fresh attention. Pace yourself by taking time to reflect, explore, and integrate before proceeding to the next step.

Becoming Aware of Your Operating System

If you have not spent time thinking about your operating system, you are probably not aware of how often it affects your leadership.

A. The first step is to notice the messages you are receiving from yourself.

- Pick a recent moment that made you question your leadership.
- Write down all of the messages that you gave yourself at that time and afterward.

B. The second step is to identify which messages occur more frequently. The more frequently they appear, the deeper they may be ingrained in your operating system.

- When you look at this list, note the messages that come up at work or in other parts of your life.
- Is there one message that arises frequently or brings up a lot of feelings for you?

- Are any of the messages you give yourself similar to those I listed earlier in the chapter for the different operating systems?

C. The third step is to observe how these messages impact you.

- How do these messages make you feel emotionally?
- How do they affect how your body feels?
- How did these messages affect your leadership at that moment?

D. The fourth step is to pay attention in the next week and see how often these messages come up. Take the opportunity to practice working with them when they appear. When they arise, take a few deep breaths and acknowledge them. Here are some ideas for how to begin work with them:

- Externalize them in some way—by writing them down, for example.
- Bring yourself into the moment by becoming aware of senses that are accessible to you: What are you seeing, smelling, hearing, touching, or sensing in your environment right now?
- Focus on the parts of you and your leadership that you appreciate.

By doing this, you are creating an ever-so-slight separation between yourself and these messages. This is the beginning of cultivating a process where you can start making conscious decisions about how you want to respond to these messages. This process is a crucial step in gaining insight into your current operating system and determining how you want to move through the world as a leader.

2

BUILDING YOUR WELL OF COURAGE

To fly, we have to have resistance.

—MAYA LIN

Without courage, we cannot practice any other virtues with consistency. We can't be kind, true, merciful, generous, or honest.

—MAYA ANGELOU

Big Acts of Courage

Leading against the current to create social change requires us to act out of courage. The courage to stand up to powerful oppositional forces, to move through our fears, to take risks, and to fight for our vision when the odds are against us. This system is called the Courageous Operating System because it takes courage to use and because it will grow your courage as you implement it. Courage comes from the Latin term *cor*, which means heart. Looking back at history, we see examples of people leading with their hearts and inspiring us with their big acts of courage.

Leaders like Ella Baker, who used her courage in countless ways throughout her fifty years of activism in her vision for the liberation of oppressed communities. In her definitive biography, historian Barbara Ransby chronicles how Ella Baker organized within grassroots communities for profound change (including for the civil rights movement, to protest the Vietnam War, and to fight for Puerto Rican independence), at times risking her life, all the while being rooted in the Black freedom movement.[1] In addition, as a Black woman, she was often dismissed by male leaders in the civil rights movement.

For example, after the success of the Montgomery bus boycott, Ella Baker, Martin Luther King Jr., and other civil rights leaders formed the Southern Christian Leadership Conference (SCLC), a new organization designed to launch similar campaigns in the South. But the other prominent leaders, all men, including King, did not have the skills or inclination to build out an organization from the grassroots that Ella Baker had. Even so, King was reluctant to hire her because she was a woman. In the end, King's colleagues persuaded him to let Baker lead the organization, but he never gave her the title of director, which was reserved for a male minister.[2]

Her leadership style radically differed from prominent Black male leaders like King and W. E. B. Du Bois, with whom she engaged frequently. Instead of positioning herself as a charismatic leader at the forefront of the movement, she used a model of group-centered leadership, where she worked directly with grassroots community members and activists to facilitate *their* leadership development and reach their potential. For example, in the early 1960s, Ella Baker worked with a group of young Black activists conducting sit-ins around the country to protest the segregation of restaurants. Other SCLC leaders, including King, wanted the students to join their organization, but Baker convinced them to create their own. She encouraged them to focus on building their leadership from the ground up collectively rather than relying on following one leader. Also, during this time, Baker grew increasingly frustrated with the way she was being treated by SCLC ministers whom she felt viewed her as a glorified secretary for King.[3] She soon resigned from SCLC and started to support the leadership of the students from the sidelines and focus her efforts on mass-based, grassroots organizations.

Throughout her activism, Ella Baker tenaciously brought her radical vision and strategies for social change to each of her efforts. At every turn, she "inserted herself into leadership situations where others thought she simply did not belong." Her unwavering courage in the face of grave injustice, her visionary spirit that fueled critical civil rights institutions, and her deep commitment to growing the leadership of others helped to build the engine that drove the civil rights movement.[4]

In our current political climate, numerous examples show leaders willing to take significant risks to fight for the liberation of frontline communities experiencing some of the greatest attacks. For instance, the leaders who risk arrest as they help their communities get access to abortion care in states that have banned these services since the US Supreme Court's June 2022 *Dobbs v. Jackson Women's Health Organization* decision that overturned *Roe v. Wade*. And leaders who receive death threats as they fight for the safety of transgender people in rural parts of the country. Student leaders who risk being expelled as they protest the war in Gaza on college campuses. Black Lives Matter leaders who are surveilled by the FBI and targeted by the police. It is heartbreaking to see how those in power in this country are responding with increasing violence, criminalization, and contempt to the courage of activists and leaders who are valiantly moving against the current.

Everyday Acts of Courage

When we reflect on courage, we often think about these big, bold acts where great risks are involved. But what about the acts of bravery that are part of our daily work? What about the courage needed to navigate each moment when multiple layers of oppression—based on race, class, gender, and ability—are bearing down on even the most mundane actions we take? What about the daily courageous decisions and actions, which are invisible to others and maybe even to ourselves, necessary to launch efforts that move the needle toward change?

Courage's most simple definition is the ability to do something that you know is difficult or dangerous. Courage motivates us to take action resulting in opposition, resistance, or significant discomfort. This definition encourages us to see the everyday acts of courage that are part of the actions and decisions we make in our daily lives. In my experience, everyday acts of courage take many forms. They can feel like jumping off of a cliff or taking the smallest step forward on a new path. They can surround me like a cloak when I enter a room as the only woman of color, or they can reside in my pocket, accessible to my touch when needed in dicey situations. They can take the shape of a megaphone or come as a whisper that only I can hear. Everyday acts of courage are the stones that make up the road we travel as we advocate for social change.

Many of us experienced these everyday acts of courage as we stewarded our organizations or teams through the crucible that was the beginning of the pandemic. I remember calling on my courage frequently amid collective anxiety, fear, and uncertainty. Each day brought new questions: How do we protect our team and the communities we serve? What kind of support can we provide our staff and their families as they succumb to COVID? How do we continue our plans now that everything has turned upside down? While we were grappling with one question, another would pop up, and we would often have to create organizational policies and procedures on the fly.

Even now that the pandemic has receded, leaders use their courage every day. Very few of us, if any, enter the job equipped with the experience and skills necessary to perform everything expected of us. It takes courage to pull up our sleeves, assess what needs to be done, gain the required skills, and then figure out how to address each of these areas, often simultaneously. We are required to tackle a multitude of efforts: launching and maintaining strategic change campaigns or initiatives, overseeing the financial health and growth of the organization, ensuring that personnel matters are attended to regularly, managing multidisciplinary and multiracial teams, embarking on multiyear strategic planning, and being accountable to the communities whom we serve and the funders who invest in our work. Sometimes, it takes courage to just get out of bed and get ready for a day we know will be filled with challenges and difficulties.

And these acts of courage can have an accumulative impact as we launch efforts to move the needle of change forward. In 2010, Forward Together, the organization I led at the time, in partnership with others, launched the Strong Families Network. Preceding the launch, I knew we were pushing against the current, facing enormous challenges I wasn't sure we could surmount. For decades, multiple factions of the Right had organized under the umbrella of "family values" to move their agendas, severely restricting the agency and freedoms of marginalized families. We wanted to take back the terrain of families from them and create conditions where all kinds of families (single parent, working class, LGBTQ+, immigrant, formerly incarcerated, etc.) could receive the rights, recognition, and resources they needed to thrive. In addition, raising funding for this ten-year, multifaceted initiative would be challenging since donors generally funded organizations doing single-issue work. At the time, donors did not tend to support long-term collaborations.

I had additional concerns about my own leadership. Did I have the skills and strength necessary to lead this initiative? Would I be able to convince other leaders who were focused on their own organizational work to join this collaborative effort? How would I effectively address the disagreements or tensions that would naturally emerge among leaders as we built this initiative together? Analyzing my doubts, I realized that I was asking, "Am I the right leader for this?"

Before we decided to launch, I spent much time contemplating this question. After a few months, I realized that the answer was really unknowable without action. The only way to discover the answer would be to call upon my courage and move through the planning and into implementation. I did not know if funders would provide resources until I did the actual work of asking. Additionally, to request funding, we would have to launch the initiative and demonstrate interest among other social justice organizations.

What started as an idea fostered by nine organizations grew to become one of the largest multi-issue strategic initiatives in the country focused on supporting families of all shapes and sizes at that time.[5] In five years, over two hundred organizational partners came together across various sectors at the intersection of race, gender, and sexuality, busting divisions to build power so all families could thrive. Over a decade, Strong Family Network partners worked to pass policies on the state and national levels to protect and strengthen families while our culture-change campaigns reached over twenty million people.

Launching this initiative took a leap of courage for all involved, along with countless other acts of courage to make change happen: the courage to go up against those in power who were responsible for the continued attacks on our families; the courage to mobilize others to join this new initiative; the courage to put forth a vision of the conditions and policies needed for our families to thrive; the courage to come together across geography, issue areas, communities, and strategies; and the courage to commit significant staff time and resources toward this new, yet-to-be-tried effort.

Examples of Everyday Acts of Courage

We use courage in many ways in our daily lives. The following are six examples of everyday acts of courage.

EVERYDAY ACT 1: THE COURAGE TO ENGAGE IN DIFFICULT CONVERSATIONS

In our line of work, we operate in diverse teams. Team members come from different cultural and family backgrounds, belong to different generations, hold various levels of power within the organization, exhibit varying work styles, and may have overlapping or opposing perspectives. Navigating these differences can be challenging, and this is by no means a comprehensive list of potential sources of conflict among us.

In this context, miscommunication, disagreements, and conflict are common occurrences. However, having difficult conversations that are constructive and productive is not a common practice in our society. It is no surprise that conflict management is one of the most sought-after skill sets among the leaders I work with.

Many leaders choose to avoid the discomfort and tension that come with difficult conversations, largely due to the fear of potential severe conflicts. It's understandable—sometimes, repair or resolution simply doesn't happen. How many of us have distanced ourselves from family members because of differing political views? How many have experienced tense conversations that escalate into disagreements, leading to colleagues refusing to speak to each other or one party being "canceled"?

When I invite leaders to think about a time when they were in a heated discussion and then ask them to tell me what their purpose was at that moment, the answer I most commonly receive is "to prove my point." I know that when I first began my career as an ED, whenever I was in an escalating disagreement, I felt that I needed to put on invisible armor to protect myself and stay firm in my resolve to stand my ground. For many of us, disagreements conjure up battle images and straightforward black-and-white reasoning: "It's me versus you, " or "Being in conflict means that we may get injured, so we need protection from one another."

I have learned the hard way that we are not taught how to be good allies to each other during disagreements and conflict. And the implications of this are critical to the success of our movement. Too often, disagreements and conflict cause disruption and collateral damage that undermine our progress in promoting social change. In the blink of an eye, we can turn from allies into enemies. I have witnessed this up close and from afar. I have been part of organizations or coalitions that have nearly self-destructed because we did not have effective tools for dealing with disagreements.

Many of us know organizations that have suffered significantly or even collapsed because of internal conflict.

Whenever I approach disagreements with a boxing-match mindset—viewing them as needing to end with one winner and one loser—I find it easier to distance myself from the other person and lose sight of who they are. Before the conflict, the person in front of me was a colleague, an ally, maybe a friend. But in moments of heated conflict, I have seen how quickly I can forget all of that and begin to view them as an opponent—someone to defeat or, at the very least, convince to come over to my side of seeing things. This is a very polarizing model of dealing with disagreements.

To deal effectively with disagreements within our organizations, we need the courage to engage in conflict not as if it is a boxing match but instead, as if it is a partnership. It takes courage to sit and listen to each other's perspectives. It takes courage to lean into discomfort and uncertainty as we seek to de-escalate situations and identify potential solutions. It takes courage to shift from our tightly held truths to make space for new perspectives. It takes courage to admit that we could be wrong. If we regard dealing with disagreements and conflicts as part of the normal work we do together, then we can view it as a partnership, a shared experience in which we have the opportunity to gain more clarity, understand the other person better, deepen our trust with each other, and come to new solutions that help both parties.

Everyday Act 2: The Courage to Lead with Vulnerability

As an executive director, I tried my best to support the staff I worked with. When I needed support, I went to others outside of the organization. I was careful not to bring any of my needs to my staff because I viewed this as inappropriately burdening them.

Several years ago, my mother, who was in the middle stages of Alzheimer's, suffered a stroke and was in the hospital for two months. My brother and I took my father to the hospital every night so that he could have dinner with my mom and hold her hand. During this time, my father grew depressed and became increasingly ill. In August, he had a series of strokes and was never the same again.

I didn't mention what was happening with my family at work because I didn't want my team to worry about me. I felt like I should be able to handle it all. However, a month after my mom's stroke, as I was driving my dad to the emergency room for the third weekend in a row, I admitted to myself that I was not able to do my job at 100 percent. It was hard for me to focus because I was so worried about my parents. Whenever there was a medical crisis, I had to drop everything at work and attend to it. I needed some time during the day to take care of my parents. This would be the first time in my career that I had asked for a reduced work schedule except for parental leave when my daughters were born.

I was fortunate to have a very supportive board that gave me the time off I needed for medical appointments for my parents. However, I was much more reluctant to tell the staff I would work less in the next few months. This was happening at a hectic time in the organization, and my working less would result in some of them having to cover for my absence at meetings or in moving projects forward. Would they resent me increasing their workload? Would this diminish their perception of me as a leader?

Even though I was determined to relay this news with stoicism, I teared up as I described the ways my mom and dad had changed and how much they meant to me. For a moment, I forgot we were at work, and I was just very present with the grief and sadness I had been feeling outside of work every day. As I looked at each of my team members, I saw deep compassion and empathy in their faces, and I felt truly held. Thanks to their kindness, I did not feel that I was a burden at all in that moment. We spent the next part of the meeting coming up with a plan for moving forward in the next few months, during which they would share some of the responsibilities I gave them. I would also check with them mid-way through to see how this plan worked and assess if they needed additional support.

After the meeting, my team members approached me separately and *thanked* me for sharing what was happening with my family. A number of them revealed that this conversation permitted them to talk about their aging parents who were also suffering from Alzheimer's or other serious conditions and what it meant to be a caregiver of parents while also raising children. Another team member approached me to say that she was more than happy to help out, given how we had all rallied around her the year before when her son was diagnosed with cancer. I saw then that allowing myself to be more vulnerable with my team fostered our collective ability to talk about their challenges and create additional spaces to support one another in meaningful ways.

How many messages do we get from our families and society that tell us we must achieve success or overcome obstacles by ourselves? Even though many of us know this notion of pulling ourselves up by our bootstraps is a harmful narrative, we are still sometimes ashamed or feel inadequate when we cannot do everything perfectly by ourselves.

I recognize that there are moments when it is not wise for us to be vulnerable, especially in oppressive or adversarial situations that make it unsafe. However, practicing embracing our vulnerability can expand our leadership in ways that are not possible when we keep our guard up. The courage to be vulnerable allows us to embrace our full humanity. It enables us to deepen our trust and our connection with others. It allows us to create and see the possibilities in situations. It permits us to ask for help. It strengthens our ability to deal with uncertainty and the unknown. It allows us to show up as our authentic selves and encourages others around us to do the same. It invites us to be gentle with ourselves and acknowledge the importance of caring for ourselves. It bolsters our ability to model leadership as it invites compassion and empathy and models to others on the team what is possible when they are open to being vulnerable, too.

EVERYDAY ACT 3: THE COURAGE TO MAKE TOUGH DECISIONS

As leaders, we will inevitably face tough decisions—choices that may not be well received, decisions others might not fully understand because only we, or a few on our team, possess the full context. Yet, these are decisions we must have the courage to stand by, regardless of the challenges they bring.

One of the most difficult decisions I made as a leader was to close our youth organizing program. This was our organization's inaugural program, which many, including myself, loved. Hundreds of young people, primarily young Asian women, had attended the program, learning how to organize and change policies at the local and state levels. It was the first, and for many years, the only program that focused on reproductive justice in Oakland. Seeing this program's impact on the young people who went through it lifted my heart. Years later, I am sometimes still stopped in the street by one of the alums telling me how this program helped them continue to fight for change as they got older in their communities.

Almost two decades after it started, the program began to face significant challenges. The long-term staff member overseeing the program moved away, and we struggled to find a suitable replacement. The people we hired often cycled in and out after just a year or two, leading to further instability. Additionally, funding for the program was dwindling, and we found it increasingly difficult to attract donors interested in supporting our efforts. These factors resulted in additional pressure on other staff members to fill the gaps left by departing employees. I realized that this situation was not sustainable for either the program or the organization. So, in consultation with the leadership team and the board, I made the difficult decision to shut down the program and let go of its remaining two staff. I sat with the decision for a few weeks and wrestled with it to ensure it was right for the organization. I knew this would not go over well with several of my staff who wanted to see the program continue.

We informed the rest of the team by transparently and thoughtfully sharing our thought process. We wanted them to understand that this decision was difficult and stemmed from various challenges the program had faced. Most of the staff understood our reasoning. However, it felt like a gut punch, especially for some of those working in the program and in the office that housed it.

The day after we announced the decision, I came into that office, and it felt like someone had just died. The remaining program staff were understandably upset and angry over the situation. I was sad, and I would dearly miss this program, which I had helped create. I did a lot of internal work on myself to process my grief about the program while also holding space for the staff to express feelings of anger, hurt, and betrayal, which were directed at me or a few others on the leadership team.

This period remains painful for me to reflect on. I engaged in significant internal work to process my grief about the program while also striving to maintain my composure and support the staff in expressing their feelings of anger, hurt, and betrayal—feelings that were sometimes directed at me and a few others on the leadership team. It took the organization several months to process and recover from that challenging time, and, unfortunately, a few of my relationships suffered as a result of the experience. I wouldn't be surprised if some of those staff members back then are still upset with me. Making that hard decision was essential for the team's and organization's health and well-being.

EVERYDAY ACT 4: THE COURAGE TO TAKE ACTION IN THE FACE OF THE UNKNOWN

At the beginning of the pandemic, leaders in philanthropy, just like leaders in nonprofit organizations, were in chaotic conditions. During those unprecedented times, many struggled to figure out the best way forward in supporting their grant partners. One program officer told me that the stress level at every meeting she attended with other colleagues was quite high as people were distraught, overwhelmed, and unsure how to proceed. Many program officers felt isolated, including those who funded our work. To support them, I brought together a group of over twenty philanthropic leaders to build community together so they wouldn't have to face similar challenges alone and provide a space where they could think strategically and collaboratively about how best to support their grant partners and the movement.

Zoom was newly becoming our collective way to meet, and I was determined to bring a mind-body approach to these sessions, even though we were not in the same room. Stressful conditions, like dealing with the COVID pandemic, trigger a physiological response that can make us feel smaller, more restricted, and rigid, both physically and mentally. When our bodies respond like this, it makes it challenging to think expansively and strategically.

At the beginning of our session, I asked everyone to take three deep breaths together, inviting them to let go of stress with every exhale. As we did this, I could feel the group's energy shift from a hectic pace of people rushing to join the session to one that became more focused and calmer. I then brought them through different interactive activities designed to connect to their courage while being attuned to their bodies.

We then discussed the types of courage needed during that time. At that particular moment, the stock market had taken a hit, the biggest since the 2008 Great Recession. This meant foundation assets were down dramatically, and trustees were scared and nervous about their endowments. Out of fear, presidents of large national foundations were decreasing their payouts to organizations and tightening their budgets, creating a climate that encouraged further funding restrictions within the philanthropic sector. If this continued, resources would dry up when leaders and organizations needed them the most. The health and lives of frontline communities were at stake. Many donors and funders were scaling down their giving when the opposite was required.

This group of funders wanted to stop this growing trend in philanthropy and instead raise the level of collective grantmaking so that organizations had enough resources to meet the new needs they faced during this time.

Nationally recognized and beloved philanthropic leader Dimple Abichandani, a long-term supporter of our work, was one of them. During our sessions, she was sitting with the question of how to summon the courage she needed to ask her board of trustees to significantly increase their annual budget for grant partners at a time when their assets had decreased more than ever before, and they were already giving out one of the highest percentages of payout in the sector. She knew this conversation would create significant tension between herself and her board members. But she was willing to go through intense discomfort if it meant that she could get more funding for the leaders on the ground who were dealing with life-and-death situations in their communities.

One of the aha moments she experienced in our time together was learning to use her breath to help her through moments of discomfort. She felt more at ease after this discovery and was more determined than ever to make the ask.

Shortly after our sessions, Dimple reported that "the board had met her embodied request with a resounding yes!"[6] Dimple would go on to write and speak about the need for foundation leaders to buck the current trend of pulling back resources during the pandemic by increasing their grant sizes, expanding to multiyear grant terms, and providing funding that offered organizations maximum flexibility.

These leadership sessions helped other participants find the courage they needed to act boldly. During our time together, a group of program officers collaborated to create a robust initiative to increase the number of rapid-response resources for their grant partners who needed a quick infusion of funding in response to the current administration's attacks. A few program officers and CEOs spoke to their board of trustees and successfully advocated for their foundations to go beyond the 5 percent payout for that year, increasing their total giving. Many of these relationships forged during those sessions remain to this day. By coming together in crisis, these philanthropic leaders found community and gathered their individual and collective courage to seek bold solutions that benefited the field. They acted individually and collectively so that an infusion of funding was released to the field in record time.

As we lead against the current, taking action can be difficult for many reasons. If we face new terrain, we might be confused about how to proceed. If the waters are too tumultuous, we may feel it's too risky to wade in. If the stakes are too high, we may feel we don't have what it takes to succeed. As leaders, we need to have the courage to step into uncertainty or the unknown together and take action individually and collectively.

EVERYDAY ACT 5: THE COURAGE TO NOURISH OURSELVES

Having the courage to care for ourselves is essential for several reasons. Leadership requires sustained energy over time. This means prioritizing care for our physical, mental, emotional, and spiritual health. Ensuring our tank is fueled up and we act in ways that contribute to our well-being will enable us to be here for the long haul. I know this is not easy to do, given our busy lives. But finding the courage to make the time can be lifechanging. I remember a participant who approached me at the beginning of a leadership session, the third in a series I was leading. As we greeted each other, she informed me how much our discussion in the second session on the importance of nourishing ourselves as leaders impacted her. In that conversation, I had asked group attendees to list one thing they could do to care for themselves that would be a game-changer in that it would significantly impact their lives. After sitting with that question, she realized it would be to take care of her heart. She was born with a congenital heart disease, which resulted in her needing ongoing monitoring and medication. Because of her busy schedule, it was easy for these tasks to fall off her to-do list. At our session, she realized that a part of her was not attending to her health because of her fear and guilt. Fear that her condition had gotten worse and guilt that she had not prioritized dealing with it. When she thought about my question to the group regarding the most significant change she could make, the image of her heart appeared, and then a picture of her dying. She knew she had to see her doctor. She was beaming when she told me that she felt relieved that her condition hadn't declined, and that she had found a caring cardiologist to whom she could go regularly. She said that this decision saved her life.

Along with caring for ourselves, we can use courage for self-preservation. This means that we don't have to be the one who always raises issues of inequity in meetings. We are not required to use our backs as a bridge for someone else's education or enlightenment or our voice as the sole drumbeat for justice at every meeting. We get to decide when and if we go out on a ledge where we might take a hit for the benefit of others.

In addition, courageous leadership does not require that we overextend ourselves. Self-nourishment means being able to set boundaries with our effort and time. We can say no to things that will allow us to say yes to the more important or meaningful things. We can retreat with our kindred spirits for solace, support, and refuge. We are allowed to rest and use our courage to nurture our hearts and well-being while also modeling for others how they can best use their resources.

EVERYDAY ACT 6: THE COURAGE TO MOVE THROUGH SELF-DOUBT

When those of us from marginalized communities take on something bold and big, self-doubt can plague us. Oppression and white supremacy create conditions where our ways of being are constantly called into question, marginalized, made invisible, or attacked. We not only fight the monster, but we do it with our hands tied behind our backs. This lack of societal or community support or outright antagonism toward our leadership can create conditions that sow seeds of self-doubt. Finding the courage to move through this is critical to our ability to lead powerfully.

If we don't recognize self-doubt, we may internalize these messages as truths about ourselves rather than understand them as simply thoughts. Once we acknowledge them, we can identify the emotions underneath them, such as insecurity, fears, or confusion. Gaining clarity about these emotions can reduce their intensity. Once the intensity is less, we can question the veracity of the messages we are giving ourselves. What evidence do we have that supports these self-doubts? What evidence do we have that challenges these self-doubts? Reflecting on past successes, accomplishments, and experiences can counter these messages. Auditing our strengths can also help, see chapter 6 for how to do this.

But our journey can't rely on self-assuredness that we won't fail or make mistakes because we can't know the future. Self-doubt comes with the territory of leadership. We can call on our courage to take the next step. Sometimes, simply taking that step can decrease self-doubt. Sometimes, it can help us learn how to handle what is coming our way. Sometimes, taking that step will help us grow to be more prepared for subsequent steps. The more we work with our self-doubt, the more we can connect to our most powerful leadership. We cannot let fear or self-doubt keep us from reaching our purpose. And if we don't get it right the first time, we will gain information that will help us be more successful the next time.

Everyday Acts of Courage in Action

Often, we combine these and other everyday acts of courage. The following are two profiles of leaders. As you read them, note the multiple acts of courage you see.

Profiles in Courage: Adriann Barboa

Adriann Barboa, a generational New Mexican, is a beloved leader. Her commitment to just and equitable policies and programs is inspiring. From starting a nationally recognized mentoring program for students of color to passing state legislation to support pregnant and parenting young people, from leading campaigns for women and families to access the full spectrum of reproductive healthcare to mobilizing community voices for quality, affordable healthcare for all, Adriann brings formidable experiences and skills to her advocacy work. In 2020, Adriann successfully ran for county commissioner for District 3 and all Bernalillo County residents in Albuquerque. Adriann has led many successful efforts to pass policies and move legislation, including the following campaign to protect abortion access.

In 2013, Adriann was one of the key leaders who helped to defeat a ballot measure that, if passed, would have restricted abortion care for later second and third-term abortions in Albuquerque, New Mexico. For more details about this campaign, please see chapter 8 on momentum. This ballot measure was initially heavily favored to win because many voters, including some from Adriann's extended family, favored these restrictions.

As a key public spokesperson, she knew her personal experiences with abortion would be covered in the newspapers and the media. She called me before the campaign almost in tears because she was concerned that she might alienate family members who didn't believe in abortion. To Adriann, family meant everything; losing family over this would be devastating. However, not using her leadership to defeat this harmful initiative was out of the question. It was a big dilemma that held significant risks on both sides.

Despite her fears of losing familial relationships and being potentially shunned, Adriann stepped into her leadership position within the campaign. She and the other women-of-color leaders had insisted that the campaign use language and talking points that spoke to the values of New Mexican families. Respect is one of those values. So the campaign referred to "respecting New Mexican women" rather than the more often-used pro-choice rhetoric that didn't resonate with Latinx New Mexican communities.

A few weeks after the campaign launched, Adriann called to tell me about an experience she'd had at a family barbecue that weekend with over fifty family members. The week before, she had been on the local news talking about the campaign, and she knew that most of her family had seen the coverage. She had gone to the party ready to defend herself and was on guard for any untoward comments. At one point, she saw one of her favorite uncles approach her. He had served in the military and held very conservative political viewpoints. She was filled with dread as he came closer. But much to her surprise, he put his arm around her and gave her a big hug. Then, he said, "I saw you on the local news, Adriann." Then he paused. "And what do you think about all these people coming from outside our state telling our families what to do? That really bugs me. I really like what you are saying. I think New Mexican women *should* be respected." Adriann breathed a deep sigh of relief. She knew that the campaign was working if her conservative-leaning Tío was coming to her to support rejecting this harmful ban. They were starting to win the hearts and minds of New Mexican families and voters.

This conversation with her uncle helped Adriann gain even more courage as she spoke to other family members who were not as supportive. An unanticipated result of this conversation was that Adriann was now even more willing to discuss the campaign with other family members, which helped them speak up. She soon spoke to her sister, who was not usually one to take a stand on political issues, especially on abortion, since she was raised Catholic. A few days later, a couple of members of her sister's husband's family, who had seen Adriann on the news, approached her sister in anger because she wasn't stopping Adriann from speaking in support of abortion. Adriann's sister, emboldened from their earlier conversation, not only stood up for Adriann, but also for the campaign.

These conversations continued, and Adriann stayed grounded and became more confident through each one. In some of these discussions, she persuaded people to vote against the ballot initiative they would have otherwise supported. If she was having a rough conversation with a family member, she had a game plan to exit the conversation and get support. She learned that she could decide when to put herself out there and when to take a break to protect herself from judgment or feeling attacked. Adriann stepped into her leadership by embracing her courage to act, her courage to nourish herself when necessary, and her courage to be vulnerable when people came toward her with judgment. Ultimately, she remained as outspoken as ever, publicly and to her family. Not only did she retain relationships with her family, but she strengthened them through the process and gave *them* new-found courage to speak up.

PROFILES IN COURAGE: TAMIEKA ATKINS

In 2016, I created a movement-building fellowship called Stepping Into Power which brought together leaders from around the country, including Tamieka Atkins. Tamieka is a leader with a fierce determination to dismantle systems built by white supremacy so that communities of color can have self-determination and freedom. A lifelong community organizer and activist, Tamieka founded the Atlanta Chapter of the National Domestic Workers Alliance, the first national labor justice organization chapter to focus exclusively on African Diaspora domestic workers. That chapter became the model for We Dream in Black. She is currently the executive director of ProGeorgia, a partisan civic engagement table.

Tamieka is never at a loss for bold ideas. However, she was frustrated because she rarely had time to think beyond her current workplan or to envision the radical future she longed for. After all, so much was on her plate. This seemingly endless work—and the stresses inherent to being Black and Brown in the United States—often caused her to feel drained and burnt out because she was never doing enough. Tamieka started as a new ED, inheriting the organization from a previous leader who was white. She enrolled in Stepping Into Power in 2018 after hearing about it from other Stepping Into Power alums and seeing in them the confidence they had gained in leading and planning by bringing their whole selves to the table.

In the first session of Stepping Into Power, Tamieka felt moved and validated when she and other leaders identified how oppression, sexism, and racist systems were impacting their leadership and work. She was transformed by the message that she and all cis- or transgender women of color *are* "enough." She explained, "I realized I don't have to work myself to death to prove I am valuable and have something meaningful to offer. It allowed me to move from insecurity and defensiveness to a stance where I can strategize better, dream bigger, and be more innovative."

She immediately began applying this message of courage to her work. During the 2020 Census, philanthropic donors expressed a heightened interest in funding voter engagement work in the South. Some of these funders had their own agendas for what they wanted Tamieka and her organizational partners to do.

Before coming to Stepping Into Power, Tamieka had experienced anxiety at the thought of receiving grant resources, which donors had earmarked for strategies she didn't fully believe in. Those of us who rely on funding understand this bind; donors have the power to dictate how organizations use their grant dollars. It is common for leaders to accept these terms from foundations to access money for their organizations.

However, after the first session of Stepping Into Power, Tamieka gained the courage to negotiate with funders. Instead of accepting their proposal for what they wanted her to do, she offered them *her* vision of funding use, which would have had much more robust results than what funders initially asked for. She knew that a lot of money was at stake, so her worst fear was that she and the coalition would lose significant funding for their efforts that year and in the following years. But she was willing to take the risk because she believed in the vision that she and the coalition shared. After a few conversations, the donors, while initially taken aback, came around and gave her the money to support her vision.

Part of Tamieka's vision for civic engagement differed from how typical civic engagement campaigns are waged. Civic engagement campaigns often treat electoral canvassers as expendable; once the campaign is done, the job ends, and workers become unemployed. She wanted to transform how workers were valued, even after the initial funds had dried up. Refusing to perpetuate a harmful campaign culture that induced burnout, she worked with organizational leaders in the coalition to retain and invest in these workers over the long term. As a result, many canvassers remained employed at their organizations through the pandemic to lead outreach and civic engagement efforts.

Negotiating with funders emboldened Tamieka to take further action with her colleagues in the field. She used part of the funding to support the workers, many of whom were parents and single moms during the height of the campaign. Canvassers work long hours, and many find it challenging to come home late and have to put dinner on the table for their families. During the height of the campaign, Tamieka gave them gift certificates to restaurants and partnered with a local collective of house cleaners to provide services. This helped decrease the amount of labor the campaign workers needed to do for their families at home, allowing them to rest and have more time with their families at night.

Tamieka and her colleagues flipped the narrative for women of color from "I am not enough" to "I deserve to be treated with dignity, and my labor at home and work must be recognized." Tamieka achieved these changes by starting with the courage to see herself, amid oppressive social messages that disparaged her leadership, as an advocate with a bold and valuable vision and strategy to offer. The courage she gained from claiming her leadership in this new way bolstered her to show funders, who held power over her resources, her vision for running the campaign differently. Her success in doing this emboldened her to work with her colleagues and create conditions for civic engagement work that were more humane and sustainable for everyone involved. And now, a few years later, Tamieka has gained the complete confidence of donors and colleagues, which has resulted in her organization and efforts growing ten-fold as she continues to make significant changes.

Courage Begets Courage

Whether we engage in big, bold acts or everyday acts of courage, we can build up a reservoir of courage. Researchers believe that courage is a muscle we can build and develop through practice.[7] If you are leading against the current, the challenge is not only to find your courage but also to *aggregate* the acts of courage you use to fuel the next steps of courage you take.

In the early 2000s, our organization experienced difficult dynamics that threatened the stability of our work. It was a very stressful time, and I enlisted the help of a few incredible consultants, including Norma Wong, who used a somatic focus in her work.

Norma, a Zen Roshi, taught me how to use my breath to engage more calmly and with greater clarity during heated discussions where, at times, people raised their voices at me or some of my staff in anger or frustration.

By working with her and the other consultants, I was able to connect to my courage and persevere through months of difficult conversations and challenging interactions until we found a way to get the organization successfully through these dynamics and on a more restorative path.

I was curious to see how this somatic methodology could strengthen our organization in the aftermath of the crisis. I wasn't sure how open the rest of my staff would be to experimenting with it on an ongoing basis. I overcame my initial hesitancy and invited Norma to join us for a day-long work retreat.

She worked with us to explore different ways we could move in formation together. For instance, she helped us understand that forming a line creates a different impact compared to arranging ourselves in a circle or moving in a V shape, similar to how some birds fly during long migratory routes.

Moving in a line facilitates progress from point A to point B much more effectively than being in a circle does. However, positioning ourselves in a circle, with everyone facing inward, greatly enhances communication within the group. The downside is that it limits our ability to observe what is happening outside the group. On the other hand, moving in a V formation allows different individuals to take the lead, depending on the needs of the situation. Rotating the lead position strategically can be very beneficial as the context and conditions of our work evolve over time. From there, we talked about how to translate these formations into different strategies for working together based on our desired outcome.

This work transformed my understanding of the importance of engaging our bodies, breathing, and movement in organizing. Moving together across the room, unified in our voice, breath, and actions, was thrilling and translated into our ability to work much more effectively long after the retreat ended. At the end of the day-long retreat, to my excitement, the staff asked for more. As our work with Norma continued to evolve in collaboration, we called this practice Forward Stance.

Seeing how well the staff initially took to this gave me the courage to incorporate it more deeply into our organization, including practicing it weekly before every staff meeting. We continued to use it, evolving it to suit the needs of a growing organization. It became one of our anchor methodologies for unifying our staff. It gave us a common language, a way of moving together across time and space, and helped us diagnose and solve problems proactively.

Integrating Forward Stance into the organization gave us the courage to introduce it in our work with other partner organizations out in the movement. During this time, the broader culture of the larger movement did not yet embrace these practices because, unlike today, these practices were not recognized as legitimate methodologies of social change work. Activists and leaders primarily interacted by sitting in chairs and engaging in discussion, often supplemented by a PowerPoint presentation or flipchart at the front of the room. I had never before observed activities such as focusing on breathing, moving around the room, or shouting together in unison in strategy meetings. I would later learn that Staci Haines and generative somatics were also breaking ground doing somatic work at this time.

I was nervous about the stigma we might face from others outside the organization as we introduced this methodology. This time, the stakes were higher as I felt that my reputation as a leader and our reputation as an organization were on the line. But I called upon my courage and took a leap of faith that if my staff and I found value in this work, so might my colleagues in the larger movement.

To my relief and some surprise, people enjoyed the experience. Of course, some took to it more than others. After the session, many leaders approached me to express how much they gained from participating in the movements together. I decided at that moment to incorporate Forward Stance practice whenever we gathered leaders. In 2007, we officially launched this effort by partnering with Norma to develop the Forward Stance Leadership Initiative, which engaged twenty-three organizations and sixty-two leaders.

As our movement-building initiative grew, interest among donors increased, and some of these donors were curious about our methodology.

At first, I was hesitant to talk about it for fear they might pull our funding. But I knew how to move through this fear by now. I became less nervous each time I talked about Forward Stance. Even though I didn't get a positive response every time, talking about it and claiming it as a significant part of our work increased my confidence.

Soon after that, I brought together a set of our core funders to experience the mind-body practice themselves for a two-day intensive. Once again, I was nervous about how they would react, but at that point, after doing this repeatedly with other leaders, I felt only about a quarter of the fear that I had when we were first starting to introduce Forward Stance. And then, when I saw these ordinarily buttoned-up folks moving together in different formations around the room, aligning their breath and motion while yelling "Aye!" at the top of their lungs together, I could see how far this work had come.

This experience taught me how to tap into and deepen my reservoir of courage. Each time I summoned my courage, I discovered I had a deeper reserve to draw from. Throughout this journey, I gained new insights into how to navigate challenges. Each time I overcame fear or insecurity, I increased my tolerance for discomfort and risk. Introducing Forward Stance to new audiences became easier as I confronted my fears of being judged. Witnessing participants benefit from our work together further strengthened my confidence.

Drawing Courage from Community

Often, we can access our courage more easily when we are connected to each other. I found this to be true for myself and other leaders during the Great Recession. At that time, many foundations had pulled back funding, which deeply impacted smaller social and reproductive justice organizations. We were concerned about our organization's ability to survive the downturn. I remember talking to one of our donors and asking for advice about weathering the economic storm. Her reply was to hunker down, to refrain from expanding our work, and to try to get through the next few years. This conversation scared me. It left me feeling trapped and small, and the conclusion didn't sit right with me. After talking with my staff, we decided to bring together a group of other leaders and discuss how to get through this economic crisis together. We came up with a plan to communicate with each other regularly so that we weren't isolated. Some of us devised contingency plans of creatively working together to reduce our overall collective expenses. We also shared our list of funding partners with each other and volunteered to make introductions for one another to help increase our collective access to potential resources.

Through this process, this group of organizations not only survived, but many of us grew our work. This growth attracted more funding. We made it through the recession because we were in close relationships with each other and because we continued to advance our work. If we were to have taken the advice of our well-meaning donor, I'm not sure if we would have survived the recession. What was asked for at that moment was the courage to lean into community and collaborative cooperation and face these daunting conditions together.

Your Turn

Start with an activity that helps you get into a state of readiness. You can use the one outlined at the beginning of the Your Turn section in chapter 1 or select one that works for you.

Noticing Moments of Courage

Here is an activity to help you recognize the acts of courage you embody on an ongoing basis as a leader:

   A. Close your eyes and give yourself a few minutes to identify a recent time you acted with courage. If you have a difficult time identifying a moment, keep in mind the definition of courage from the *Merriam-Webster Dictionary*—the mental or moral strength to venture, persevere, and withstand danger, fear, or difficulty—or look at the following image of everyday acts of courage to see if it sparks a moment for you.

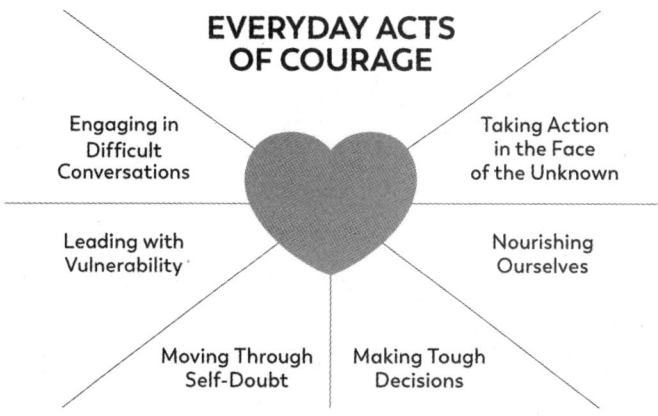

Eveline Shen, Diagram designs: Amy Wu, duende.us

B. Write down your memory, then answer the following questions:

- Before you acted with courage, what were your fears? What were you most concerned about? What was at stake?
- What helped you move through that moment? Were there any people or resources that supported your act of courage?
- What did you learn about yourself from this experience? About your ability to move with courage? Did anything surprising come up for you?
- What can you bring from that experience to help you with future acts of courage?

Spending time reflecting on moments of courage helps you become better at recognizing your own acts. By tracking your courageous moments, you can highlight the insights and growth you've gained from these experiences, empowering you to take even bolder steps of courage in the future. If we are unaware of our everyday acts of courage, we sell ourselves short. If our bravery, persistence, and ability to take a stand in the face of significant risks remains invisible, it makes it difficult to keep building those muscles. Increasing our awareness of courage enables us to embrace it fully and treat it as a resource that can continue to grow and fuel our social change.

Sharing Stories of Courage

Sometimes, courage is more challenging to see in ourselves than in others. I often pair up leaders to help them identify moments of courage. Try this activity with a partner or in a small group:

A. Give yourselves a few minutes to identify a recent moment when you used your courage to move through your fears or self-doubt. If you're having difficulty recalling a moment, refer to the graphic of everyday types of courage from the previous activity, which was created to help stimulate your memory.

B. Once you have your moments, pick someone to go first and tell their story. Each person will have three to five minutes to share. It's important to time this so each of you has equal time. As the listener, try to identify the different types of courage you hear from the storyteller. Often, you'll be able to recognize multiple acts of courage, some that even the storyteller might not be aware they are using. You may want to take notes so you remember what you noticed.

C. After each of you tells your story, the listener will share all of the types of courage they heard in that story.

D. After you both have told your stories and shared the types of courage your heard, answer the following questions together:

- What themes of courage came out in both stories?

- What strategies did you each use to move through any fears or self-doubt?
- What lessons can you learn about courage from hearing and telling your stories?

We often can overlook the courage we possess, but sharing our courageous moments with others encourages us to pause, reflect, and acknowledge our acts of bravery. By recalling these experiences, we can honor and celebrate our achievements as well as others around us. Additionally, listening to the stories of others can help us recognize the courage within ourselves that we might have missed or inspire us to take future acts of bravery.

Connecting with Your Courage

The following is a process that can help connect you with your courage:

A. Notice when you feel emotions like fear, hesitancy, shyness, self-doubt, or lack of confidence that prevent you from moving forward easily.

B. Acknowledge and welcome these feelings. Pushing them away or ignoring them can make them come back stronger.

C. Develop a curiosity about them: What are they protecting you from? What are they trying to tell you? Do they originally stem from someone else?

D. How is this moment calling for your courage? Given the circumstances, does it make sense that these feelings are coming up? Do you still want to move forward? If so, what kind of courage can you call forth to take the next step?

E. What will help bolster your courage? Are there things you can do or additional support you can seek to help you put your courage into action? Keep in mind that even if things don't unfold as expected, you can still learn and grow from the experience.

Connecting with your courage in this way gives you the space to notice it, even when it is hidden from you or when you aren't accessing it. Often, courage is right below the surface of our emotions of fear, self-doubt, or something similar. Accepting and welcoming these feelings allows you to explore them and creates space for you to step into your courage and enable it to grow.

3

FINDING THE RIGHT PURPOSE

I am who I am, doing what I came to do

—AUDRE LORDE

. . . which causes me to wonder, my own purpose on so many days as humble as the spider's, what is beautiful that I make? What is elegant? What feeds the world?

—LOUISE ERDRICH

Claiming Purpose as a Guide

I was managing a crew of five community organizers early in my career. For the first two years, we had stable funding, and I strove to build a team culture in which each member felt supported to do their best work and collaborate with a high degree of trust. However, in year three, the executive director informed me that I would have to cut $30,000 from our budget because of an unexpected budget gap. It was terrible timing since we were slated to move much work in the next six months. Additionally, each of the team members was making a positive contribution.

She asked me to think strategically about how to do this so our work would be least compromised. I asked other managers for guidance, and they suggested that the most effective option would be to lay off one of the part-time team members since their salary roughly equaled the amount we were short. Another manager suggested I make my selection based on who had the least seniority to make things "fair." This was the first time I had to make staffing cuts, and I found it personally painful and potentially dehumanizing to everyone concerned.

My heart was heavy knowing the impact this decision would make, not only on one of my team members but also on us. In a challenging job market, it would be difficult for them to land another position quickly, especially one with health insurance. We would also be left struggling to fill the void from the absence of one of our team member's unique strengths, experiences, and capacities. In addition, losing a team member would decrease the group's morale and potentially negatively impact our collective efforts.

Sometimes, there is no choice but to lay someone off, but I didn't want to settle for that. I wanted to see if a better possibility would work for us. One of my purposes as a manager was to cultivate an environment where each member felt supported and invested in each other's success. So, I searched for another solution. I proposed to the team that we share the amount to cut across each of our salaries. If we shared the burden across the team, with those of us making higher salaries taking a more significant cut, everyone could keep their jobs. I was unsure what their response would be to this idea of shared sacrifice. I didn't know if having a decrease in pay would be too much for any of them to make ends meet. But this decision aligned best with my purpose as a manager.

I would only move forward if everyone agreed to this. I spoke to each of my team individually. I wanted them to give me an honest answer without worrying about how others might judge them. It turned out that each of them accepted the proposal without hesitancy and with gratitude that we would all be able to keep our jobs and that the team would remain intact. Even though our salaries were lower than the previous year, the team's spirit rose, and trust deepened as we carried out the work together.

Many of us know how to set and reach our goals at work. Goals are concrete, usually with measurable outcomes. Setting goals is different from identifying your purpose. Purpose includes your deepest intentions, what drives you as a leader, and your core values. It is the answer to the question of why you lead. As social change leaders, we can use purpose as our guide through challenging waters that threaten to take us off course. But there are many ways to identify our purpose. Arriving at the proper purpose starts with avoiding purpose pitfalls.

Purpose Pitfalls

Our work lives are often hectic, with much more on our plates than we can manage. We frequently move quickly and are under many demands, easily resulting in us falling into a purpose pitfall. The following are four purpose pitfalls to avoid.

Pitfall 1:
Jumping to Action Before Identifying Purpose

I once took a call from a highly regarded national leader who was notoriously hard to reach. A little starstruck, I was excited that she had sought me out and was ready to help her however I could. Our conversation focused on her asking me to invite other leaders in our national network to a conference she was organizing. I hung up feeling good about being able to support her. However, over the next week, I realized I had a request for her too. The policy director on my team had told me a few weeks ago that she was hoping to get this leader to support our campaign but needed help to get through to her. If I had taken the time to identify *my* purpose in talking with her, even briefly, before our call, I would have remembered this request and not have missed this opportunity to engage her.

Unfortunately, during our work week, we often encounter situations in which we are disconnected from our purpose. How often have we hosted or been invited to meetings that don't have clear outcomes or aren't facilitated productively? How often have we spent too much of our day focused on administrative or personnel issues and not enough time on the critical strategic questions our organization grapples with? This happens when we spring to action before we are clear about our purpose.

Pitfall 2:
Choosing a Purpose That Moves Us In the Wrong Direction

Focusing solely on short-term wins without considering long-term consequences may lead us away from where we ultimately want to go. Put another way, short-sighted strategies may yield immediate benefits but can result in us taking a path that doesn't serve our greater purpose.

For example, a colleague of mine joined a coalition with others working on a local ordinance to protect all immigrant workers from discrimination. The city council was willing to pass the ordinance only if undocumented workers were excluded from the policy because it was an election year and some of the council members worried that they would lose votes if they were seen supporting undocumented immigrants. It was the end of a long campaign; everyone was tired. Many activists could see that passing the policy was within reach. After a heated debate, the majority of the coalition decided to remove undocumented immigrant workers from the policy, and it ended up passing unanimously.

There was a big celebration at the end. But the victory felt hollow to some, including my colleague. Even though this could be considered a short-term win, the decision to leave undocumented communities out resulted not only in significant divisions within the coalition but also perpetuated one of the most vulnerable communities having no work protections. When we focus on achieving a purpose in a way that aligns differently from our core values, we often end up undermining our success over the long term by replicating the oppression we are seeking to change.

How often have you been a part of a big win, whether a campaign, a completed project, or an event that ends up causing collateral damage along the way? Maybe you observed staff suffering from burnout due to excessive overtime work or colleagues turning away from each other in anger because everyone was so focused on the immediate win that they didn't think about the long-term consequences of overworking staff or tending to relationships along the way. We can be so focused on achieving these short-term wins that we can undermine our longer-term success.

Pitfall 3:
Choosing a Purpose That Is
Urgent but Not Important

As a leader, I have been drawn into urgent situations without connecting them to my purpose. One time, the staff and I were preparing for a big meeting with over seventy people from around the country. Anyone who has done event planning knows that troubles can erupt as significant events like this approach. The day before, I was preparing my opening remarks when one of my staff members rushed into my office to let me know that the printer had stopped working, which had halted the production of participant materials. She also told me that the caterer had accidentally put our meeting down for the following week and was not prepared to bring food the next day. I immediately started problem-solving. Hours later, we located a printer in one of our partner organizations in the same building and found another caterer to step in. However, by then, it was near the end of the day, and I had not made any progress on my opening remarks. I frantically worked late into the night, which meant that I was sleep-deprived the following day. I came to the session nervous and depleted; the result was that my opening remarks fell flat. Looking back at that situation,

I now see that the more prudent action would have been for me to assign one of my senior staff members to do the troubleshooting so that I could successfully focus on my purpose of setting an inspirational tone for the participants and the rest of the day.

Urgent problems can seem so demanding that sometimes it's even hard to take a breath and make a conscious strategic decision before responding. Our never-ending to-do lists hound us through our waking hours, demanding immediate attention. At one point in my career, I habitually walked into the office in the morning, sat down, and immediately answered emails. I aimed to get through the fifty-plus emails waiting for me so the senders would see I responded promptly. I have since realized that there are better uses of my time. Research has shown that most of us are at our best in the morning because our minds and bodies are fresh and ready. And many emails can wait until later in the day. We will get more bang for our buck if we use our morning mental and physical capacities to focus on matters requiring depth or expansiveness of thought and effort rather than to answer every email that comes in overnight. My mornings are now reserved for significant meetings, strategic work, and writing so that I can leverage my best thinking. Although I spend a few minutes scanning my emails at some point in the morning to see if I must answer any important and urgent ones, I reply to the bulk of my emails later in the day.

Pitfall 4:
Choosing a Purpose That Is Not Bold Enough

I once worked with Jimmy, a young Latinx leader who was heading up a statewide coalition to pass a comprehensive sex education bill in their state. The coalition members had been securing a legislator to sponsor their bill. Over the last year and a half, they had already met with several who had turned them down.

One day, a call came through from the staff of a state senator. The staff member told Jimmy that the senator would like to serve as the bill's sponsor. Jimmy and his team were excited about the partnership and immediately accepted the senator's invitation. At one point, they discussed possibly adding a funding provision for the implementation. Still, the senator was afraid that if they did so, she wouldn't get enough support from other legislators who might prioritize the need for fiscal tightening, and thus defeat the bill.

The bill went back and forth from committee to committee, and each time it made it to the next phase, Jimmy and his team breathed a sigh of relief. In addition, they brought two busloads of parents and students to the state capital, who spoke passionately about the need for the curriculum in schools. After weeks of debate, the bill arrived at the governor's desk and was signed!

Unfortunately, because the bill lacked implementation funding, the curricula was put on hold, and none of it reached any schools. Looking back, Jimmy and his team realized that they should have pushed the senator to include a funding provision. If they had done so, they would have included a robust strategy for engaging one-on-one with other legislators to persuade them to support the bill. Even if they had ultimately lost, Jimmy and his team would have been in a better position than they were after the bill passed, as they would have built many more relationships with legislators. This would have set the necessary groundwork for more successfully passing future legislation with funding for implementation.

Now, let's turn our attention to purposeful leadership mindsets.

Developing a Purposeful Leadership Mindset

Developing a purposeful leadership mindset can help you avoid purpose pitfalls and stay connected to purpose at every turn on your journey. We cannot afford to settle for purposes that prevent us from offering our greatest gifts.

I used to reserve thinking deeply about purpose for significant challenges or major crossroads in my life. Now, I have adopted a mindset where I view any moment as an opportunity to connect to purpose as a leader.

When you adopt a purposeful leadership mindset, you always have an internal GPS handy. This GPS can help you identify which level of purpose you want to focus on for whatever situation you are facing.

Finding Purpose at Multiple Levels

Imagine seeing the landscape of time in your life unfolding from this current moment. As we move through our lives, it helps to answer the question, "What is the purpose of my leadership?" on several levels: the *far-term time horizon* where you focus on a more extended time period of your life; the *near-term time horizon* where you focus on the current moment; and the *mid-term time horizon* where you focus on a time period somewhere in between. Working at a far-term-horizon level, you can identify your long-range purpose. For example, you might choose to focus on the upcoming two decades or the rest of your life. If you are working at a mid-term-horizon level, you can center your purpose for the upcoming few years. Meanwhile, if you are working with your near-term perspective, you can identify the purpose for the conversation you plan to have in the next hour. Developing a purposeful mindset helps us navigate these time horizons more easily, allowing us to make adjustments as we align our purpose at various levels. Ideally, our near-and mid-term purposes should support us in achieving our long-term ones.

Far-Term Time Horizon

When I left my job as an executive director after twenty-two years, it was the first time since high school that I didn't have another job lined up. Departing executive directors commonly choose three options: 1) Become the leader of another organization, 2) become an independent consultant to help organizations, or 3) take a position within philanthropy. I was not interested in any of these when it was my turn to leave. In addition, I knew

Eveline Shen, Diagram designs: Amy Wu, duende.us

I had accumulated a number of skills over the last two decades and could apply them in many different situations and contexts. But I also knew I needed to pick a focus, and I wanted to pick something aligned with my values, strengths, and passions. So, I asked myself the following questions:

- What would bring me joy as a leader for the upcoming decades?
- What did I want my leadership legacy to be when I retired?
- In the time I have left to give, where could I make the most significant impact using my talents and strengths?

The answers to my questions led me to a clear purpose for the next twenty years: I wanted to support BIPOC leaders to step into their power as they navigate complex challenges and confront an oppressive terrain. My purpose was threefold: First, I planned to foster a movement culture that welcomed and supported leaders from all walks of life and that offered an expansive and diverse set of experiences and skills; second, I planned to create spaces in which leaders could come together, be in community with one another, and support each other to step more fully into their power; and finally, I planned to coach leaders hungry for deeper transformation.

These aims will guide me for the decades to come. To this day, I am grateful for the clarity I found at this far-term time horizon because it showed me a path where there was none before.

Mid-Term Horizon

After I gained clarity about my longer-term purpose, I knew I could easily create a work plan for the mid-term time horizon in all three areas. From there, I could lay out my strategies for the next two to three years. I decided to create a set of resources, including this book, which would influence our movement to embrace a greater diversity of leaders and a greater range of support for leaders who are not straight white men. I was also excited to deepen my curriculum on each component and develop new trainings on the Courageous Operating System, which I went on to implement with new sets of leaders across the country. And finally, I focused 30 percent of my work on coaching to work with leaders on a deeper individual level.

Here is another example of how I used mid-term-horizon purpose setting in a different context. Early in my tenure as an executive director, one of my staff came to me for advice about two people she was supervising who were in conflict. Initially, I was going to focus on a near-term purpose—one that would get her individualized support immediately. My first thought was to suggest that she consider a conflict-resolution workshop or find some good books on conflict resolution. I planned to brainstorm with her on many ways to address the conflict. She could pick the strategy that most aligned with her.

Before I jumped into this discussion, though, I took a step back and tried to broaden my view to include the rest of the organization. In my experience, when one team member has a specific need, they are often not the only one. I was curious to see if addressing conflict was something that other people on my staff would be interested in. I polled staff directors who provided supervision and found many of them were also struggling with helping their team members deal with conflict. Armed with this new information, I decided to pick a purpose at the mid-term horizon and focus on bringing conflict-resolution support to both this particular staff member and to the rest of the team. This purpose allowed me to have an impact on building the team's capacity, and it also increased staff investment and commitment to a culture that directly resolved conflict.

Near-Term Time Horizon

In addition to identifying our purpose in longer-range planning, working with purpose in the current moment is beneficial. Being aware of our ground-level purpose helps us figure out how to navigate through our day-to-day activities and align our decisions and actions with our mid- and far-horizon goals. For example, setting my far- and mid-horizon purposes for my career change guided my daily decisions regarding how I spent my time. I was clear that leadership was the lane I would stay in. So, when people came to me with requests for strategic planning or network building, I could immediately decline the invitation and refer them to other people who specialize in these strategies. This made my life much easier, eliminating time I would have otherwise spent trying to make a decision.

I have since helped other leaders connect to their near-term purpose. I was coaching a leader in philanthropy who was feeling distressed about a weekly staff meeting she had to attend right after our session. She was preparing to leave for vacation at the end of the week and felt like she needed every second to accomplish all of her tasks. The staff meetings, coordinated by the CEO, were not run as efficiently as she would have liked, and she wished she could spend that hour and a half in other, more productive ways. When I asked her to tell me about her purpose in those meetings, she stopped and looked at me. Even though we frequently talked about her purpose and role as a leader, she rarely attended those staff meetings with a purpose in mind. However, given the invitation to think about it, she realized that she could use this meeting to do several things connected to her mid-term-horizon-level purpose.

She was worried about one of her staff members whose father had been in the hospital for the past week. Although she had spoken to that staff member over the phone, this staff meeting would allow her to talk with him in person and see if he needed additional support. In addition, she had originally planned to email a couple of colleagues to review the questions she had for a grant partner, but she realized that she could address those questions at the end of the staff meeting instead. This would enable a real-time discussion, saving her time and helping her build stronger relationships with her colleagues.

By spending a few minutes focusing on her purpose for the upcoming staff meeting, she recognized that she could complete several items on her to-do list ahead of schedule. She entered the meeting feeling much less frustrated.

Reflecting about her purpose for that particular staff meeting inspired her to think of ways she and her team could use those meetings more effectively. After returning from vacation, she gathered her team to brainstorm how they could leverage these meetings to advance their work. Together, they developed a list of strategies, which included requesting time on the staff meeting agenda to provide updates and receive feedback on ongoing projects, and seeking support and buy-in for new initiatives. Over time, the culture of these meetings evolved from passive participation to a more proactive and purpose-driven engagement.

Including Yourself in the Purpose Picture

We can focus our efforts when choosing purpose in many ways. For example, we can look to the needs of those surrounding us and use our purpose to address them. We can listen to stakeholders' demands and use our purpose to assuage them. Too often, we leave ourselves out of the purpose picture. In my own work and in my support of others, I have found it critical for leaders to include themselves when deciding on significant purposes. When we put ourselves in the purpose picture, we can:

1. Connect to the values that are most important to us at that particular moment to ensure that our actions align with our beliefs.

2. Integrate our passions into our work.

3. Link it to our vision for the future.

4. Identify and leverage our particular strengths.

By centering ourselves in purpose in this way, we can unlock our ability to lead with authenticity and power, as the following examples show.

Including My Strengths and Passions in Purpose

When the opportunity arose to become an executive director, I initially hesitated because I knew it would take me further away from the day-to-day programmatic work I loved. After taking the position, I remember sitting in my office trying to figure out my primary focus in this new role. I made a chart of the leadership gaps that needed to be filled in the organization: fundraising, budgeting, personnel issues, and administrative work. I decided to make the purpose of my work plan in the first year to fill some of those gaps.

Despite my best efforts, I grew unhappy and unsatisfied because the work wasn't feeding my passion. I wasn't focusing on my strengths, which were the more people-centered and programmatic parts of the job. My staff weren't responding well to what I was doing. I was becoming resentful of being an executive director and of my leadership role. I was not succeeding in my leadership because my greater purpose was not connected to my vision, strengths, or passions. Instead, I let the needs within the organization determine my purpose.

I faced great challenges as I was learning and growing into the position. However, after gaining my footing, I spent increasingly more time focusing on my purpose differently. I thought about where I wanted to take the organization and the larger impact I wanted to make, based on the organization's mission and capacity. As I gained clarity about my larger purpose and the impact I wanted our organization to make, I was more able to reignite the passion that I had before I became an ED. I wanted to shift the organization's focus from primarily research and health to utilizing organizing and leadership development strategies to help young Asian women gain the resources they needed to thrive. I aimed to change statewide policies that affected our communities and collaborate with other organizations to amplify our impact and voice for Asian American women and girls. I felt a strong connection to a mission that truly mattered to me. Centering my larger purpose reminded me that administrative and fundraising tasks are simply strategies to help achieve my bold vision of making change and building a strong and vibrant organization. When I spoke to funders about this vision, they were so inspired that they began giving us grants to support our work. With this funding, I was able to hire additional staff to alleviate some of the financial and administrative responsibilities from my workload, allowing me to focus on the things I loved.

From my experiences and from working with others, I have seen the value of identifying a leadership purpose that connects directly to our passion and strengths. There is no one way to be a strong leader, and our collective efforts benefit from each of us being able to tap into the unique set of contributions, interests, experiences, and wisdom that we bring. Our social change ecosystem increases its power if we can be our best selves and do our best work by putting our unique footprint on the job.

Angie Addresses Overlooked Urban Indigenous Communities by Including Her Values and Lived Experiences in Purpose

I met Angie DeLille when she enrolled in one of my leadership trainings. I was immediately struck by how purposeful and driven she was to make changes for Indigenous communities across the state. Angie is Ojibwe from Lake Manitoba First Nation and is the Director of the Office of Indian Policy for the State Department of Human Services in Minnesota. She has also served on the State of Minnesota Board of Social Work since 2008 and is, along with her partner, the proud parent of eight children. She is a life-long marathon runner and has completed her twenty-third race as of the writing of this book. Simply put, Angie is a trailblazing and formidable leader.

Angie was born in Winnipeg, Canada, during the Sixties Scoop when social services were routinely kidnapping Indigenous children from their families and placing them up for adoption into non-Native homes in that country and the United States. When Angie was less than a year old, she, her older sister, Julia, and older brother, Michael, were stolen from their family. Her aunts and uncles would later tell her that it was like they had just vanished one day.

She and her brother and sister were separated and put in foster care in Canada until she was four. Her experience with her foster family was horrific. It wasn't until she received childcare training for one of her summer jobs in high school that she realized how bad it was. She learned that parents were not supposed to punish toddlers by withholding food and that they weren't supposed to yell at little kids and blame them for having accidents. She discovered that parents were expected to hold their babies and give them lots of hugs and that it wasn't normal to be locked in your crib at night.

Fortunately, the people who adopted Angie, Michael, and Julia were nothing like her foster parents and provided a wonderful, loving home. They helped Angie track down their birth family and reunite them. From then on, Angie and her siblings had two families into which they were fully integrated, and they would go back and forth between their birth family and adopted family seamlessly.

Growing up, Angie experienced what it meant to be Native in urban communities and the devastating impacts of colonialism. At school, there were a small number of Indigenous students, but they connected frequently, not feeling accepted within the educational system or among the white kids. They didn't have as much access to their cultural traditions as their peers who lived in tribal communities. Life was challenging, and she witnessed friends and family who were incarcerated and struggled with addiction, some dying from overdose. All of her siblings have been unhoused at some point in their lives. She attributes this to the lack of services and infrastructure for urban Native young people.

Angie got her social work degree to provide clinical mental health services to her community at a local clinic. There, she learned the power of combining traditional Native healing practices with Western clinical work. For example, when some of her clients, who were dealing with addiction, did not respond to therapy, she would send them to traditional healers who led naming ceremonies. There, these clients could connect to their native language and ancestors and receive critical information about themselves. She saw clients completely change their trajectories from this experience. They came back with a much stronger sense of self and belonging and of being known. From there, they were able to continue successfully with Western therapy.

Angie brought these experiences with her when she became the American Indian mental health coordinator at the Behavioral Health Division of the Minnesota Department of Human Services. In 2018, she drew upon these experiences to provide critical leadership in passing state-level legislation for the first-ever funding of Indigenous mental health healing practices. Angie worked with American Indian Mental Health Advisory Council members (consisting of leaders from tribal and urban American Indian mental health programs) to testify to state legislators at various hearings. She also met with diverse community and mental health stakeholders to garner support for the policy. As a result, the policy passed with no opposition and resulted in $2 million in annual grants for the next five years. Governor Tim Walz was so impressed with the results that he extended this funding indefinitely.

Her department recognized Angie's leadership, and she was offered several promotions. She is now the second-highest Indigenous staff member at the State Department of Human Services. She continues to bring her values and lived experience to inform her leadership purpose. Early in her tenure as the director, she attended a meeting hosted by Governor Walz's office, which included Native urban leaders and state commissioners. These leaders were frustrated because they were consistently not getting chosen for funding opportunities to support the services they provided, which included healthcare and substance abuse services for unhoused urban Indigenous communities in Minnesota.

Angie left the meeting ill at ease and curious about the amount of funding that the state agency was providing for urban Indians. She worked with the directors who oversaw contracts and asked them for the number of resources allocated to this population. The contract director returned to Angie and showed her the extraordinarily low number. It was so low that it wouldn't even provide a dent in addressing the increasingly wide health disparities of urban Native communities, compared to non-Indigenous urban communities. When Angie saw the number, she burst into tears of grief. Grief for the friends and family members who had suffered and died because they didn't have access to the services they needed. Grief for realizing that her community in urban areas was invisible, even to the department that was supposed to look out for them. As the incoming director in that department, Angie felt accountable for correcting this issue of chronic underfunding for her community.

Angie was determined to find resources for urban Indians in Minnesota. At the time of this writing, she is working with her grants department to expand their requests-for-proposal (RFP) process and make it easier for urban partners to receive funding. She also searches for other ways the department and the federal government can provide additional resources. She is working to educate the entire agency about the differences in need between urban and tribal communities. She helps officials across the state understand how magnified the isolation is for Indians who are living in cities and falling through the cracks. By putting herself at the center of her leadership purpose, Angie is making significant contributions to ensure that the State Department of Health Services no longer neglects a critical community in Minnesota and that it can get much-needed services and resources.

Hillary Shuts Down ICE by Focusing Her Leadership Growth and Family in Purpose

Hillary Brooks is a queer mixed-race African-American Ashkenazi Jew who currently works as the controller at Disability Rights Advocates. She is the only parent of her daughter Willa and one of the fiercest mama bears I know. Hillary and I know each other from working together when she was our organization's finance director. After leaving our organization and becoming an associate director, Hillary enrolled in Stepping Into Power. One of the things I appreciate about Hillary is that she brings a social justice outlook to every role she takes on.

Throughout her activist career, Hillary has preferred to provide her leadership internally by focusing on overseeing the financial systems and operational infrastructure of organizations. However, after experiencing the massive attacks on immigrants initiated by the Trump administration after the 2016 elections, she felt compelled to grow beyond her comfort zone and be more visible as a leader.

She was especially upset by how the administration was targeting immigrants through incarceration and deportation. After the 2016 elections, protests erupted across the country. Hillary brought Willa to a couple of them, but they stopped going because Willa was having a hard time participating because of her extreme anxiety and sensitivity to sound. Large, raucous crowds and unfamiliar new situations were scary to her.

So, Hillary wanted to organize something that Willa could participate in. Hillary ran into her old friend Laura at Kehilla Community Synagogue, the temple to which they both belonged. They used to do clinic defense together in the 1990s, but now, in their mid-forties, they did not want to do more of this mode of activism in addition to the hours-long protests. They decided to talk with Reverend Deborah Lee, executive director of the Interfaith Movement for Human Integrity, who had been leading spiritual vigils every month at one of the county detention facilities in Richmond, California. Deborah encouraged them to join her effort to shut down the detention center as it had a big contract with Immigration and Customs Enforcement (ICE). The West County Detention Facility partnered with ICE to house an average of two hundred undocumented immigrants at a time under terrible conditions.

Together, Hillary and Laura decided to co-organize a monthly protest based out of Kehilla, calling it Let Our People Go at the West County Jail, demanding the release of these undocumented immigrants. Their purpose was to engage activists and their families in this effort to call attention to the injustice happening in this facility.

So, from 12 to 1 p.m., Let Our People Go was at the facility every second Sunday of the month. They engaged children by having an art table and invited activists to sing and do cultural activities with the kids. Hillary and Laura ensured that the event was accessible, setting it up in a place that didn't involve people needing to use stairs and ensuring that everyone who needed one had a chair. They also invited different organizations to read poetry, speak, and engage with the group about the importance of working on this issue. They always opened with a circle, inviting any family members of people held at the detention center to speak. Hillary and Laura used this as an opportunity to ask for donations for these families and to connect them to legal and other resources.

When they started, about twenty people came. But as the Trump administration escalated its attacks on immigrants with the so-called Muslim Ban and increased acts of separating undocumented parents from their children, protesting became a growing public interest, and more participants attended. In June of 2018, over a thousand people came to protest the treatment at the facility, which now included allegations of sexual misconduct and rape of two detainees by a veteran of the Sheriff's office who worked there. Almost a year later, over four thousand people came, bringing a lot of media attention. A few weeks after that, the facility shut down the detention center and did not renew its contract with ICE. The detention center was now one of hundreds across the country that were shut down by people protesting ICE.

Daroneshia Helps Black Trans Women in Alabama by Centering Her Courage and Vision in Purpose.

Daroneshia Duncan-Boyd is the founder and executive director of TAKE (Transgender Advocates Knowledgeable Empowering) Resource Center in Birmingham, Alabama. She is bold, visionary, and exuberant. I will never forget that after an intense group discussion on the impact of oppression at one of my leadership sessions, she proclaimed, "Whatever they do, they will never take the joy out of me."

Daroneshia was born and raised in Alabama. From a very early age, she describes herself as a nurturer. Taking care of her family and community is a core value that resides within her. This value drives her desire to dedicate her leadership to serving her community.

As an unapologetic Black trans woman, she has faced many challenges in her life, including sexual violence, workplace discrimination, and exclusion from church and community. After being denied housing services, she said to herself, "Life should not be this tough. How can I help Black trans women who are trapped in this system of discrimination and oppression?"

Daroneshia envisioned a different world, one where her community would have access to what they needed: safety, a job with a living wage, food, healthcare, and housing. Fueled by this vision of helping other Black trans women in her community, she convened a group in 2013 at her dining room table. What started as a bimonthly support group blossomed into community-building activities that spread to outreach at local parks and community centers.

One of her many strengths is raising money for efforts she believes in. Once she secured seed money for her vision from local donors, Daroneshia traveled from conference to conference and started networking with funders to raise even more money. Her strong negotiation skills helped her turn a $20,000 grant into $50,000.

Four and a half years later, Daroneshia's vision of a resource center found its home in a tiny 585 square foot office. When the opening of the center was announced in the media, there was a backlash of racist and transphobic sentiment from community members. However, Daroneshia, armed with great courage, persevered. She went on to run the TAKE resource center in Birmingham's East Lake neighborhood, offering a one-stop shop for Black trans women to receive therapy sessions, support in accessing health services including HIV and reproductive care, clothing for job interviews, medical bill assistance, free food, and a safe space. In addition, Daroneshia wanted to make sure that Black trans women didn't have to transition alone. TAKE connected participants to professionals to provide them with hormone replacement treatments while also helping them through the step of changing their name and identification to start their new lives.

Daroneshia raised enough money over the next few years to move TAKE into a larger location and eventually buy their own property, which is now close to 5,000 square feet. This is enough space to house their administrative office, a full kitchen, and the multitude of services they provide for participants from all over Alabama and neighboring states to access what they need for a better life. The programs and services TAKE offers continues to expand and now include peer support for transmasculine folx, emergency housing, voter engagement, and the Monica Roberts Freedom School for Black trans leadership.

But Daroneshia is not done yet. She wants to find funding to build affordable housing and a community center where TAKE can hold large gatherings to bolster and strengthen her community. Amidst all of this, Daroneshia still finds her joy. In November 2024, she was crowned Miss Renaissance Opulence, a pageant promoting community service by Atlanta-based Renaissance Kares. She continues to serve her community in incredible ways, while looking and feeling absolutely regal and fabulous.

Your Turn

Get into a State of Readiness

You can use the relaxation activity outlined at the beginning of the Your Turn section in chapter 1 or select one that works for you.

Identifying Purpose at Different Levels

Here are some questions you can ask yourself at each level (far-term time horizon, mid-term time horizon, and near-term time horizon) to identify your purpose.

First, identify which level(s) of purpose you want to work with. Look at the questions under the levels you choose and sit with the them for a while. Pick the ones to answer that you think will be the most fruitful for the situation you are facing.

FAR-TERM TIME HORIZON QUESTIONS

- What is my life's mission as a leader?
- What am I most excited about accomplishing as a leader in the next ten to twenty years?
- What do I want people to say about my leadership when I am gone?
- What brings me the most joy as a leader?
- What is the sweet spot where my strengths, passions, and values meet?

MID-TERM TIME HORIZON QUESTIONS

- What are the two to three things I am most excited to accomplish in the next few years?
- What role can I best play in supporting my team for the next year?
- What new learning or growth area will catapult my leadership to the next level?

- How can I use my wisdom, passion, and strengths to solve a problem that has emerged?
- How can I bring fun and meaning to my work right now?
- How can I take better care of myself physically, emotionally, and spiritually in the coming year?

NEAR-TERM TIME HORIZON QUESTIONS

- What do I want to get out of the phone call I will have this afternoon?
- What do I want to model for others at my next meeting?
- How can I embody my values as a leader in this moment?
- What are the difficult truths I need to tell the team member struggling in front of me?

If you were able to identify a purpose for all three levels, check to see how they are aligned with each other and if you need to make any adjustments.

Avoiding Purpose Pitfalls

Once you have your purpose, you can go through the purpose pitfall checklist to make sure that you are selecting a purpose that

- ✓ Brings you further towards the right destination
- ✓ Is important and meaningful, not just urgent
- ✓ Is aspirational enough
- ✓ Includes your vision, passion, and strengths
- ✓ Aligns with your values

Adopting a purpose-driven mindset has provided me with significant clarity regarding my short- and long-term goals, allowing me to make a greater impact with less effort. I encourage you to cultivate a practice of rigorously selecting your purposes, enabling you to more easily identify your North Stars and achieve the impact you desire, all while ensuring that your journey aligns with your values, strengths, and passions.

Putting Yourself in the Purpose Picture

Once you have your purpose at the level you have chosen, it's important to bring yourself into the process. You can do this at any level of purpose setting. The following are some questions you can use to help with this integration. This activity aims to determine whether your chosen purpose hits enough of your leadership sweet spots.

- How does this purpose connect to my mission as a leader?
- How passionate do I feel about this purpose?
- Will this purpose help me achieve something meaningful?
- How does this purpose resonate with my core values?
- How does this purpose leverage my strengths?
- How will this purpose help me grow as a leader?
- How will this purpose get me to where I want to go in the long term?

4

CULTIVATING SUCCESS

Never let the people who despise you define you.

—ANITA HILL

Around us, life bursts with miracles—a glass of water, a ray of sunshine, a leaf, a caterpillar, a flower, laughter, raindrops. If you live in aware-ness, it is easy to see miracles everywhere.

—THICH NHAT HANH

Success and Failures

Our society treats success and failure as a binary dynamic: You either win or lose the race; you pass or fail your test; you are victorious or defeated in a campaign. As leaders for social change, operating in this either-or perspective means that given our challenges, we will likely be on the losing side more often than not. But we can transform our understanding of success and failure by cultivating success on our own terms and by constructively working with failure. If we can do these two things, we will see that success and failure can provide pathways to achieving our purpose. The following two chapters focus on how to work generatively with success and failure.

The Multiple Dimensions of Success

When we embark on a significant endeavor, our primary goal is often to succeed. It's easy to view success as a linear process: moving from point A, our current situation, to point B, where we achieve our objective. However, reaching success is rarely that straightforward. We frequently operate in complex environments that interact and evolve over time. If we perceive success in such a simplistic manner, we risk overlooking opportunities to cultivate it in various ways.

Instead of viewing success as a linear path, let's imagine it as a vibrant garden. In this garden, I cannot focus solely on individual plants; I must nurture the entire ecosystem and consider a variety of factors. What types of plants and flowers grow well together? Which locations are best suited for them? What do the weather, light, and soil conditions allow? How will the garden withstand changing circumstances, such as a drought?

I also need to reflect on my role as the gardener. What capacity do I have to nurture this garden successfully? What kind of garden would bring me the most joy? Do I see it as part of a larger ecosystem that supports local bees and birds? What aspects would make this garden worth the ongoing time and effort it requires? By contemplating these questions, I can better understand the diverse facets of success for both my garden and myself.

Likewise, taking the time to examine the various dimensions of how we relate to and define success can enhance our leadership impact and contributions. This deep exploration helps us identify and cultivate a broader spectrum of success that aligns with our missions, integrates our individual and collective visions, and resonates with our core values. So, let's start by exploring the following dimensions of success:

- Being aware of how oppression shapes how we regard success.
- Cultivating success for ourselves as we lead against the current.
- Integrating our individual and collective vision for success.
- Aligning success with our core values.
- Celebrating success.

Dimension 1: The Impact of Oppression on Success

I have found it helpful to reflect on how oppression affects how I view and experience success. Throughout my career, I have been humbled and inspired by BIPOC leaders who continue to fight for justice for their communities while having to navigate discrimination and immense hardship from the oppression they face. I'm thinking about Indira, a queer Indigenous reproductive justice leader who advocates for her communities to have access to clean water without having any health insurance for herself; Mannie, a mixed-race nonbinary disability justice leader who tended to those in need during the pandemic but who couldn't afford to pay for the caregivers *she* needed; and Jazmine, a Black trans justice leader who has helped hundreds of trans women get off of the streets while also facing violence within her neighborhood and transphobia from cisgendered social justice activists. When we look at success, we must include our ability and daily efforts to navigate systemic oppression. Sometimes, just surviving the day is a story of success.

Oppression can shape our relationship to success by placing intense pressure on us to perform at higher levels than our counterparts who have much more societal privilege. I have a friend who works for a large advocacy organization with a $20 million budget. The organization is run by a white man, and they work on various civil rights issues. My friend coordinated a project focused on communities of color, doing similar work to our organization. One day, over lunch, we chatted about the upcoming grant proposals our organizations were submitting to the same foundation—one of the largest in our region. I had just come from a meeting with our program officer at the foundation, who told me how happy they were with our work. We were asking for a renewal of $150,000 for our organizational work. My friend's organization was requesting $300,000 for her project work.

Our nonprofit had been receiving funding from this foundation for a few years, and we were gearing up to submit a lengthy proposal describing in detail the seven to ten activities we would implement for the year with their funding. When I asked my friend how her organization was preparing for their proposal, she told me that she had to submit only a few paragraphs, giving a general idea of what they would do with the money without specifying *any* particular activities. It was assumed that this foundation would give them $300,000 yearly because, in my friend's words, "They trust us."

I was shocked. The project she oversaw was smaller in scope than our proposed work, and yet she received twice as much money and had to submit much less paperwork. It would be a relief to know that we could rely on $300,000 of funding year after year without spending hours preparing a case for funding each year. I wondered what it would be like to secure the "trust" of this foundation so we could have flexibility in how we spent the resources based on the emerging needs of our communities and work, rather than having to project our deliverables in detail a year ahead of time.

That was a number of years ago. Since then, I had the fortunate experience of building relationships with many program officers and foundations who funded us for numerous years. Yet even with this track record, as a woman of color leading an organization of primarily women and gender expansive people of color, I felt the ongoing pressure to overachieve and continuously prove the worthiness of our work and efforts.

In the United States, women-of-color-, trans-, and nonbinary-led organizations receive far less funding than organizations led by white men or white women. One funder I spoke to estimated that less than 3 percent of all funding goes to organizations run by women of color, even less to those led by transgender leaders. Simply put, we are often asked to do more with far fewer resources—and we have to do more to justify receiving those resources. When foundations continue to see these large, established institutions, run primarily by white men or white women, as organizations they can trust, we remain in a system where we must fight to get in the door and, once there, continue to prove our ability, to make an impact. This sets up a culture for us as leaders to feel that we are never doing enough and must maintain a perpetual sprint to accomplish more while receiving only the scraps of what other institutions are getting.

THE SHRINKING IMPACTS OF INTERNALIZED OPPRESSION

Oppression works in insidious ways. It affects how we think about ourselves. Harmful and unfair messages we internalize from society or our communities diminish us and our effectiveness. Oppression can limit our vision of success and what we think is even possible. Because of this, so many of us experience imposter syndrome at some point in our leadership from messages telling us that we are not supposed to lead, that we are not good enough, or that we are not deserving of success. Even after decades of working proactively to combat such messages, I find they can still sneakily undermine how I think about success.

I recently spoke with Staci Haines, a highly regarded national author and leader on somatic practice and trauma. We discussed strategies for reaching more leaders in the field. She shared her recent accomplishment of leading a multiple-session online class which she had capped at five hundred participants and encouraged me to think about this as an option in my work. My first reaction was excitement for her and the participants she reached and for the positive impact this would have on the movement. Despite her encouragement, my following response was to dismiss the idea of doing something similar for myself. The notion of engaging that many people in a single session had never crossed my mind. Until then, I had primarily focused on smaller groups, which allowed me to go deeper with participants. The thought of reaching such a large audience was beyond my sense of what was possible for my leadership programs.

Fortunately, I had a chance to revisit this reaction. The following day, I spoke to another friend and colleague of mine, Michael Balaoing, a successful communications coach who has worked with thousands of people around the world. He and I have worked closely together on leadership trainings over the years. He also encouraged me to consider ways to expand my work and reach a larger audience. Still feeling the after effects of my conversation with Staci the previous day, I started to say no. However he pointed out the growing demand for experiential learning environments similar to those I create in my online training with forty participants. Our discussion helped me open the door to the possibility of scaling my work. Whether designing a training for that many people would be beneficial for my approach was still uncertain, but I realized that I had dismissed the possibility before even allowing myself to consider it. Those deeply ingrained messages I received growing up to stay small and invisible, which I integrated into my coping strategies for staying safe, were still influencing the possibilities I saw for myself.

Once I became aware of how internalized oppression was limiting my ability to think about success, I permitted myself to interrogate this as a possibility. I started asking myself these questions: How *do* I want to scale my work to meet the needs of more leaders? What are the benefits of doing a large online class and reaching more people and what are the tradeoffs? How would I work with people who have graduated from this large online class? Once I began grappling with these questions, I could think about what success could look like before any self-imposed boundaries limited my view.

If we can't envision something, it's often more challenging to even attempt it. Giving myself permission to consider a large-scale training as a possibility made me realize it could be an effective way to offer an introductory series. This approach would allow me to reach more people who are new to the Courageous Operating System and give them a glimpse of its potential benefits. Afterward, any participants interested in exploring further could join my more intimate programs, where we could collaborate more closely. This introductory series could also serve as a valuable part of my pipeline for reaching potential leaders eager to learn more about the system.

I began researching how to make this happen and am actively building my capacity to take this next step. This situation reinforces the idea that when I downplay my successes and fail to acknowledge them, it signals a need to examine how oppression is affecting me internally.

Dimension 2: Redefining Success for Ourselves

Even when addressing internalized oppression, we may encounter other barriers to embracing success. As leaders moving against the current, the term itself may be loaded for us. Once, when introducing the importance of thinking about success in a leadership session, I received some resistance from several participants. "We don't like that word, *success*," they said. "It is oppressive." I was initially stunned because I was conducting what I thought was a straightforward activity to help them identify concrete outcomes of success they wanted to achieve as they moved toward their purpose. As I listened to their objections, I realized that they were using a definition of success that included all the trappings of what our society deems as success: valuing a lifestyle based on the extraction of resources from low-income communities and the environment. To them, "success" meant that their communities would lose. No wonder they didn't want to claim this version of success.

I then asked them to discard society's definition of success and envision the kinds of success they would want for their communities. This led to a rich discussion that included images and values that they associated with success. Here is a partial list of what participants came up with:

- Clean drinking water and good air to breathe
- Affordable healthcare access for people with disabilities, including funding for caregivers
- Redistribution of wealth and power

- Reparations
- Affordable childcare and education
- Freedom from gun violence
- A living wage
- A path to citizenship for undocumented families

Our discussion, which integrated their values and mission as social change leaders, enabled participants to embrace success much more readily. That session taught me that if we don't take the time to acknowledge the ways in which society defines success in terms of amassing wealth and power, we let our opposition co-opt the term. Another challenge in identifying outcomes of success is when we rush to achieve our purpose without being clear about the kind of success we seek.

When introducing the need to deepen our understanding of success with leaders, I often conduct a group activity, asking participants to spread themselves evenly around the room. I tell them that the purpose of this activity is to walk across the room and touch the wall opposite them and from there, go and touch the remaining three walls within fifteen seconds. This is enough time for everyone to succeed regardless of their ability and mobility. I shout, "Ready, set, go!" and everyone rushes around the room, sometimes colliding with each other in their haste to reach the walls. So focused on their goal, they're oblivious to those around them, and the atmosphere becomes chaotic and loud.

Afterward, I ask them how they are feeling physically. Many are out of breath because they have moved so quickly and are more anxious than when they started. When I ask them to raise their hand if they achieved their purpose, everyone's hand goes up. I then ask how many people looked at each other's faces as they passed by to get to the walls. How connected did they feel to each other during this process? In the many times I have done this activity, only a few participants replied that they intentionally tried to make eye contact with people as they passed them by. The overwhelming majority are so focused on completing the task that they are only aware of themselves and regard the people around them as obstacles to avoid.

But now I give them another opportunity. I tell them that they will have the same challenge of touching the four walls with the same parameters in the next round. But this time, they must make some connection with the people they pass. To maintain some time pressure, I shortened their allotted time to twelve seconds. This time, when I say, "Ready, set, go!" there is a calmness in the room. While still moving at a relatively quick pace, people have slowed down considerably from the first try and are mainly moving silently. They decrease their speed so they can acknowledge each other as they pass, and the room has much more of a group sense of caring and regard. They can all complete the task even in a shorter amount of time. After they are done, when I ask them to share their feelings, most reply that they feel more grounded, connected, and seen. Many of them are smiling and say they feel happy.

Finally, I give them one last challenge, with the same purpose. But this time, I ask them to move together as a group. In other words, they are not to complete the task individually but they are to find a way to complete it as a group, with each member still touching the walls. They still have twelve seconds, but they can't talk to each other.

Groups successfully approached this in several ways. All of them start by taking a few moments to communicate nonverbally and experiment with different formations. Some groups form one line that winds around the room, while others divide into four lines and complete the exercise working in tandem. Some groups form teams that pass through each other as they move across the room. Regardless of their specific formation there is a sense of togetherness that was not present during the other previous attempts. I conduct this activity to demonstrate that even though the purpose of the activity was the same each time, the outcomes of success varied widely, depending on what they were prioritizing and paying attention to.

We can take many paths as we move toward our purpose. Thinking through what successful outcomes look like for us will help us act and make decisions that cultivate the success we desire.

This lesson can be applied to any endeavor we pursue. For example, a staff celebration event can be organized in many ways. If time is of the essence, we might select a very experienced team leader with a vision for the event who knows how to effectively and quickly delegate tasks. If, on the other hand, we want to use this as an opportunity for team building, we could bring together a group of people from various departments within the organization who don't usually have a chance to work together and task them with figuring out how to create and implement the event. Thinking about what success would look like beforehand gives us criteria to determine how we proceed toward our purpose.

Dimension 3: Integrating Our Individual and Collective Vision for Success

Taking the time to explore our individual and our team's collective vision of success enables us to create a much more comprehensive way to conceptualize it. I once worked with a reproductive justice mixed-race queer leader, Pam, who was anxious to start preparing for her end-of-year gala. She was daunted by the amount of money they were trying to raise, and she dreaded the amount of work she and her staff would put into it. When I asked her what success looked like, she immediately said, "Oh, that's simple—I need to get $100,000 in the door from this event."

"Is that your only measure of success?" I asked.

"Yes!" she replied.

I then asked her how she would feel if she could reach her fundraising goal, but the gala was not well attended. And how would she feel if the majority of the money was raised from corporate donors who were keeping the city from building low-income housing for the communities she served? And would it feel successful if they had neglected to invite key community members? She quickly got the picture that she had initially neglected to consider aspects that were a part of her vision of success.

Next, I invited Pam to close her eyes and envision the event surpassing her wildest expectations. I gave her some time to think about the following: Who was in the room? What were they doing? What was the energy like? Who was the spotlight on? When she opened her eyes, she was beaming with a huge smile. She pictured a room full of vibrant, kind, and loving people buzzing and excited about being together. Instead of having to do the thirty-minute keynote, which she was not looking forward to preparing for, she could cut her speaking time in half and use the rest of the time to have her staff speak about the victories they led over the past year. She was excited at this opportunity to thank the donors who made critical contributions and wanted to update them about how their funding had helped grow the work. I saw her sense of dread turn into excitement, and she started talking much more animatedly as she created a new list of potential successes for the event, which included:

- Building community and deepening connections between donors, staff, colleagues, and community leaders.
- Deepening stakeholder investment in the organization throughout the rest of the year.
- Creating an agenda that was festive and fun that highlighted the voices of staff and community victories.
- Focusing on significant donors who contributed to the community in positive ways.

After our meeting, Pam was so inspired by this process that she reached out to the board chair and the staff in charge of the event to elicit even more indicators of success that she may not have thought about. The staff spoke about the opportunity to use vendors and entertainment from within the communities they serve, along with honoring a key community elder and a young leader who played critical roles in one of their successful campaigns of the year. The development team expressed some trepidation about doing all the heavy lifting of inviting donors and hoped that other teams could pitch in. The board chair, who was leaving, wanted to use this event to introduce the new board chair to key donors. As the conversation progressed, the board and staff grew more excited about the event and its possibilities. From that discussion, we added another set of success measures:

- Using local caterers and musicians to provide food and entertainment from the community.
- Honoring and celebrating some of the key leaders from the community.
- Calling on board and staff to share the load of inviting donors.
- Introducing the new board chair to all of the organization's stakeholders at the event.

In a short period, Pam went from defining success in a very limited way—simply to raise $100,000—to thinking about success in a much more expansive way. Using a process that required her to think about success in terms of herself, her staff, and her board, she now had a much richer and broader definition of the word. In addition, she gained a collective understanding of what the key stakeholders wanted from this event and increased engagement and investment from her staff and board. Without this process, these opportunities would have likely remained untapped. And finally, this process gave Pam, her staff, and the board a chance to think about success beyond the event. They identified successful outcomes once the event was over, including closer relationships with donors, less burnout experienced by the development staff, public acknowledgment of the transition at the board-chair level, and Pam having time to prepare for the next big event. By giving herself some space and dedicated time to think about success, Pam's contracted thoughts about the event blossomed into a much richer vision.

Dimension 4: Aligning Success with Our Core Values

One of the most important reasons to reflect on success is to ensure that the process of achieving purpose aligns with our core values.

ALIGNING VALUES AND SUCCESS
CASE STUDY

In 2017, Forward Together worked with a coalition of organizations to help pass the Reproductive Health Equity Act (RHEA). RHEA helped Oregon become the first state to require insurance companies to cover the full spectrum of reproductive healthcare for any person, regardless of their gender identity, citizenship status, or type of insurance. Treatment covered by RHEA ensured that all Oregonians could access the full range of preventive reproductive health services, including family planning, hormone therapy, abortion, and postpartum care. In response to the passage of this bill, anti-abortion advocates struck back, and in 2018, Oregon faced Measure 106, which attempted to overturn RHEA. Forward Together was on the campaign's steering committee to defeat Measure 106. Team member Kalpana Krishnamurthy led our efforts, along with Michele Ruffin, the field director. Integrating our values into our work was a core tenant of what being a women-of-color-led organization meant for me and the senior leadership team. This campaign was no different.

Kalpana is a highly respected, seasoned reproductive and social justice leader with impressive victories under her belt. As the helm of our organizing effort, she made sure to lead with our organizational values, which deeply shaped how our campaign was run. Kalpana centered four values that informed the process of how we achieved victory and helped defeat Measure 106.

VALUE 1
Centering communities of color who have been historically left out of conversations on abortion

The conversation on abortion has been typically very polarizing, and the messages used by activists to protect abortion access often include content that does not speak to the experiences of communities of color or low-income communities. For example, my immigrant mother from China, who believed in access to abortion, didn't resonate with the pro-choice right-to-privacy rhetoric ("keep your laws off of my body"). Up until very recently, nonbinary and trans people were utterly shut out of the discourse that focused on "a *woman's* right to choose." Moreover, up until about fifteen years ago, the values and beliefs of voters of color on abortion were not even researched by campaigns that were solely focusing on white, middle-class women, leaving all other impacted groups out of the picture.

Forward Together's focus for this campaign was on reaching voters of color, and we wanted to do so by employing messengers who reflected the communities we were trying to reach. Kalpana and her staff saw the opportunity to hire canvassers from communities of color and LGBTQ+ communities and bring their voices and lived experiences into the campaign. For example, canvassers are typically asked to use a script or a set of talking points to speak to prospective voters. Most of the time, these scripts are developed by campaign staff and not the canvassers themselves. Kalpana believed the canvassers needed to be part of shaping the script so that they could feel connected to what they were saying.

She and her team invited the canvassers to articulate their connection to abortion through discussion and writing. By connecting to their own experiences and those of their siblings, partners, and aunties, they were able to talk about abortion from a place of empathy rather than with any sense of judgment. Kalpana and her team centered the lived experience of canvassers of color by regarding them as respected messengers and by enlisting them to shape the content of messages delivered to prospective voters in the campaign.

VALUE 2
Going for the short-term win while also setting our communities up for long-term success

At that time, Forward Together was building a base of support on key issues that impacted communities of color, including abortion, immigration, and LGBTQ+ justice. While we wanted to defeat Measure 106, we also wanted to use it to expand our support base over the long term. That meant we needed to build deeper relationships with prospective voters that would last over time and through other campaigns. In a typical campaign, canvassers knock on voters' doors, quickly assess where they stand on the issue, and leave. The usual goal is to connect with as many people as possible in a day by making these quick transactional contacts with prospective voters. However, this way of interacting is not conducive to building trust. Kalpana knew that we needed to do something different if we were going to focus not only on the short-term campaign but also on our vision of success in building long-term power in communities of color. So, under her and Michele's leadership,

Forward Together became one of the first organizations we knew of at the time to use a methodology of deep canvassing on the issue of abortion in a ballot measure campaign. Using this methodology, canvassers led with empathy, and their primary goal was to build a relationship with prospective voters by listening to their values and lived experiences and engaging them on issues. By having in-depth conversations with community members in which they felt listened to and cared about, we found that we were often able to help them connect their story to the issue of abortion access and find their reasons for voting no on Measure 106 as well as engage them in our future work.

VALUE 3
Supporting the organizing team

In a typical campaign, canvassers are treated like cogs in a machine, pushed to reach as many voters as possible regardless of the human cost. Kalpana and Michele worked diligently to support the leadership development of each member of the canvassing team who didn't have the required skills but was eager to learn on the job. They treated the canvassers as key players by supporting them through daily team meetings to ensure they had what they needed to do their job successfully, including reworking their scripts based on what was working and what wasn't. They brought Forward Together's culture of learning into the team by including opportunities to hear from seasoned leaders who could support their growth and ongoing feedback about what they were doing well and where they could improve. This deep investment in their growth enabled the canvass team members to increase their capacity and refine their skills.

VALUE 4
Ensure that the campaign operated with a set of shared values that benefitted all of the partners

Campaigns are usually run by an executive team comprising the leadership of each core organizational member. Typically, within these executive teams, organizations have to "pay to play," meaning that the organizations with the most significant amount of money to spend obtain the greatest decision-making power. This results in larger organizations, like the ACLU or Planned Parenthood, with many more resources controlling the campaign process. In comparison, the smaller organizations, which are usually more connected to the communities most impacted, are left out. To create a different set of values for the campaign to run, Kalpana called for a meeting with the head consultants and executive team to help define shared core values of the campaign that could help mitigate power imbalances among the coalition members. This did not mean that they didn't prioritize winning—a decisive win was seen as a core strategy to bolster necessary support for abortion in Oregon and was one of the campaign's core values. Two of the values they identified were that 1) each organization could choose the strategies they felt were the best ways to reach their communities, and 2) as a group, they would make space for discussions during the campaign when there was disagreement. Establishing these values enabled the executive committee to resolve conflicts when making hard decisions. For example, during a budgetary meeting in which some executive team members didn't want to do additional research on Latinx voters because it was too costly, the executive team made time for a deeper discussion. Returning to their agreement on shared values gave them clarity that they needed to spend the additional money on researching Latinx voters so they could have effective, persuadable messages to reach this community. Along with these messages, our team also found leaders from the national and local farmworker's movement like Dolores Huerta and local Latinx leaders like Ramon Ramirez and Reyna Lopez to show broad support for abortion within the Latinx community and help to get out the Latinx vote.

The campaign won with 65 percent of voters handily defeating Measure 106. However, because Kalpana and her team integrated these core values into their work, there were many great successes beyond the campaign victory. Post-election polls revealed that Latinx voters were more supportive of abortion than we had anticipated, and the prospective voters we approached through our deep canvassing were more likely to turn out to vote on election day than voters from the same communities with whom we didn't talk. Forward Together now had new members to work with in future campaigns, not only on abortion but on other issues impacting communities of color. In addition, we were able to develop, value, and support a set of dedicated staff and grassroots community leaders.

Dimension 5: Celebrating Our Success

As leaders moving against the current, we rarely receive ample recognition for our actions. Part of the reason is that for many of us, recognition is not why we do this work. However, even when we accomplish our goals and achieve what we have planned and strategized on for months or years, how often do we acknowledge the successes even to ourselves? And when we reach our purpose, regardless of how big or meaningful, how many of us move right on to the next "thing" on our list without skipping a beat? How often are we asked to talk about our successes?

In my group leadership sessions, I ask people to identify a recent accomplishment they are particularly proud of. I ask them to reflect on what it took to achieve their success, what impacts resulted from their success, and what this success says about their leadership. I then divide the group into pairs, where each partner has a chance to share their story of success. Often, for over half of the participants, this is the first time they have ever talked about this moment. Many people in the group have never spent time reflecting on their accomplishments. And very few participants systematically build in time to acknowledge and celebrate the success they experience.

After the activity, participants often discuss the power of sharing their success. Reflecting on their stories helps them recognize the vision, skills, and fortitude they possess. They frequently remark on the courage it takes to achieve their purposes successfully. Group members report that sharing their story with another leader helped them claim their success in deeper ways. And participants are excited to celebrate their partner's success story with them. They are inspired by what their partner shared. Leaders relay that hearing their partner's story not only brings forth a deeper understanding of the challenges they face but also instills increased self-compassion for what they have overcome.

Our success will likely not be written about in newspapers or history books. We, ourselves, have been conditioned through patriarchy and white supremacy to dismiss our accomplishments too. We need to find ways to acknowledge success along the way. Celebrating on your own and with your team and stakeholders is a powerful way to internalize your individual and collective achievements and accomplishments, which helps nurture your confidence and courage as you move toward your next purpose. Success should not be defined by those in power. We are doing vital work critical to the future of our families, our communities, and this planet. Honoring our accomplishments is nourishing and necessary for our ability to continue forward. Recognizing and celebrating our success is critical to our leadership because doing so fuels current and future endeavors.

Your Turn

Get into a State of Readiness

You can use the relaxation activity outlined at the beginning of the Your Turn section in chapter 1 or select one that works for you.

Defining Success For Your Leadership

A. Close your eyes and imagine it's twenty-five years from now and you have left a successful legacy as a leader. Ask yourself the following:

- What were some of the most meaningful contributions I made?
- What qualities do people associate with my leadership?
- How did I successfully deal with adversity?
- Who was with me along the way, and who is with me now?
- How did I celebrate, and what am I doing now to honor my legacy?

B. From your reflections, is there anything you want to integrate into your leadership journey now so you can move toward achieving the success you desire twenty-five years from now?

C. Is there any metric of success that you are currently holding onto that you can release because it doesn't align with your vision and values?

Cultivating Success In Your Work

Identify an upcoming project, situation, or focus within your work. Identify a purpose for this effort. Looking at your purpose, answer the following questions:

- What is your vision of success as you achieve your purpose?
- What does success look like in the short and long term?
- How would key stakeholders define success for this purpose?

- What core values do you want to keep in mind as you achieve your purpose?
- How do these values shape how you view success in terms of outcomes and processes?
- What does success look like in terms of your leadership as you achieve your purpose? What skills do you want to master? How do you want to show up?

The answers to these questions will help you determine which strategic pathways are best for achieving your purpose.

Celebrate!

You can celebrate success in many ways. The most important thing is that you do it!

Here are some of the ways you can make time to recognize success when it happens:

- Take time to reflect and honor what it took to achieve success. Do this by yourself and with your team and stakeholders. What did you appreciate most? What did they learn? Where did they shine? What are you most proud about? What challenges did they overcome? What can these successes bring as you all move forward?
- Do something fun and creative to honor the victory. Hold a party; put together a timeline that shows each step of the journey to success; enjoy a meal together and have each team member share what they most value from the journey.
- Take time off to rest in recognition of the effort it took to succeed.

5

TRANSFORMING FAILURE

Though we tremble before uncertain futures, may we meet illness, death, and adversity with strength, may we dance in the face of our fears.

—GLORIA ANZALDÚA

Failure is a greater teacher than success.

—CLARISSA PINKOLA ESTÉS

Embracing Failure as Part of the Landscape of Leadership

Failure is a loaded word in our society, steeped in stigma. If we come from marginalized communities, failure can be seen and felt as an indictment of our leadership and who we are as people. Internalizing the stigma of failure created a potent drive within me to avoid it at all costs.

In my twenties and thirties, I pushed myself to succeed because I always felt I was not good enough. When I did fail, I saw it as a reflection of who

I was as a person. If I dropped the ball, I was incompetent. If I missed a deadline, I was irresponsible. If I didn't accomplish my goals, I was a disappointment. Internalizing these messages about failure kept me from dreaming bigger, from attempting to be bolder, and from getting up more quickly after I got knocked down. It took me a while to understand that the mere *anticipation* of failure negatively affected me, even in the most benign circumstances.

A friend of mine who is a personal trainer once challenged me to do as many pushups as I could. I immediately responded, "My record is thirty, so I will go to thirty-one." "No," he replied. "Please continue doing pushups until you can't do them anymore. That way, you will see what your body is capable of. When you train to failure, your body gets stronger."

While I understood this concept intellectually, I struggled with it. For me, going to failure meant that I would experience not being physically able to complete a pushup at some point, and in that moment of failing to straighten my arms, I would feel weak and demoralized. I wanted to have a goal that was a stretch for me but one that I could reach. I tried negotiating again, this time with a higher number. This time, I said I would do thirty-five. My friend resisted my attempt and encouraged me to try and see what happened when I worked to failure. I reluctantly agreed, and as I did the pushups, I noticed that the internal voices of judgment and fear were very loud: "My arms are already shaking at fifteen; I can't look weak in front of my friend!" "I have to make it to at least thirty-five, or something is wrong with me." I held my breath and tried to conserve my energy to increase my endurance. This made me even more tense so that I could do only twenty-five pushups. I had failed, and I felt defeated.

In this case, I could laugh at myself because the stakes were so low. After I had rested a few minutes, my friend asked me to try again and see if I could relax and welcome whatever came. I had nothing to lose because I had already done miserably. I tried again. This time, the voices of fear and judgment were a lot quieter, and I focused on being in the moment and breathing and relaxing my body. At some point after pushup twenty,

I lost count, and I continued to focus on the motion and movement—up and down, breathing in and out. I kept going until my arms couldn't lift my body anymore, and then I collapsed and lay on the ground for a minute because my arms were so tired. When I looked up at my friend, he told me I had done thirty-two pushups. But instead of focusing on the fact that I beat my record, I was struck by the difference between the two experiences.

The first time, consumed by fear and judgment of failure, my body became rigid, I felt stressed out and performed more poorly than usual. But the second time, when I felt like I had nothing left to lose, I was more present in the moment. I realized I could use my breathing to support my physical movements—something I had never thought to try before—and my body was more relaxed. On top of that, I had fun fulfilling the exercise. Whenever I worked out after that, I experimented with my breath and relaxation, which has helped me strengthen my body as I do pushups. I would never have learned this if my friend hadn't challenged me in this way.

Doing pushups was a relatively low-stakes proposition compared to what I faced at work. However, this experience demonstrated how my fear of failure restricted my efforts and, ironically, kept me from reaching success and growth.

In our leadership journey, we will experience multiple ways of what we judge to be failing. This includes times when our efforts result in outcomes that aren't what we had hoped, when we cannot overcome challenges, and when we wish we had done something differently in hindsight. Being leaders moving against the current means that we are often in unfavorable conditions with a high probability of such failures. We have chosen a route that, by its very nature, poses obstructions and hazardous surroundings as we reach our destination.

As leaders, we want to succeed. The irony is that many of us who are leading against the current tend to brush off our successes, often without acknowledging them, while our failures or perceived failures stick to our backs like Velcro. Many of us carry our failures around like weights on our shoulders that can get even more burdensome when we use them to continue beating ourselves up, afraid to take them off our backs and hold them to the light of day. Throughout the years, I have challenged myself to turn toward failure instead of running away from it. Failure does not come easily to me because of all the messages I have received about failure from society. However, using my courage to explore it more fully has helped me reconcile my relationship to failure and learn how to use it to help me move toward my purpose.

When Oppression Removes Failure as an Option or Sets Us Up to Fail

Before we explore failure more deeply, I think it's important to discuss how systemic oppression can create conditions that either eliminate the option to fail or set us up to fail.

When Failure Is Not Seen as Part of the Equation

"Failure is not an option." I can't count how often I have said this to myself when leading a new project or tackling a big challenge. This scenario is akin to navigating through the turbulent current threatening to swamp us at every turn as we struggle with a leaky boat and have only one shot at successfully reaching our purpose.

I remember when I was a relatively new executive director. Our organization, Asian Communities for Reproductive Justice, was doing well, and we had just successfully transitioned from our old name, Asian Pacific Islanders for Reproductive Health, to more accurately reflect the communities we were serving and the strategies we were using. But we also were facing growing pains around our staffing and infrastructure. During that time, one of our program officers scheduled a meeting with me to talk about our grant being renewed for another year. She had also been an executive director some years prior, and I was looking forward to speaking with her about some of my challenges. I was hoping she could share some words of support and advice. Because she was one of two women-of-color program officers funding our organization, I assumed I could be more forthcoming and authentic than usual.

The phone call started friendly enough as she asked about my health—I was pregnant then with my first daughter. I told her I was experiencing intense morning sickness, which she commiserated with as she, too, had had nausea when pregnant. I remember appreciating the connection we were having. Then, the conversation pivoted to my giving her an update about the work. I had spoken just a few sentences about it when she interrupted me and said, "This is all well and fine, but I want to talk about your name change. This is the third time you have changed your name, and I don't think it was a good idea because it gives the impression that your organization is unclear about its mission. You are a small organization just starting to get national recognition and don't want to blow it. This is not how you gain the confidence of big donors!" Her words felt like a slap in the face! We had previously communicated with all our donors about our name change decision and rationale and got approval from almost all the major stakeholders. We had solicited questions from invested parties about our new name five months before changing it so that we could address any concerns. Not once through this process did she share any reservations.

Additionally, while we wanted feedback from our donors about our new name, the decision to make the change rested with the board and staff. She was overstepping her role as a foundation program officer. My confusion turned to anger as I now had to defend our decision and process.

She went on to advise that I should wait to announce our name change for another six months to provide us with more time to think about the decision and perhaps reverse it. As we continued the discussion, she pressed even further and said that she was taking a risk investing in women-of-color-led organizations like ours. She talked about another leader in the field with whom she was upset because their staff was experiencing a lot of turnover. I then realized that at the root of her discomfort with our name change was how vulnerable she felt at her foundation. She was one of the few women of color on staff. She thought that she was putting her reputation on the line by funding smaller grassroots reproductive justice groups, and she was communicating to me that it was imperative that we not fail. I surmised that if one of the groups she chose to fund ended up struggling in some way, it would reflect poorly on her, and she might face repercussions from the leadership of that foundation. Although I disagreed with how she approached me, this new understanding enabled me to be compassionate about her situation and see the pressure she was under.

A year later, she approached me and apologized. During our conversation, she shared that her supervisor had been pressuring her about her decision to increase funding for women-of-color-led organizations. Unfortunately, this would not be the first partnership I would have with a woman-of-color funder working at a foundation whose efforts to support BIPOC-led efforts would be intensely scrutinized.

When We Are Set Up to Fail

At the time of the writing of this book, a critical national discussion is underway over what awaits many Black women elected to office or hired to lead nonprofits or businesses that experience the glass cliff. The *glass cliff* is a term first coined by University of Exeter researchers Michelle K. Ryan and S. Alexander Haslam and then substantiated by other researchers.[1] It refers to a trend of promoting women and people of color to head companies and institutions that are in crisis or weakly performing. They receive little or no support once they get into these top positions. They inherit multiple crises and face hostility toward their leadership from not only opponents and competitors but also supposed colleagues and allies. They are expected to perform in these conditions, creating greater outcomes than their white or cis-male counterparts with no second chances.

Claudine Gay, former president of Harvard, was put in an untenable situation while testifying at the December 2023 Congressional hearings without adequate support from Harvard. As part of the ongoing anti-DEI backlash facing corporations and institutions, wealthy donors and conservatives seized upon this as an opportunity to paint her hiring as part of a "diversity initiative," implying she was unqualified for the position, and then substantiated their claims with accusations of plagiarism. A Harvard independent panel concluded that there was "no violation of Harvard's standard for research misconduct," and she promptly admitted and corrected her mistakes.[2] She was still subsequently fired, becoming the first woman and Black leader of Harvard University with the shortest tenure of any president. Gay, in her *New York Times* op-ed, contextualized her experience as part of a more extensive series of attacks to discredit public institutions and their leadership with the goal of "unraveling public faith in pillars of American society."[3] In glass-cliff situations, it is critical to make visible the forces of white supremacy and patriarchy that are at the root of this failure.

Exploring the Benefits/Fruits of Failure

The previous examples demonstrate two ways oppression can affect our experiences with failure. Now, let's focus on when failure can bring some hidden gems that may not be initially apparent. Sometimes, failure is not the terrible ogre it might initially appear to be. Sometimes, it can even help us move toward our purpose. I invite you to explore three ways to work with failure: understanding that our initial perceptions of failure may not be correct; finding ways to build our skills through failure; and identifying failure as a path to new ways of doing things.

When a Failure Is Not What It First Appears to Be

The change we seek is complex and continues over the long term. This means that our experiences, which we initially see as failures, may be part of a larger picture; they will take time to reveal themselves to us. A well-known Chinese parable believed to have originated in the second century BCE illustrates this beautifully. Once upon a time, a Chinese farmer lost his horse. The neighboring farmers came to console him, saying, "That is too bad," to which the farmer replied, "Perhaps." The next day, the horse came back with seven wild horses. The neighbors gathered around him and, this time, said, "That is great!" to which the farmer replied, "Perhaps." The following day, the son attempted to ride one of the wild horses and fell off, breaking his leg. His neighbors came around that night and said, "That's too bad," to which the farmer replied, "Perhaps." The next day, the soldiers were rounding up young men to join the army, but they rejected the farmer's son because of his broken leg. The neighbors gathered for the last time and said, "That's wonderful," and the Farmer replied, "Perhaps." This story reflects the Taoist philosophy that life is too complex to tell if an experience is "bad" or "good." This also translates to outcomes we experience around our efforts. What may seem initially like a failure may be a success, and vice versa.

Several years ago, I was invited to apply for a prestigious fellowship. I was excited about it because it came with resources for professional development that I wanted to use to expand the scale and scope of our work to the national level. I also looked forward to building relationships with other leaders in the four-week-long retreats that were part of the fellowship. I spent a lot of time carefully working on my application. I spoke to one of the previous recipients of the fellowship, who told me that I had a good chance of receiving one of the five slots they had available. I was so happy when they offered me a phone meeting with a panel of interviewers. At one point, they asked me a question about my strengths.

On a whim, I decided to focus on and demonstrate my facilitation skills by asking each person on the call to think about a time when they were successfully leading an effort and share some of the conditions they experienced that were critical to their success. I was confident I could facilitate this process within the time it would have taken to answer the question. I knew this was an unconventional tactic in a traditional interview, but I thought it was worth taking the risk so that they could see one of my strengths in action.

Even though we were on the phone, I could sense that the group was reluctant to engage. Although they did participate, I could feel the energy shift during the interview from that moment on. I kicked myself afterward for not simply answering the question and was not surprised that my application was rejected. I was disappointed that my judgment had failed me. This experience stung for a few weeks. I kicked myself for taking a risk that didn't pay off, which resulted in not having resources that could have made a big difference in moving our work forward.

A week after my rejection notification, I started revising my work plan for the rest of the year and saw that not being part of the fellowship would free up some time within my schedule. I decided to use that time to focus on how to grow our work. That was the beginning of a process that led me to engage in multiple conversations with executive directors across the country who were hungry to work together. At that point, I decided to create a strategic initiative that would bring leaders together to grapple with key questions we were each facing and to find ways to collaborate. Eight organizations were part of the resulting EMERJ (Expanding the Movement for Empowerment and Reproductive Justice) program. This initiative tripled in size within six months. It continued to grow rapidly, garnering exponentially more public attention to the issues we worked on than my organization could have achieved alone.

I had no way of knowing this at the time, but failing to receive the fellowship helped me succeed in launching a project that was critical to our long-term goals. Ironically, my facilitation skills, which I was berating myself for using during that failed interview, were among the key strengths I used to bring other leaders together to build this project. This experience and others like it have taught me to avoid immediately labeling an outcome as a failure when something doesn't go as planned or when I face an outcome that I don't initially desire. If I can be open to whatever outcome transpires, it allows me to move forward without spending toxic energy beating myself up.

"Failure" as Skills Building

Let's continue to explore examples of experiences that may initially look like failures but ultimately become beneficial to our purpose. When I think about my personal development—from riding a bike without training wheels in kindergarten to landing my first job out of college after submitting my resume to multiple organizations, to learning how to parent—not getting things "right" the first time has helped me figure things out. When a baby is learning to walk, would you consider their first attempt, which results in them falling down, a failure? No, of course not. In order to walk successfully, the baby must first develop coordination, leg and foot muscles, and balance. And as is the case with the baby, each "failed" attempt, each wobbly step, is necessary and should be viewed as part of the process.

Early in my career, a friend of mine, the executive director of a small organization, created a strategic planning process and asked for my assistance. I had initially suggested that my friend hire a consultant who could provide much more expertise in this area, but my friend's organization didn't have any resources, so I agreed to help her. The organization, focused on ending gender-based violence, was transitioning from a sole focus of educational forums to advocating for policies at the state level. She and I created a method to engage the staff and board. We hoped that by making the plan together, everyone involved would be fully invested in the success of this plan. To our surprise, the planning process went relatively smoothly. Afterward, everyone expressed excitement and confirmed they were completely on board with this new direction. My friend was thrilled with the results, and I was happy to have been able to help them move into this new phase. Six months into their plan, the work stalled. Some of the staff started resisting the original plan. Staff who were trained as educators had a steep learning curve in understanding the legislative process and felt unprepared to help the community members they served testify in front of legislators at the state capital. The morale was low, and some staff members threatened to quit.

I volunteered to help, feeling like I was to blame for creating a failed strategic planning process. I was determined to help the staff figure out how to move forward. In talking with the staff, we realized that the professional development training we had put into place at the beginning of the plan needed to be longer and more comprehensive. We revamped the training to include sessions before each legislative visit so the staff could voice any concerns or fears and get support beforehand. The ED of the organization also debriefed with the staff after every visit so that they could talk about what went well and track their progress. The organization instituted a protocol in which the staff who were more comfortable with advocacy would mentor and provide support during the legislative visits to the less comfortable staff. Over time, to my relief, these interventions, along with others, started working, and the staff was successful in reaching its purpose of transitioning its core strategy.

The challenges and bumps we experienced in this process provided me with valuable lessons and skills that would strengthen my ability to lead strategic planning processes. I learned that whenever an organization is experiencing a shift in its core strategies, even if it appears that everyone is initially in favor of it, it is critical to build support within the plan's first year. The strategic planning process must anticipate staff discomfort or resistance if they are asked to let go of how they used to do things and adopt new skills and behaviors. This was the first of many times I would lead a strategic planning process. And each time, I would gain skills that would help me strengthen my efforts for the next time. Many of the challenges I faced were complex, and some were not predictable, so the only way I could gain these skills was by trying to deal with the missteps so I might be more equipped next time.

Over the years of working on honing many strategic planning processes, I have concluded that strategic planning for a five-year period is ineffective because it is too long to account for the high level of uncertainty and complexity that our organizations face. Three years is the outer limit, and even that depends on the conditions at hand. For example, during the pandemic, given the unpredictability of what we were facing, I led my staff through a six-week planning process.

Along with building my skills, failure has helped me evolve as a leader. Experiencing deep organizational conflict pushed me to find ways to mitigate disagreements within our organizational culture, such as somatic practices and nonviolent communication techniques. Hiring multiple team members who turned out to be a grave mismatch for our organization taught me the importance of having a rigorous interviewing protocol. Unsuccessfully winging a presentation showed me that preparation works much better for me than improvisation when I'm trying to give an inspirational talk.

Failure as a Path to New Ways of Doing Things

Along with helping our leadership evolve, failure can create new pathways for our work as we move toward our purpose. Recently, I was coaching Alexis, an African American nonbinary deputy director of a state-based reproductive justice organization, who was struggling to help their organization get through a budget crisis. Their biggest donor had just announced that this would be the last year Alexis's organization would receive funding from them. This would create a 12 percent reduction in their income stream for next year. Alexis and the executive director of the organization were determined to retain everyone's job, but it would mean that each team's budget would be reduced. As they attempted to talk about the implications of the budget cuts, each team director within the organization started to become very protective of their own team resources. Within a few weeks, so much tension had grown that many directors were not speaking to each other. Alexis saw this as a failure of their organizational culture and was despondent about how to resolve the tensions.

I asked Alexis to tell me how they would like the directors to deal with the crisis. They explained that they wanted the team directors to come together to think about what was best for the organization as a whole rather than only focusing on their piece of the pie. Alexis wanted them to see the benefits of thinking collectively rather than competitively. We explored what organizational dynamics might contribute to this current situation.

One of the things Alexis realized right away was that how their organization created annual budgets helped exacerbate the current dynamics among the directors. The directors would work with their teams each year and make a plan for the upcoming year. After creating their plan, they would draw up a budget to support it. The directors would then submit their individual budgets to Alexis, who would consolidate them.

This budgeting process occurred at the end of the fiscal year when many other things were also happening at the organization, including job performance reviews, holiday celebrations, and other end-of-year activities. Because there was always a time crunch, Alexis would negotiate with each director individually if they sought to make any changes. Nowhere in the process before the organizational budget was finalized did any of the team directors see the team budgets of their peers. In addition, Alexis realized directors needed training to help them collaborate to craft an organization-wide budget.

Another aspect of their organizational culture included friendly team competitions throughout the year. This included fundraising challenges, where each team competed to see who could reach the most individual donors, and all-staff retreats, which often included teams playing games against each other. They also had a staff spotlight every quarter for the staff member who reached an important goal in their work. The team with the most spotlighted members was given a prize at the end of the year.

In our coaching sessions, Alexis began to see how ingrained competition and team spirit were in their organizational culture. So, Alexis and the executive director made equitable cuts across the teams to get through the current budget crisis without exacerbating team divisiveness. But they also immediately began to change how they did their annual budgeting process. They started two months earlier the next year and included an orientation and training for the directors on thinking about the organization's overall needs and goals. They brought financial consultants to train the directors to help them think about strategies for building a sustainable organization through challenging funding times. Alexis was excited to see that the team of directors was very engaged and that the staff was starting to think more organizationally rather than just from their perspectives.

I worked with Alexis and the ED to talk with the directors to develop creative ways for staff to build relationships across teams during the all-staff retreats. They decided to do some activities focused on cross-team building and collaboration, including crafts and a ropes course. Over the next year, they worked to decrease the volume of team competition while still engaging in fun activities that helped build relationships. They eliminated the team spotlight tradition and replaced it with a practice of team directors appreciating members from other teams to model cross-team collaboration.

By the end of the following year, Alexis was pleased with the results. Directors were working much more collaboratively and building relationships across teams. The team directors were more deeply involved in creating the organizational budget, which helped them be more flexible and understanding when their team had to make cuts to their budget; they had seen how it benefited the organization as a whole. One unintentional but welcomed outcome was when team directors started expressing appreciation of members on other teams. This helped to enhance trust across teams, which fostered greater collaboration. Looking back, Alexis commented that the internal conflicts opened their eyes to ways their organizational culture could improve, and their organization was now greatly strengthened by the process.

Working with Failure

As my relationship to failure has changed, I have seen how valuable it can be. Failure provides data and information to help us learn and grow. Failure helps us achieve success. Failure might also pave the way to accomplishing what we never would have reached for otherwise. We must create room to make mistakes, test things, and try something new.

There are often no easy templates when we are engaged in social justice work. Creative solutions mean we will be taking risks, trying new strategies, and testing innovative ideas. When I regard failure as a possibility, I can deal with it more effectively when it arrives, learn from the experience, and use it to achieve my purpose. Here are four ways that I have found helpful in working with failure:

1. Exploring failure before taking action.

2. Using failure to propel forward.

3. Mining failure for hidden gems.

4. Creating environments to embrace and recover from mistakes.

Exploring Failure Before We Take Action Toward Our Purpose

Giving ourselves the opportunity to examine failure proactively *before* we begin to achieve our purpose can be beneficial in several ways. It can help us see potential roadblocks or challenges that we may not be thinking about, identify strategies for dealing with these difficulties, and determine what we can or cannot control.

After a decade at Forward Together, the board granted me a sabbatical leave. As it turned out, the year I planned to take the sabbatical was also the year that our development director and program director took parental leave. Fortunately, we could plan so that only one of us was gone at a time. Six months before the first leave happened, we did extensive meeting planning to ensure that the organization would continue running as smoothly as possible. We reviewed the work plans of each team and adjusted them to accommodate each of our absences. We also identified modified supervision and organizational structures that would enable our staff to get the support they need and allow them to communicate with each other effectively. We discussed ways for each staff member to gain increased leadership skills during this time, and almost every staff member was given this opportunity, with an accompanying increase in compensation. In the next planning step, I brought the staff together, and we used our mind-body practice of Forward Stance to simulate what could go wrong. We often used Forward Stance to help identify problems and potential solutions because we found that tackling a problem using physical activities frequently brought certain things to light much more quickly than just talking about them.

For this activity, I asked the staff to stand in a large circle.[4] I brought two cases of bottled water and set them down beside me. I instructed the staff to think about each water bottle as representing a project we were working on. I picked up a bottle with my left hand and transferred it to my right hand. The staff member standing to the right next to me would then grab the water bottle from her left and transfer it to her right hand. The person standing to her right would do the same, and the water bottle would continue to travel counterclockwise around the circle in this manner until it got back to me. But of course, we had much more work than just one project, so we needed to add many more bottles. Right after the staff member to the right of me grabbed the first water bottle, I immediately picked up another water bottle and sent it in the same direction around the circle. We kept going until we reached the limit of bottles our group could successfully pass together without dropping any.

Once these bottles were moving along the circle nicely, I told them I would step out of the group, simulating when I would take my sabbatical leave from the organization. When I was ready, I silently stepped out of the circle. Only the two staff members next to me realized I was leaving, and bottles ended up dropping on the floor because the group was passing the water bottles at a speed that couldn't quickly accommodate my absence.

We immediately realized we had to make some changes to accommodate my leaving. After much trial and error, we succeeded by making several behavioral changes. When I was ready to leave the circle, I would loudly signal to everyone that I was going and wait for them to look my way. The group immediately slowed the pace of passing the water bottles way down. When we were all ready, I took the two water bottles I was holding with me so that the group would pass fewer water bottles than when I was in the circle. This adjustment in behaviors enabled the staff to continue passing the water bottles successfully around the circle.

The next part of the activity involved me returning to the circle, simulating my sabbatical's end. We had learned from the previous experience, and when I was ready to re-enter the circle, I announced that I was about to do so. Everyone in the circle looked in my direction. They slowed the pace down so that I could enter. The first time I tried entering between two staff members, there was not enough space for me to step in between them. Also, we didn't realize that the whole circle would have to expand to accommodate my presence, and the circle became an awkward shape, which meant that some water bottles were being passed more quickly than others. This uneven pacing resulted in a few water bottles being dropped. With this failure, we learned that the staff needed to take time, even before I entered the circle, to make the pacing and spatial adjustments necessary for me to join.

This activity helped us create a protocol for when a staff member took an extended leave of absence. This protocol included ensuring that everyone on staff was clear about their departure date, that preparations were being made to slow down the pace of the work as the staff member was leaving, and that the collective workload was appropriately decreased to ensure that nothing would fall through the cracks. When it was time for reentry, all staff would be sent a signal a few weeks ahead to make the necessary structural and pacing changes to accommodate this member's return. So, even though the incoming member was bringing increased capacity for the group to hold more water bottles, the transition required slowing down and making sure the organization and staff were in a formation to bring them back on.

Doing this activity was an aha moment for all of us. Even with the most meticulous planning, we would have to slow down as each of us left and rejoined the team. We would also have to identify work that could be put on hold during our absences. Before we attempted this exercise, we had yet to think of slowing down both when someone left the team and when they returned. In its wake, we also realized we had underestimated the amount of work we needed to postpone while one of us was gone. This experience showed us how each transition required more attention and care than we had previously imagined.

After doing this Forward Stance work to diagnose potential pitfalls and ways we might fail, we began the final planning stage. Proactively working with failure involved a series of meetings with the executive team in which I asked them to list everything that could go wrong. I told them to include their greatest fears. Here is a partial list:

1. Staff would be unclear about how decisions would be made.

2. Donors would withdraw funding because of poor economic conditions.

3. Internal disagreement would not be resolved.

4. The political situation on the national level would shift in the upcoming elections, encouraging even more attacks on reproductive justice, and we would be unprepared.

5. Some of our programs would fail to move forward because of disruptions in our already established connections with our partner organizations.

After looking at this list, I asked the team to divide the items into two categories: items we had influence over and those beyond our control. Items 1, 3, and 5 in the preceding list went under what we could control. Items 2 and 4 were identified as beyond our control. Identifying what was not under our control when considering failure was crucial for a few reasons:

Focus on what matters. By recognizing what we couldn't control, namely the behavior of funders and the results of the upcoming national elections or the funding climate that resulted, we could instead direct energy and resources toward the items we had significant influence over. After these sessions, the program staff saw the value in continuing to build deeper relationships with our local partners, strengthening our staff's investment in our collaborative work at the state level, and curtailing any thoughts about developing new work at the national level.

Maintain perspective. Previously, this team had been planning in earnest to ensure that nothing would fall through the cracks and that, hopefully, we would be able to move forward successfully dealing with *any* challenges that arose. Identifying the areas that the team didn't have control over gave us an important reality check. We learned that we might be unable to prevent or mitigate some challenges. Our operations team came up with the idea of building in designated times for each of our organizational departments to identify any potential challenges that were bubbling up to the surface. The executive team could then consider these as they revisited what they had control over and what they didn't, and they could then move their work accordingly. This would allow us to accomplish two things:

Reduce stress and anxiety. Simply putting the items into these categories relieved us of stress. We realized that when we focused on things that we didn't have control over, the anxiety continued to build and had nowhere to go. By categorizing and clarifying the challenges, team members were able to release much of the anxiety they were holding over items 2 and 4. For example, the development team realized they were not to blame if the funding climate worsened due to economic conditions or the trustees' whims.

Gain clarity. Understanding which outcomes were beyond our control allowed us to approach failure more clearly and objectively. In addition, I decided to bring in additional resources, in the form of consultants and board members, who could continue to help the executive team in their capacity to deal proactively with failures while I was gone.

All of the planning around failure helped our staff not only survive the year with three of us gone at different times but get stronger during it. The sabbatical was a transformative experience for me, and I am grateful for it. It allowed me to spend time with my family, and I supported our school district by writing grants and getting funds for LGBTQ+ families. I deepened my spiritual and wellness practices and got my creative juices flowing by playing the piano, and I returned feeling rested and restored. In my meetings with each staff member the week after I returned, I expected them to tell me they were ready to hand back their increased leadership responsibilities. However, to my surprise and delight, all but three staff were interested in maintaining their new level of leadership because they found it rewarding and meaningful. We maintained and built off many of the structural, operational, and programmatic changes we made, including creating a deputy director and an executive assistant. These positions were fundamental to my ability to expand the organization, including success-fully launching Strong Families, our most significant national initiative during my tenure.

Using Failure to Propel Your Efforts Forward

As the previous example illustrates, working proactively to prevent failure helps increase your chance of success. But what happens if you are facing a likely failure? Many of us have worked on efforts that were highly likely to fail due to a lack of popular support or because we were going up against an opponent with great resources or power. In these cases, it is critical to identify how we can build toward our long-term goals, even if we fail to get the short-term win.

I coached a leader whose organization was running a campaign to defeat a ballot measure that would, if passed, restrict abortion access. She knew going in that the odds were not in her favor. However, she worked with the coalition to identify secondary goals they could gain in the campaign, even if the initiative passed. These included:

- Increasing their base of members willing to work on future abortion access issues by 20 percent
- Developing ten new relationships with organizations willing and able to educate their constituencies about voting for abortion access
- Attaining five new major donors willing to give $10,000 or more to future abortion access campaigns
- Building a core of twenty leaders across the state who could be effective spokespeople for abortion access within communities of color, LGBTQ+ communities, and immigrant communities
- Developing an infrastructure that could unite the organizations together for their next effort to secure abortion access in future campaigns

Developing these goals helped them see that even if they lost the campaign, they could still make critical progress toward long-term support on issues of abortion access. In addition to identifying these campaign goals, they also discussed a failure pitfall many had experienced in previous campaigns. They knew that conflicts often arose in high-pressure situations like this campaign. So, they created a memorandum of understanding (MOU) that each member organization of the executive committee signed, which created a process for more equitable decision-making and resource sharing.

These efforts were very fruitful because, as the campaign was underway, the MOU created an effective protocol that prevented significant disagreements from escalating and mitigated conflict when key challenges arose. The organization did lose the campaign, but by a much smaller margin than predicted. Because they were successful in all but one of their secondary goals, the coalition grew stronger by increasing the number of stakeholders and securing additional resources and public support for future campaign wins.

Mining Failure for Hidden Gems

Along with proactively exploring failure *before* we take action, facing it *after* it happens can also reap great benefits. Turning toward our failures takes courage. But if we can take the time to revisit our failures, we can find hidden gems that will help us transform our experiences of failure into opportunities to move toward our purpose. And we don't have to do it alone. I have engaged in this process alone but have gotten the most insight when doing it with others. Often, in moments of crisis, agitation, or disruption, we may not fully grasp or even accurately remember the conditions and challenges we faced when we failed. Having a supportive partner to walk with us as we reexamine what happened can help us be more grounded so we can see with greater clarity.

During this process, it is also critical to note how power and oppression might have impacted the situation. White supremacy and patriarchy provide challenges to our success in multiple ways, and we need to name and address these dynamics when they are present rather than blaming ourselves for not being good enough. We've all experienced this. You say something new and vital in a strategy session with the team. You get ignored. Maybe someone else restates what you say a few minutes later, and now they receive a significant positive response. When this kind of thing happens, it is easy for us to fault ourselves for not speaking more forcefully or for not expressing ourselves more eloquently. But it is also likely that in those contexts, our comment might not have been received, even if we were the most skilled communicator in the room.

REVISITING FAILURE
A CASE STUDY

The following case study is an example of how I helped a leader find hidden gems using these steps:

1. Revisiting the moment

2. Conducting a reality check

3. Finding opportunities to move toward your purpose

4. Identifying lessons learned

A few years ago, I was working with Ellie, a queer woman of color who wanted to help young people in the Asian Pacific Islander (API) and Latinx communities organize at the school-board level to introduce more ethnic studies classes in the school district. As part of that work, she brought together a group of principals from the local high schools in her district to hear directly from these young people about their vision for ethnic studies courses. The group was made up of six principals and five youth. Of the six principals, three were straight white men, two were men of color and one was a white woman. Ten minutes into the discussion, to Ellie's shock, one of the principals made an off-the-cuff sexist and homophobic remark, jokingly referring to Ellie's mannerisms and clothing as being "butch and dude-like." Feeling demeaned and seething internally, Ellie was thrown off of her game. She decided not to address the comment and moved forward with her agenda as the man who had commented smirked.

Right after this meeting, Ellie came to me. She was distraught and felt much less confident about her facilitating skills. I asked Ellie if she would be willing to revisit the session, beginning with sharing her feelings. She was initially reluctant to do so; she judged herself harshly and didn't want to put herself back in that moment. Part of what we face as women, nonbinary, and trans leaders of color is that when we experience failure, our feelings of shame and anger go especially deep. I let Ellie know that revisiting experiences of failure is critical to moving forward and that we would do this together. After taking a few deep breaths, she shared with me that she had left the group enraged at the principal for making the remark but even more furious at herself for not handling the situation better and not being a "better role model" for the youth in the room.

We focused the first part of our discussion on the systemic forces in the room. Ellie shared how the remark knocked her off balance. Listening, it was clear to me that Ellie had created a narrative from the incident about her inadequacies as a leader. She could have walked away from the meeting, understandably upset at the person who made the remark, without feeling that this experience reflected on who she was as a facilitator or a model to the young people. However, she had taken on responsibility for his lack of judgment and professionalism. But we know in moments like this that as women, nonbinary, and trans leaders of color, we rarely emerge unscathed, and we are often our own worst critics. This internalized oppression is something that we can learn to resist.

Ellie and I talked about how harmful and toxic that remark was not only to her but to other queer folks who happened to be in the room and that it was a way to assert heteronormativity power and privilege. In addition, the principal's remark triggered Ellie's memories of middle school when she had been teased for the way she looked and had suffered homophobic attacks from her classmates. We took a moment to process the emotions that were coming up for her related to her past experiences. After incidents like this, it is essential to take the time to express our feelings and unpack all of the dynamics of oppression at play. As Ellie talked, her self-doubt and shame began to dissolve, leaving more space for us to continue exploring what had happened.

Revisiting the Moment

During damaging experiences like this one, so many things happen simultaneously that it can be confusing or overwhelming. I asked Ellie to reflect on the moment to gain clarity and understanding. I did this with Ellie by asking her to think back to when the comment was made and then tell me how she *wished* she had responded.

After a minute she said, "I wished I had some pithy comeback that would have put him in his place. But then, when

I thought further, I remembered that I didn't say anything at that moment because I didn't want to alienate some of the young people in the group, who looked up to the principal who had made the remark. I also held back because this principal is in charge of the largest high school in the district and has a lot of influence over the school board. I didn't want to say anything amid my anger that would undermine our efforts." She sat quietly for a moment, realizing that she hadn't frozen up the way she thought. Instead, she had made strategic choices.

Researchers have found that our memories are not reliable. A group of researchers who interviewed people about their experiences after 9/11 found that 40 percent of the people they studied shifted their recollections considerably over time. Researchers have also found that we remember events through narratives we tell ourselves.[5] Ellie beat herself up after the meeting because her memories had shifted to align with a narrative she had begun about herself that told her she was not brave enough to speak up when insulted by the principal. But in that split second, she had made a strategic decision to let the comment go instead of blurting out a response in anger or surprise, which might have resulted in her being alienated from the principals. Her epiphany was that she didn't fail at that moment and might make the same decision again. This critical realization helped Ellie disrupt the negative narrative she was starting to spin about herself as a bad leader. Instead, she began creating a new narrative about being a facilitator who, when faced with a surprise verbal attack, could assess the moment, possess the discipline to withhold an immediate response, and make a strategic decision with long-term impacts in mind while having the bravery to continue facilitating the agenda.

Conducting a Reality Check

This was a great deal of progress for Ellie. But we weren't done. After all, part of learning about failure is checking and seeing if your worst fears of failing are actually true. I asked Ellie, "How does this realization about what happened change your feelings about your impact on the young people in the room?" At that moment, she realized that she had succeeded in her purpose of going through the agenda with the principals and discovered that she had an additional purpose of serving as a model for the group of young people. She hadn't identified this previously, and this purpose had become visible once she slowed down the process and revisited what had happened.

At this point, Ellie still felt uncomfortable about the situation because, even though she now understood why she hadn't addressed the remark, she was worried that the youth would think she was condoning being silent when confronted by people in power. "I am trying to teach them how to be courageous in front of the school board, and then they see that I couldn't even respond to an off-hand remark from the principal?"

I asked Ellie if she had spoken to any of the young people from the meeting yet. She told me that she had canceled the meeting scheduled for the next day because she was so embarrassed and needed time to reclaim her confidence. "So, you don't know what the young people are actually feeling about what happened?" When she heard my question, she smiled and admitted that she had come to some pretty harsh conclusions about herself as a role model based on her fears of being judged without any evidence from the youth themselves. With my encouragement, she agreed to suspend judgment until she could talk to them.

Finding Opportunities to Move Toward Your Purpose

Ellie scheduled a follow-up meeting with the students so she could debrief with them. Ellie was surprised that the young people offered support and compassion instead of scrutinizing her. They were appreciative and relieved to have the chance to talk about what happened at the meeting with the principals. The comment was hurtful and offensive to them, and they were concerned about how Ellie was doing. In addition, two of them shared that they had left the meeting feeling bad for not speaking up to the principal who made the comment. *They* felt guilty that they didn't have the courage to intervene and that *they* had failed Ellie.

Ellie was shocked to see that the students experienced the same pattern of self-blame that had impacted her. However, after going through our coaching session, Ellie now had the tools to lead a discussion in which the group revisited this experience, reevaluated their initial assessment of themselves, and proactively identified ways they could respond if something similar happened to them in future interactions with the administration.

After meeting with the group of young people, Ellie and I looked at future meetings she would facilitate with the principals and explored any additional lessons she had learned from this situation that might help her. She decided that one lesson was that she needed to proactively deal with this principal by the time they were to meet again. But she didn't want to do this alone, nor did she think it was her responsibility to educate that principal about issues of homophobia or sexism. I asked her if there were any principals in that group with whom she had a good relationship. She identified one, Candice, with whom she worked on a task force of student leaders and school administrators that met monthly to look at school safety and diversity policies. We then devised a plan for Ellie to meet with Candice to find ways for Candice to educate the principals about homophobia and sexism. Ellie was excited about the plan, which would be a way to build a stronger relationship with Candice, who, she hoped, could be a good advocate for the youth.

Identifying Lessons Learned

Ellie also learned to be prepared for comments like this in the future. She decided that before facilitating any new group, she would build in questions about their experience and competency around issues of homophobia and sexism, as well as other "isms." She would then use the findings in her assessment to develop strategies to work with the group to prevent or be prepared to handle situations like the principal's remark. These strategies included Ellie setting a culture within the group that dissuaded people from making these comments, identifying a person from that group who could intervene and hold the group accountable for addressing homophobic or sexist comments, and creating responses to those kinds of comments that hold the person accountable while also moving the agenda forward. In extreme circumstances, she would think about even declining to work with the group if there were too many red flags.

Thanks to our discussion, Ellie's understanding and narratives about that moment with the principal had transformed from feelings of failure to seeing her strengths and how to use that moment to move her agenda forward. She shifted from wanting to hide and not think about that moment to being grateful for the opportunities it offered her. By moving from a place of self-blame and shame to adopting a learning stance, Ellie was able to reap the rich learnings that come from "failing."

By leaning into the failure and learning from it, Ellie emerged from that situation, which she had initially chalked up to being a miserable failure, with greater clarity, a firm plan for moving toward her purpose, and more confidence in her leadership.

Creating Environments for Us to Embrace and Recover and Learn from Our Mistakes

The previous examples of failure speak to when things don't go as planned or when we fall short of predesignated goals. But what happens when we make a mistake and do something wrong? To err is also part of being human and a leader.

In the past, when I made mistakes, I would beat myself up repeatedly for not doing better. I used my mistakes to define who I was a leader. (For this section, note that I am not referring to egregious mistakes that result in violence, neglect, or unsafe conditions. For those kinds of mistakes, it is critical to stop what is happening and get help immediately. Numerous books and trainings on restorative justice are good resources for helping us through these processes.) Here, I want to focus on how we create environments for ourselves so that we can learn from our mistakes and are unlikely to repeat them in the future.

I remember when I was asked to present to a network of donors. I had been trying to get in front of these donors for years and finally was invited to speak at their annual conference. I had prepared diligently by research-ing their interest and honing my talking points well ahead of time, getting feedback from a couple of people I knew within that network. I created a dynamic presentation, starting with an interactive activity to grab their attention, great visuals, and a video. When the day came to present, I was nervous but pumped and ready to go. I got up on stage, and everything went smoothly at first.

Participants reacted very positively to the exercise I started with, which got them moving around the room and talking to each other. My opening remarks went well and grabbed their attention as I spoke about our inno-vative work in partnership with these outstanding leaders. I walked across the stage, saying, "But enough from me. I want you to hear directly from these incredible leaders about the impact they are achieving in their com-munities this year." I went over to the laptop to play the slide show, and to my horror, I realized that I didn't have the correct version.

The slide show I had was an unfinished previous version without any videos loaded onto it. Suddenly, my vision got very narrow, and I started panicking. I had not prepared any additional content to fill the next twelve minutes when the videos were supposed to be playing. When I apologized to the audience about not having the videos, my speech came out in spurts as I tried to paraphrase what the leaders said on camera. Trying my best to wing it, I knew what I was doing was a poor rendition of what would have been a powerful set of presentations by the leaders themselves. I walked off the stage feeling like I wanted to disappear into a corner.

Right after I was done, I immediately picked up my belongings and left. After going over and over how the mix-up had happened, I remem-bered that I had saved the most recent version on my desktop computer at work and had not updated to the last version on my laptop. This careless mistake cost me a big chance to impress these funders, and all the hours and effort I had spent preparing were wasted because of my error. I also was frustrated that I hadn't handled the situation better. I should have been able to recover quickly and improvise because I knew the material and the content of their speeches so well. I should have been able to come up with an engaging way to get my point across even without those videos. I was deeply disappointed in myself all around.

I never reached out to that network again because I was so mortified and felt that I didn't deserve a second chance. Looking back now, with years of public speaking under my belt, I wish I could go back to my younger self and talk her through what happened. I would let her know that giving speeches is nerve-wracking for most people and that it is understandable that she might have a difficult time bouncing back immediately in front of two hundred people. According to the National Social Anxiety Center, the most common fear is public speaking—ahead of death, spiders, and heights.

I would help her remember that the first part of her speech had gone well and that she was able to keep the audience's attention, even getting them to laugh at the jokes she had sprinkled in. I would then talk to her about having a system next time where she double-checks to ensure all her materials are in order before she leaves the house. I would brainstorm what she could do when things don't go as planned, such as acknowledging to the audience what is happening and taking a few deep breaths to calm down and ground herself, giving her time to think about the best way to move forward.

I would also encourage her to remain in the room afterward. At the time, I had assumed that audience members would not be interested in speaking with me because of my mistake. If I could do it over again, I would have stayed in the room, connected to my courage instead of focusing on my shame, and engaged with audience members. Who knows, I might have been able to engage a few people in a conversation, and that might have led to more interest in supporting our work further down the road. Finally, I would encourage my younger self to continue to reach out to the network to see if there might be other opportunities to speak with donors. Even though I made a mistake, it wasn't an offensive one that people might remember forever. Who knows, I might have denied myself other opportunities to get funding because I shut the door and never looked back.

Research on child development has shown that shouting at or punishing a child for making a mistake can prevent them from listening or learning. This is also true for adults. When we treat ourselves with compassion and kindness and take responsibility for our mistakes, we will be much more successful in achieving our purpose of learning from our mistakes and attempting to avoid making the same mistake again.

As leaders working for social change, we will encounter many situations where outcomes will go differently than planned or where we will make mistakes and suffer failures. Rather than running from them, we can acknowledge them as ever-present possibilities that could bring value and help us move closer to our purposes. Failure can serve as a potent teacher, offering incredible opportunities to learn, innovate, and develop skills, and it can propel us closer to our destination. By exploring the multifaceted nature of failure, leaders can gain insights into their experiences, gain new strengths and strategies, and enhance their effectiveness and impact. Ultimately, by acknowledging failure as an inherent part of the journey, leaders can navigate challenges with grace and emerge stronger, driving continuous improvement and sustainable success.

Your Turn

Get into a State of Readiness

You can use the relaxation activity outlined at the beginning of the Your Turn section in chapter 1 or select one that works for you.

Exploring Your Relationship with Failure

Before working with failure, it can be helpful to know how you hold it. This set of exercises can help you understand your relationship to failure.

WHAT MESSAGES HAVE YOU INTEGRATED ABOUT FAILURE?

Think about messages you have gotten from society, your family, and your community about failure.

- Write them down on a sheet of paper.
- Circle the messages that you have incorporated into your thinking.
- Reflect on the messages you circled. How do they affect you? Are there any that you do not find helpful?

HOW DO MESSAGES ABOUT FAILURE IMPACT YOU?

A. Take a piece of paper and write at the top "When I fail, I feel . . . ." Write down everything that comes to mind.

B. At the top of another piece of paper, write down "Failure tells me . . . ." Write down your responses to that statement.

C. Look at the answers to both prompts in steps A and B and circle the answers that are positive and/or constructive. How do they help you move through failure?

D. Notice the ones you didn't circle. How do these hinder your ability to move through failure?

These activities are designed to bring up your feelings, thoughts, and fears—both the ones you have experienced and the ones you might face in the future. See if you can start to relate to failure with more curiosity, interest, and intention rather than fear, avoidance, or self-deprecation. Doing this on an ongoing basis can change your relationship to failure and help you work with it more productively.

Working with Mistakes

The following is an exercise I have conducted with leaders that helps them practice working with mistakes of any kind, with the exception of those that involve egregious abuse or violence. I invite you to try it now:

A. Close your eyes and think about a significant mistake you have made. As you think about that mistake, remember the messages you gave yourself, especially those that were the harshest. Write them down. After that, take a few minutes to write some reflections about how hearing those messages makes you feel.

B. When you are finished, picture one of your best friends, someone you love dearly. Imagine that they made the same mistake and were coming to you for support. What messages would you give them? Write those down. Do you see differences between the messages you gave yourself and those you gave to your friend?

When I have done this exercise with others, almost everyone's two lists are very different from each other. The first list has messages that tend to be demeaning, unforgiving, belittling, or denigrating. The second offers more supportive, constructive, compassionate, and helpful messages. It becomes clear to the participants that the two sets of messages are different because they were constructed with different purposes. The message they gave to themselves was focused more on punishing and shaming. The messages they gave to their friend were focused on helping them to learn and grow and supporting them to repair the harm.

We are often our greatest critic and can be downright cruel in our self-messages. If you gave your friend the messages you reserved for yourself, would your friend keep coming to you for support? The answer is probably no, because cruel and harsh messages between friends would likely end the friendship. We need to treat ourselves the way we treat our friends. We need to give ourselves unconditional love, even when we make mistakes.

Let's go back to the mistake that you identified earlier and proceed with the purpose of learning and growing from it.

A. Close your eyes and gently hold that mistake. Now, hold yourself with regard and unconditional love, knowing that you are not your mistakes.

B. Remember that mistakes are part of life. We are not perfect beings, so mistakes will happen. I have seen how perfectionism becomes a corrosive force that encourages us to mold ourselves to a standard (using values of the dominant culture) that is simply not attainable.

C. Give yourself time to breathe and become calm. It is difficult to gain perspective, get the courage we need to repair any harm, or learn from our mistakes when we are in crisis mode.

D. Encourage yourself to acknowledge the mistake from a place of kindness and compassion. If you are having difficulty doing this, imagine, as described previously, that you are talking to a friend who made the same mistake and see if that helps.

E. Identify what you can do to repair the situation and make amends if the situation warrants.

F. Now think about what you want to tell yourself to help you learn and grow from the situation so you don't repeat it.

G. Identify some times in the future when you can put what you learned into practice to build the skills necessary to move away from this mistake.

If you are like many of the people I've worked with, the messages you give yourself when you embrace yourself with unconditional love are much more compassionate, self-affirming, and valuable than when you come from the place of the harsh critic. When we give ourselves the spaciousness to be human, to make mistakes, to trip and fall for a moment, we are much more able to recover, learn, and grow from the experience, increasing our ability to do something different the next time and become an inspiration for others to do the same.

6

POWERING UP YOUR LEADERSHIP

Power is not brute force and money; power is in your spirit.

—WINONA LADUKE

I shall plant my hands in the garden. And I will grow.

—FORUGH FARROKHZAD

Supercharging Your Leadership

The stakes are high as our communities face an increasing number of threats, like climate change and serious challenges to democracy caused by the rise of authoritarianism and a growing consolidation of power among elite groups around the globe. The world needs us to function optimally, and *we* need ourselves to function optimally. Leveling up our leadership and leveraging our inner resources is critical to our success.

There are several aspects to powering up our leadership. The first component is *creating a dashboard of our leadership needs*. Too often, we neglect our leadership needs because we dismiss them as unimportant or peripheral to our efforts. But the opposite is true—when we address our leadership needs, we can function much more effectively over the long term and are less likely to succumb to burnout or defeat.

The second component is *accessing and growing our internal resources*. Our set of internal resources includes our values, personal strengths, skills, and lessons gained from past experiences. These inner resources propel us forward through the challenging current.

The third component is *activating our superpower of self-growth*. When we learn from and develop new capabilities through challenging situations, we become stronger with each experience. We can use these obstacles to build our resilience and enhance our ability to tackle future challenges. Every difficult situation becomes an opportunity for growth and transformation.

Component 1:
Assessing and Addressing
Your Leadership Needs

Needs. I used to cringe at the word. Leaders are not supposed to have needs. We are here to help others, not focus on ourselves. The last thing many of us want to do is think about our needs. Having needs also makes many of us feel vulnerable or deficient in some way. But having needs is part of being human. Denying that we have needs as leaders is akin to ignoring the warning lights in our cars that signal that we must pay attention and address what isn't functioning correctly. We understand that general maintenance is expected when we have a car. Our cars must have their oil changed regularly and undergo ongoing tune-ups to run smoothly.

**Set of
Internal
Resources**
- Moral Compass
- Strengths
- Experience

**POWERING UP
YOUR LEADERSHIP**

**Leadership
Needs**
- Baseline of Support
- Meaning
- Thought Partnership and Guidance
- Professional Development
- Spaciousness
- Restoration
- Celebration

**Superpower
of Self-Growth**
- Self Reflection
- New Skills, Tools, Behaviors
- Practice and Integration

Eveline Shen, Diagram designs: Amy Wu, duende.us

Similarly, focusing on addressing our leadership needs helps us function effectively over a longer period. In this chapter, I refer to needs that support our capacity to fulfill our role and responsibilities as leaders. It is also essential to address our personal needs, which I will cover in the next chapter.

Creating and Assessing Your Dashboard of Needs

Our leadership needs are invaluable because they point to what we must work on to function more optimally. Instead of discarding or ignoring them, we can create a dashboard of these needs to help us start addressing them. Working with our needs in this ongoing way allows us to create conditions to move upstream, maintain our balance, move with peak efficiency, and contribute over the long term. From my experiences as a leader and coaching other leaders, I've gathered some gauges we can pay particular attention to on our dashboard.

GAUGE 1: BASELINE OF SUPPORT

Leaders need a baseline of support to do their jobs. It is not easy being a leader moving against the current. They need to be entrusted with sufficient confidence by those around them to fulfill their roles effectively. They need time to learn and to be given the grace to make mistakes. Of course, leaders are accountable for their actions and deeper trust must be earned. If mistakes are continuously made or if it becomes apparent over time that the pace of learning is not commiserate with what is necessary to do the job, then, perhaps the leader isn't a good fit for the position. However, if a leader is surrounded by stakeholders who generally mistrust them from the get-go, then their success will be severely hampered.

GAUGE 2: MEANING

As leaders, we spend a lot of time on tasks that don't fulfill us. Dealing with ongoing personnel problems, difficult organizational dynamics, or financial emergencies can sap our energy and morale. And on top of these tasks, we face formidable challenges as we make the external social changes we seek.

We need time to find meaning in our work to stay motivated to continue our journeys. By making an ongoing effort to connect with our purpose, our core values, our relationships with those around us, and the lessons we are learning, we can continue to deepen the meaning of our work. Finding meaning increases our inner resolve, supports our moral compass, and increases our emotional and spiritual well-being.

GAUGE 3: THOUGHT PARTNERSHIP AND GUIDANCE

In addition to this baseline of support, high-functioning leaders need people around them whom they trust for assistance, problem-solving, and guidance. Great leaders in history, from Ida B. Wells to Martin Luther King Jr. to Yuri Kochiyama, didn't act alone. They had people around them who provided strategic support and counsel. Leaders need to have a trusted

DASHBOARD OF LEADERSHIP NEEDS

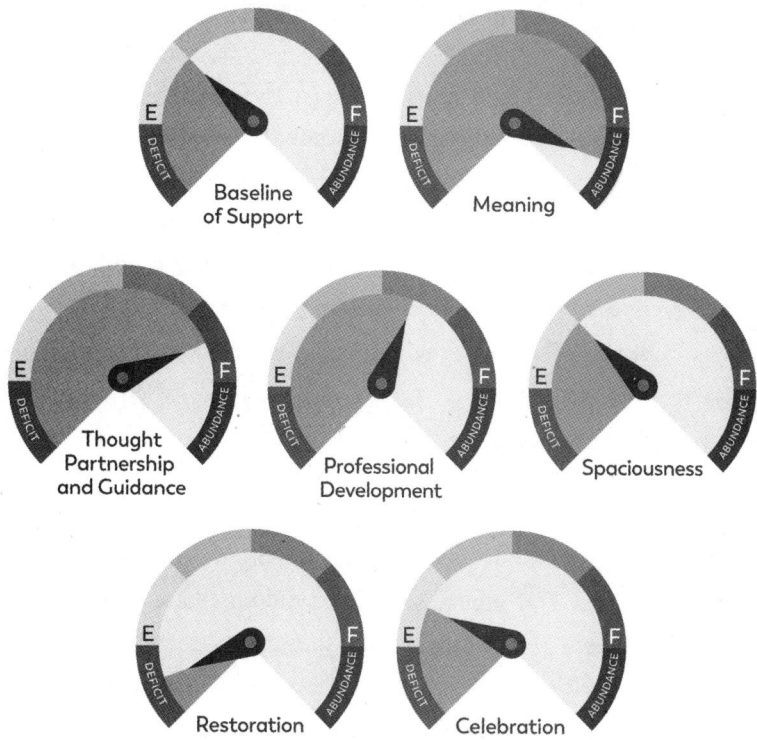

Eveline Shen, Diagram designs: Amy Wu, duende.us

circle of advisors, which includes team members upon whom they can rely for thought partnership, support for holding the collective work together, and aid in identifying threats and opposition. They also need people who will challenge them with compassionate honesty to help them evolve into better leaders.

GAUGE 4: PROFESSIONAL DEVELOPMENT

Leaders need to grow and continue to develop their skills. This includes opportunities for professional development, mentoring, and coaching. They will continue to address complex and formidable challenges, so their leadership capacity needs to build and evolve accordingly. They need to learn from their mistakes, harvest the lessons from each experience, and improve their ability to handle the unknown.

GAUGE 5: SPACIOUSNESS

It is easy for leaders to get caught in the weeds and the day-to-day demands of their work. Leaders need spacious time in their work lives to focus on visioning, strategizing, grappling with gnarly dilemmas, and finding inspiration. These functions often cannot be completed within an hour or two or squeezed in between a gaggle of meetings. Sometimes, these functions require a leader to take downtime without any specific focus. Some of the answers to my most significant problems have come when I have given myself a day off from meetings to think expansively.

GAUGE 6: RESTORATION

As leaders, we need time to for rest and restoration. This means ensuring that our day-to-day and year-to-year work rhythms have ebbs and flows. Research has shown that taking breaks throughout the day or vacations during the year enables people to be more creative and achieve better results. Being able to restore ourselves means having the time to enjoy our lives more wholistically, whether that means connecting with family and community, deepening our spiritual practice, or relaxing and genuinely taking time off from daily demands. Having time to restore ourselves allows us to become better leaders and encourages those around us to do the same.

GAUGE 7: CELEBRATION

Leaders need time to celebrate their individual and collective victories. As I mentioned in chapter 4 on cultivating success, too often, after reaching a big goal, leaders forgo acknowledging the effort and courage it took to achieve it and move on to the next one. Taking the time to celebrate victories helps leaders integrate lessons they learned along the way, value themselves and those around them, and replenish their grit and courage for the next endeavor.

Mai and Her Dashboard

Every leader I have coached and supported has greatly benefitted from paying attention to addressing their own needs. For example, I once worked with Mai, who was asked by her organization's board of directors to become the executive director when the current ED, a white woman, left after a seven-year tenure. Mai inherited an organization that was not set up for her success. The primarily white board had close relationships with the former ED, and they were used to how she had related to them.

The former ED, who was trained as a lawyer, felt very comfortable debating issues with the board. Mai was an Asian-Latina immigrant, English was not her first language, and she came from a country where external debate about issues, especially if it was seen as a critique of those in power, was not encouraged. Mai's communication was much more soft-spoken, though she was clear about what she wanted to do and how to get there. The board viewed her "softer" communications approach as a weakness and often interrupted or spoke over her at board meetings, undermining her leadership.

In addition, Mai wanted to focus more of the organization's services and advocacy work on immigrant and LGBTQ+ communities, two constituencies that were part of the organization's mission but that the former executive director had overlooked. Worried that the organization would lose funding if it changed the focus of its primary constituency, the deputy director was not initially supportive of Mai's intentions.

The organization was also running a deficit, so Mai spent the first nine months working seventy hours a week hustling and successfully raising enough money to get their funding in the black. When she and I spoke, she was running on fumes, feeling burnt out, unsupported, and questioning her ability to lead the organization. Mai felt she was failing on the job and wished she was more like the leader she replaced.

We discussed whether she was a good fit for the organization. I asked her, "What do you need as a leader to succeed?" Initially, she was taken aback. "This isn't about what *I* need; it's about what the *organization* needs!" We revisited her initial conversations with the board when she was hired. When we looked at the outcomes they wanted from their next leader, Mai fit the bill. As we talked it through, we concluded that she had the experience, skills, and talents to move the organization forward successfully. So, the question became how the organization could better support her leadership so she could make her greatest contributions.

Mai's initial response is common among executive directors, especially those from marginalized communities. We are not trained or encouraged to think about our needs or desires. Instead, we look at the organization's needs and dive right in, trying to plug every hole we can, even if it is at the expense of our well-being. But there will always be too many holes to plug. Instead, we make our most significant impact if we step back and explore where we are most excited to dig in and what kind of support we will need. Then, we can focus on the needs of the organization that match our strengths, skills, interests, and desires as a leader. Once we know where to focus, we can find other people to help fill the remaining needs.

In our following conversation, I asked Mai to think about what she struggled with in the organization and write down whatever came to mind. Here is some of what she wrote:

- Deep fatigue from running in place and not feeling productive enough
- Anger and frustration at the lack of support from the board and staff
- A belief of being unsuccessful

I next asked Mai to think about how she would ideally like to see herself in this position and to describe to me what was happening, "I see myself waking up excited to go to work because I know I will be able to accomplish many things with my great team," she told me. "My board members are checking in with me and asking how they can support me.

I have senior staff skilled at leading the work, and we all work together to achieve our collective goals. My work has meaning because we are reaching the people most in need," she concluded.

We created her dashboard of needs, similar to the dashboard of needs graphic I just introduced. In checking her gauges, she noted that many were pretty low, including her baseline of support, availability of thought partners, spaciousness in her schedule, and conditions for her to grow in this position. I then asked her to identify potential solutions that would increase these gauges in the short and long term. She came up with the following:

- Spending less time doing administrative work
- Working with a board that supported her leadership
- Building a more robust working partnership with her deputy director
- Being able to increase fundraising capacity that would bring in more critical resources for the work and the team

I worked with Mai to develop a plan to meet these needs so she could fully step into her leadership. At that time, Mai's organization didn't have enough resources to create a new position, but she did have a staff member leaving to return to graduate school. Mai used the money earmarked for that staff member to create a new position that would do all of Mai's scheduling, take over some of her administrative work, and do some of the easier grant writing.

We also worked on a series of interviews for Mai to conduct with each board member to assess their willingness to become the chair and partner with her to explore the possibility of expanding their programming into other communities that fit their organizational mission. We identified potential consultants that Mai and the board chair could bring in to help facilitate a retreat and developed a series of meetings to reset the board's culture and recruit new board members excited about Mai's leadership and vision.

Mai also decided to spend more time with her deputy director, first to gain his trust and hear more about his concerns and then to establish a strong partnership to work together to address these concerns. Finally, she identified a longer-term goal of raising more money by hiring three staff members to support the organization's administrative, fundraising, and programmatic functions as it grew.

As Mai implemented her plan, we would check in periodically on her needs dashboard, making adjustments along the way. It was not always smooth sailing. For example, at the beginning of Mai's tenure, a small group of board members kept questioning her leadership at every turn and requesting that she provide lengthy documentation for every key decision she was making. Mai was so demoralized and frustrated that she was thinking of quitting. We spent a few sessions developing an exit strategy so that Mai would know that she could leave, which gave her peace of mind. The board consultant led a meeting with the board, creating time for each member to share their appreciation for Mai's leadership. The consultant presented which executive decisions were appropriate for the board to approve and which decisions Mai could move forward with. The consultant then solicited questions from board members about upcoming decisions that Mai was making that were in the category of board approval. Fortunately, this meeting set a precedent for creating a more positive tone of support for Mai and establishing clear decision-making boundaries between her and the board. Another turning point emerged when two members who constantly questioned Mai left the board because they had reached their term limits.

Mai persevered through the following year, working strategically to make the changes she sought and continuing to develop trust with more members of her board and staff. Afterward, she told me that the most powerful lesson she had learned was that when she met her needs, the rest of the organization benefitted.

Her team was able to fulfill its mission more robustly by serving immigrant and LGBTQ+ communities. For example, in resetting the culture, the board and executive team became much more open to different communication styles, which fostered greater contributions from individual members. Increased collaboration resulted in higher staff retention and a stronger reputation within the community, making recruiting new staff easier.

Mai felt more supported in being authentic in her leadership and was able to use many more of her strengths to benefit the organization. This created an environment that encouraged other team members to do the same, and the organization achieved results that wouldn't have been possible otherwise.

Three years later, Mai had a board chair who was invested in her leadership and vision, a full-time executive assistant, and a much stronger relationship with her deputy director; she was about to hire a program director to oversee the expansion of their services to newer communities. She ran the organization from a place of resilience and vision as she continued to pay attention to meeting her leadership needs.

The gauges I identified in this section are the ones I use most frequently with myself and with leaders I work with. Feel free to add your own if you see any missing that will help you track the critical needs that fuel your leadership. If your gauge is close to empty, you will need to give yourself time to meet that need and address it. Mai focused on two of those gauges (Thought Partnership and Guidance and Meaning) before she could start addressing the other gauges (Baseline of Support, Professional Development, and Spaciousness).

One final note: If enough of these gauges are empty and you have no way of changing them given the current environment, you might want to take a moment to think about an exit strategy, as the conditions are not likely a good match for you and your leadership. Staying too long in conditions that prevent you from addressing these needs can have harmful consequences. Sometimes it is better to leave a leadership position if it continues to deplete your energy or causes damage to your physical and emotional health and well-being.

Component 2:
Knowing and Growing Your
Set of Internal Resources

When I think about how very few world leaders today genuinely have the best interests of the people they serve at heart, I feel utterly discouraged. But when I look at the leaders I know who are fighting for a different world and better conditions for all of us, my heart is filled with inspiration and gratitude. As leaders, we have so much to offer. These assets, which include our *moral compass*, our *strengths*, and the lessons we have learned from our previous *experience*, make up a set of internal resources we can utilize to achieve our purposes. When we are in challenging situations where we are taking bold steps, doing something for the first time, or working in a high-stakes situation, feelings of inadequacy can arise. On an ongoing basis, it is critical to remember, contribute to, and access our set of internal resources.

Using Your Moral Compass

Our values guide our actions, commitments, and behaviors. Our core values inform how we want to show up as leaders and serve as the moral compass for how we move. They are a tremendous asset within our set of internal resources as they illuminate which pathway we choose to get from where we are to our purpose. At any given moment, we can make many choices and take various actions, and if we don't use our moral compass, we can be pulled off course.

As we move toward our social change goals, our core values can ensure we treat those around us with care and dignity—even if they don't respond in kind. Our values can encourage us to deal with power and decision-making so that our team members feel appreciated and respected, even if they are not the final decision-makers. Shared values can promote a team culture that prioritizes trust and deep collaboration to help get through moments when strategic alignment doesn't exist. They can guide us through complex situations with more ease as they are deeply connected to our long-term purpose and overall mission in life. Our core values help us hold ourselves and each other with accountability and compassion through our mistakes. They can also foster a commitment to continued self-growth, to clean up any collateral damage for which we are responsible, and to bring our best selves, even in the most challenging situations.

CORRINE'S WINDING PATH TO VICTORY

Corrine Oqua Pi Povi Sanchez is the current executive director of Tewa Women United (TWU), located in the ancestral Tewa homelands of Northern New Mexico. TWU's mission is to end all forms of violence against Native women and girls and Mother Earth and to promote peace in New Mexico. Corrine is a nationally recognized leader within the field of sexual assault prevention and trauma-informed care. I have known Corrine for over fifteen years, had the privilege of working closely with her when she came to one of my leadership programs, and collaborated with her through our strategic initiatives. Time and again, I have seen how she relies on her moral compass to guide her through complex situations.

In the mid-2000s, Corrine successfully applied for and received an extensive Health Resources and Services Administration (HRSA) grant for adolescent health from the federal government. It was the first set of resources dedicated by HRSA for tribal communities. At over $1.5 million over five years, this was one of the most significant grants TWU had received. Even though the grant focused on teen pregnancy prevention, Corrine had a much more expansive vision of using the money. Proponents of teen pregnancy prevention programs focused solely on changing adolescent behavior by stigmatizing them, especially teens of color. Corrine believed this was not an appropriate way to empower young Native people who had survived a generational legacy of genocidal war waged against their people. She was determined to use the resources in ways that aligned with this understanding and with TWU's core values to help promote the health, safety, and overall well-being of Native youth in her tribe and in neighboring Indigenous communities.

In the first year of the grant, each funded organization had to go through a planning process with community stakeholders to help them select one of twenty-four curricula that HRSA had predetermined. Unfortunately, out of these curricula, only three had been tested within tribal communities, and none were created by Indigenous communities. During their planning process, Corrine and her team conducted multiple focus groups with parents, grandparents, young people, and LGBTQ+ Indigenous youth to assess the types of curricula that would work the best. They also consulted with other Indigenous organizations that had developed curricula for tribal communities, including Wise Women Gathering Place, founded by Alice Skenandore, a tribal member from the Lac Courte Oreilles band of Ojibwe.

At the end of the planning year, HRSA administrators convened a phone call to get an update about the process and where TWU was landing. Corrine was extremely nervous going into the call. Coming into such a call with a counterproposal was unprecedented. Corrine saw the opportunity to leverage these incredible resources to benefit Indigenous youth and communities in many ways. She wanted to test out innovative curricula that centered her community and also develop the leadership of the young people they served. She also sought to increase TWU's capacity to promote body sovereignty and healthy sexuality for Native girls and women. TWU was one of the first organizations to use the term *body sovereignty*, defining it as the "right and responsibility to have complete and unfettered control of one's own body." Corrine and TWU wanted to use the program to shift tribal culture to regard having full agency over their bodies as an integral component of political and land sovereignty for Native peoples. The stakes were high for this discussion to go well.

On the call, the administrators invited Corrine to start the meeting by sharing highlights and giving them any essential updates. When it came time for Corrine to reveal which of the preselected programs TWU was going to implement, she explained in depth her decision to use Alice's and TWU's curricula.

She was met with silence. Corrine, anticipating this tense pause, breathed deeply and waited. One of the administrators then told her that he would look into the program she proposed but that they needed more time. For now, they still wanted her to choose one of the preselected programs. Corrine calmly told them this would not work because none of those programs matched TWU's community values. One of the administrators retorted, "Are you saying that you are refusing to abide by our procedures?"

At this point, Corrine asked herself if she and TWU could walk away from this money, totaling $1.5 million. She looked down at her notes, which reminded her of all the conversations she had had, and she pictured the community stakeholders, advisors, and other reproductive justice Indigenous leaders who were standing with her vision of possibility for their young people. She felt emboldened by her moral compass. She replied, "After following the methodology and criteria *you* gave us, we identified a curriculum that deeply aligns with our culture, values, and mission. This is a tremendous opportunity for us. I applaud you for centering tribal communities. Won't you partner with us to implement this innovative program created by and for Indigenous communities?"

After she spoke, she was met with another moment of silence. But this time, the administrators let her know that they would have to discuss it and would get back to her. An hour later, they replied with an email informing her that she and TWU could proceed.

The program was a big success and was implemented in public, charter, and tribal schools in the local area. Corrine and her team continued to press for what was culturally appropriate and aligned with her values every step of the way. Instead of working with an evaluator who was unfamiliar with their community, they found a local evaluator within the community. This evaluator worked closely with TWU to develop culturally responsive metrics. In this process, Corrine and TWU program managers gained valuable evaluation tools and frameworks to bring to other parts of their work to make visible the positive outcomes they generated within their communities. They also trained young people from the community to develop their leadership as facilitators so students could learn from those who looked like them and spoke the same language they did. Parents became big advocates of the program. They saw how it taught their children to discuss their body parts with dignity and pride, as opposed to the shame and stigma that came from generational trauma and sexual abuse, plus a legacy of genocide, colonization, and patriarchy. By the end of the first round of funding, TWU's program, known as the A'Gin Healthy Sexuality and Body Sovereignty Project, became nationally recognized and honored multiple times by HRSA administrators.

HRSA awarded Corrine and TWU an additional two cycles of five-year funding. But for the third cycle, conditions were different. With the election of Trump, the HRSA bureaucracy had changed, and TWU found that meeting the changing HRSA requirements was confusing and onerous. With the advent of the pandemic, schools went virtual, which meant that TWU's program also had to adapt. Along with the disproportionate health and economic toll COVID took on Indigenous communities, TWU also experienced significant staffing changes, losing key program directors and managers. These were not conditions under which TWU could successfully implement the resources.

During this challenging time, Corrine made the difficult decision to return the money for the third cycle. This time, her core value of taking care of her staff and setting TWU up for success during these unprecedented times gave her clarity that the funding was not worth stretching her staff too thinly and compromising the program's quality. Corrine knew this decision would immediately impact TWU as this was still one of their most significant grants, and she was also worried about what giving money back would mean for their reputation. Even though she knew this was the right decision, a part of her was afraid that others would see it as a failure and question TWU's ability to do the work. Rarely do organizations take this step of returning resources because of the burden it creates to replace the funding and because it might result in other donors interpreting this as a sign that the organization no longer needs support.

However, as soon as she informed HRSA of her decision, she felt relief. Over time, she saw that her decision created an opportunity for TWU to move forward. Being free from the government grant's restraints meant they had complete flexibility to evolve and adapt the program to the community's current needs. In addition, not having to administer the grant gave Corrine more time to reflect on the current needs of TWU and their communities. Instead of being a sign of failure, Corrine's courageous decision to return the funds set them up for future success!

During their thirtieth anniversary, TWU celebrated paying off their small office building. However, with the growth of their programs, they needed more space for the staff to hold their programs. One summer day, a staff member found out about a building that was perfect for them that was up for sale. Corrine called on her bold spirit and emailed her most supportive funders. The next day, she received a response asking her to confirm that this was what she wanted for TWU. The following day, she received word that she had the resources to purchase their new home. Corrine and TWU are a shining example of what happens when you dare to use your moral compass as a guide.

Connecting to Your Strengths

Along with our values, our set of internal resources contains our incredible cache of strengths. Strengths are what we do often, what we do well, and what we love doing. Using our strengths increases our level of impact in multiple ways. One of my favorite things to do is to help leaders connect to their strengths. If we are aware of our strengths, we can leverage them for a more significant impact. Even though we each have strengths, many of us need to take more time to focus on them. Perhaps this is because we don't get much external encouragement to do so. Knowing our strengths enables us to leverage them when needed, but it also helps us further develop them to be even more effective in our leadership.

TELLING THE STORY OF MY STRENGTHS

I first got acquainted with the notion of strengths when I attended a three-month leadership training to support executive directors led by Rich Snowdon and Michelle Gislason, two gifted facilitators and coaches. They asked us one at a time to tell a story of the best moment in our leadership. As I told my story, the others in the group wrote down any talents and strengths they heard on 3×5 cards—one item per card. When I was done, I was given the stack of cards they made. I laid them before me and was asked to reflect on all the strengths people saw in me. Then, the rest of the group members took turns with the same exercise.

I still remember the profound impact this activity had on me. As a woman of color who was also very tied to the Chinese cultural value of humility, I rarely talked about my strengths. I would have previously characterized this activity as bragging, which was taboo in my gendered and racialized socialization. But with the kind support of Rich and Michelle, I emerged from that experience with a glow. It was deeply gratifying to experience other leaders not only naming my strengths but appreciating them with such excitement and care.

This process also helped identify some of my strengths that I wasn't even aware of. For example, Rich saw a strong ability to connect with people in my story. I identified as someone who enjoys people, but up until then, I had not thought much about what happens when I bring people together. After reflecting on the story I told them about building my first team, I could see the strength of connection I had used. I enjoy bringing people together to work for a common cause. I hadn't thought of this as a strength. However, this activity made me aware of how I can set up conditions that bring team members with diverse life experiences together to find chemistry and collaborate. Telling my story helped me become aware of the effort I use to strengthen the glue between teammates and colleagues by designing various team-building activities, spending time getting to know each person, and helping people around me feel seen and valued. From that moment, I was excited to embrace this as one of my strengths, and it has become a core talent that I use almost every day in my leadership work.

I received so much from this experience that I now regularly use this activity in my leadership sessions. It not only supports the storyteller in identifying their key strengths, but it also makes it possible for them to transform by telling their story.

For example, Anna was a participant in my Stepping Into Power fellowship. She focused her strength story on a recent community mobilization she had led to protest healthcare cuts. She had identified twenty immigrants, including five undocumented women, who were willing to speak out to legislators about their experiences and the need for healthcare. Under her leadership, her organization had the highest turnout of community people among the fifteen organizations that participated. As she told the story, her demeanor changed, her voice grew more animated, her face showed great excitement and passion, and her shoulders visibly relaxed. The transformation continued as she received feedback from the small group listening intently to her story. Her cards included: "brave; courageous; able to make an impact; fantastic organizer; deeply connected to community and grassroots organizations; able to move people into action; change maker." I noticed tears in her eyes as she saw her strengths pointed out by other leaders. She told me later that this was a pivotal moment for her as her leadership was recognized and celebrated by other leaders in the movement. It allowed her to fully develop her strengths with exponentially more confidence and power than ever before.

STRENGTHS FROM OUR CULTURE

Our strengths don't exist in a vacuum. Sometimes, we develop them through encouragement from our families and cultural backgrounds. What isn't mentioned in traditional leadership training on strengths is that they can be influenced and shaped by our cultural norms. It's important to reflect on our strengths using the lenses of race, culture, and other identities to help us understand ourselves better and make choices about how we use and relate to these strengths.

When I look at my set of strengths, I see that some come from the cultural values I grew up with. For example, the state of harmony is significant in Chinese culture. This value was ingrained in my childhood development and shaped how I learned to deal with conflict. However, because Western society values dealing with conflict in a particular way, I didn't readily recognize it as a strength—I had mislabeled myself as being conflict avoidant. But now, I see that I don't run from conflict and instead face it squarely using a set of strengths to help me navigate it in a way that works well.

Growing up, I didn't witness much fighting between my parents. I rarely saw them argue in front of my brother and me. At Saturday's Chinese school, they taught us the importance of harmony. Peaceful coexistence was important in our families, communities, and society for progress to happen. But in our family, this harmony was active, not passive. I knew my parents disagreed at times but would work things out behind closed doors or when we were in bed at night. So, I learned from them that you have to work at harmony to achieve it. It happens when people move through the disagreement and tension with a commitment to finding a positive resolution. I grew up seeing my Chinese immigrant parents resolve their differences with each other, with other family members, and with their friends and coworkers in ways that preserved the relationships and maintained harmony.

And so I learned that disagreements can often create beneficial results with enough effort and trust. Throughout my life, I focused more and more on treating tensions and arguments as opportunities to develop greater understanding, deeper trust, and potentially new solutions while avoiding escalation and disruption of the relationship.

Disagreements and conflicts abound in our workplace. When I think about the people I've worked with who were born in different places, speak various languages, come from various family formations, have survived violence and trauma, and hold multiple social identities, I understand how easily miscommunication and misunderstandings can happen without anyone intending them to.

Proactively moving toward harmony means that before I enter a discussion, I work to clarify what *I* want to get out of it. If I don't take the time to do this beforehand, my default is often defensive. Giving myself space to identify my purpose allows me to step back and recognize my end goal. Sometimes, I want to be heard, and that is enough. Other times, I want to discuss different options with the other person. Understanding my purpose helps me know my bottom line—what I am willing to negotiate and what I'm not.

Another goal I have is to try to understand the purpose of the person I disagree with. Ascertaining their purpose can help me see things from their perspective and gain new insights or see possible solutions that I might not have seen or considered from just considering my own point of view. If this is truly a partnership, I need to hold both of our purposes simultaneously to reach a win-win solution.

Lastly, one of my primary purposes is to stay connected to the person, even when we actively disagree. This is critical because when I don't embody this connection, if the discussion escalates, I can enter fight, flight, or freeze mode, which isn't helpful if I want to preserve ultimate harmony. I want to move toward tending and befriending, which will help me maintain my connection.

The strength of maintaining connection is something I have developed as an anchor practice when I'm in active disagreement with someone. When I disconnect, it is easy for me to start to draw lines in the sand between us and pepper the other person with harsh and sometimes unfair judgments. When I let this happen, I can lose my incentive to work through the challenges to resolve our differences. Treating the other person with unconditional empathy helps me step into their shoes and see the situation from their perspective, and it is from there that I automatically gain insights that I haven't seen. I work to listen with exquisite intent to truly understand their perspective before articulating mine. I've learned to maintain an open heart toward the person I disagree with as I remember their humanity and see their strengths.

One of the things I have experienced through conflict is that I always have more to learn. Our behaviors are just the tip of the iceberg when it comes to what we bring to any situation. We often carry incorrect or only partially true assumptions about others. When I disagree with another person, I do my best to confirm that my core assumptions are accurate by asking clarifying questions to help me understand their underlying motivations and the values that drive their behaviors.

But there are things I can learn about myself, too. For example, if I react strongly during a disagreement, I can ask myself if any part of my reaction is influenced by past experiences. If it is, I can work on separating those past emotions and processing them more fully. This helps me respond more clearly in the present situation, allowing me to handle the disagreement with greater clarity and emotional capacity.

Strengths from Fighting Oppression

Sometimes, we cultivate strengths in response to overcoming challenges from oppression. For those of us who come from marginalized communities, the oppression we face gives us ample opportunity to develop or shape our strengths as part of our coping mechanisms.

My strength of relentlessly practicing is a double-edged sword for me because it is partly rooted in internalized oppression. This strength was borne out of a survival strategy and fueled my perfectionism. The racism that I faced growing up caused me to internalize the message that I wasn't inherently good enough. One of the ways I coped with this was to keep practicing things until I did them very well. If I did well, other people would see me as worthy and valuable. Through the years, this drive to excel through practicing new skills has served me well because I have progressed in many different areas. But it also has hurt me because at the heart of my efforts is this sense that I must keep repeatedly proving myself to be seen as worthy.

Over the last decade and a half, I have worked hard to address these patterns of self-loathing and see the rich gifts I have to offer as a leader. I've learned the importance of being gentle and appreciative of these double-edged strengths because they have helped me survive the oppression that I have experienced. But I also acknowledge that I need to explore my motivation for using these strengths so that I don't perpetuate self-harm and instead move only from a place of deep self-value.

I know my inherent worth now. I still enjoy practicing new skills, but when I find myself striving to excel in something, I pause and look for my underlying motivation: Is this something I want to do because I enjoy it, or am I trying to prove myself again? If it is the latter, I question whether I can proceed in a way that supports my self-worth rather than one that is driven by my fear of not being worthy.

Leveraging Past Experiences and Lessons Learned

Another crucial component of our internal resources is the wisdom we gain from past experiences. We, as leaders, don't face each new goal as a blank slate. We bring our previous experiences, accumulated knowledge, and lessons. But sometimes, these resources are easy to forget. It used to be that whenever I tackled something I had never done before, my default mindset was to erase my prior experiences and lessons learned and overlook the skills that were relevant to the purpose at hand. As a result, I always felt like a beginner, which, in fact, I wasn't. This mindset eroded my confidence even before I started.

When I'm working with a leader taking on a new project and feeling daunted, I ask them to do an internal audit of their previous experiences, knowledge, and skills to see what they can directly apply. For example, let's look at the situation that Malika faced.

Malika is a seasoned leader of a long-standing organization that works with currently and formerly unhoused families and individuals. In this case, Malika wanted to run a capital campaign to raise $1 million to buy a building for her organization. As we started our coaching session, I asked her to rate her confidence in achieving her goal. She gave herself a 3 out of 10 because she had never run a capital campaign before, and this was bigger than the annual budget she had to raise. Not surprisingly, she was intimidated by the task. She told me she didn't know if she was up to the challenge.

Malika and I began working on mapping the skills she brought to the table. I started by asking her to list the skills necessary to succeed at this campaign. She listed the following:

- Crafting a great pitch
- Tracking the financials
- Creating a campaign with a timeline and benchmarks
- Connecting to donors of high wealth
- Building strong relationships
- Developing materials to share with donors
- Asking for money

Once she completed this list, I asked her to rank herself for each skill according to the following: 0 = I haven't done it before; 1 = I have used it once or twice but don't feel good at it; 2 = I use frequently and am decent at it; 3 = I use often and am great at it.

Here was how Malika ranked herself:

- Crafting a great pitch (2)
- Tracking the financials (1)
- Creating a campaign with a timeline and benchmarks (2)
- Connecting to donors of high wealth (1)
- Building strong relationships (3)
- Developing materials to share with donors (3)
- Asking for money (2)

We saw that Malika had identified two skills as strengths that she often used: developing materials for donors and building solid relationships. In addition, she had three skills—asking for money, crafting a great pitch, and running a campaign—that she could continue building upon. So even though Malika hadn't run a capital campaign, she had skills and experience that she could work with—something she hadn't realized before our coaching session.

I then asked her to list any previous experiences that might be similar to leading a capital campaign. She identified the following:

- Raising money from foundations
- Asking for money from major donors
- Asking for donations for her niece, who needed a bone marrow transplant
- Running a charity event for her local church
- Running a campaign to pass a local policy ordinance

Next, I asked her to tell me a story about a successful experience that had brought her joy. She spoke to me about when she had been part of a campaign to raise money for new classrooms for her children's school. She had just moved to her neighborhood two years earlier and didn't know anyone. As a result of participating in this campaign, she made new friends, created relationships with key administrators in the school district, and felt proud about raising more than the initial goal that she set for herself. When the campaign was over, she felt a sense of ownership over the school where three of her kids go now.

After this, I asked her to tell me about some lessons she learned from that effort that might be relevant to leading a capital campaign. She listed the following:

- Build relationships before I ask for money.
- Listen to the donor to identify what they care most about so I can speak to their interest.
- It takes time to raise money and build relationships.
- Working with a team is more fun than asking for money alone.
- I will get more noes than yeses, but I will still get yeses.

- I won't get any money if I don't ask.
- I will build lasting relationships that benefit the organization over the long term, even if people initially say no.
- Getting support after getting a no will help my resiliency.
- It's essential to revisit and evaluate my progress midway through the campaign and then make adjustments.
- Getting one big donor attracts other big donors.
- All I need to do is start with one ask.

Looking at this list, Malika realized that even though she hadn't worked on a capital campaign, she was not starting from scratch. After completing our session, Malika was relieved and found new excitement as she was now armed with the skills and experiences she could leverage to help her succeed. When I asked her to rate her confidence level now, she rated it 7. Malika went from a 3 to a 7 in one and a half hours simply by recalling what she could bring to the table. This exercise helped her remember that she already had a wealth of knowledge and skills she could draw upon to launch this big campaign, even though it was a first for her. We also discussed her getting support from experienced consultants, as capital campaigns can be challenging.

Component 3:
Activating Your Superpower of Self-Growth

Imagine if you could emerge from any situation you face in your leadership with increased capacities and core strength. This can happen with an ongoing commitment to and practice of growing yourself as a leader. Leadership is developmental. As human beings, we have remarkable potential to learn from our experiences. Here are three key strategies that I have found helpful to continuing my self-growth as a leader:

Ongoing Self-Reflection: Every day, I take a step back and reflect on how I am responding to recent events, conversations, and developments in my life. This allows me to see the parts of myself that are triggered or reacting in ways that are not beneficial to me and/or others. I then try to explore my behavior and emotions with compassion, curiosity, and as little judgment as possible. Doing this helps me understand myself better and identify perspectives and habits that I can let go of because they are no longer serving me.

New Skills, Behaviors, and Mindsets: Once I see what isn't working for me, I can start to explore ways of responding that will be more favorable and life-enhancing. For example, as I was searching for ways to respond to stress more effectively in my life, I turned to meditation and qi gong to calm my nervous system. I also have found that writing down my fears and worries helps to dissipate them so I can think clearly and more strategically without getting in my own way. Self-reflection revealed that in challenging situations, my default mindset was to find ways to control the problem to get the outcome I wanted. Replacing that mindset with one that acknowledges where I do and don't have control has resulted in my experiencing less suffering.

Practice and Integration: Changing behaviors and mindsets that no longer serve us is usually not easy. They have probably been with us for a long time as we have adopted them to help us cope with life's challenges. Becoming aware of them, understanding that they are no longer useful, and identifying different ways of responding takes courage, patience, and self-compassion. But unfortunately, we can't stop here. We need to remove those old, deep patterns and replace them with new ones. The only way to make this happen is to practice these new skills, behaviors, and mindsets regularly and start to integrate them into our lives. No matter how much motivation I had, change only happened when I found a way to practice my meditation, qi gong, and writing regularly. Some of the changes happened quickly and some didn't manifest until a year later. Only after intentionally carving out time in my day and week to do ongoing practice was I able to start to see more profound change.

Self-growth is our superpower because it enriches our leadership in powerful and transformative ways. We can use it to emerge from many situations with even greater capacities to deal with what may be around the corner. It enhances our leadership by increasing our self-awareness, deepening fulfillment in our pursuits, and expanding our opportunities to lead in ways that benefit ourselves and those around us. Here are two examples of leaders who have used self-growth to expand their leadership power.

Blanca Creates a Big Win for Her Teams

Blanca is an immigrant from Brazil and a parent of two kids. She leads campaigns for climate change and was recently promoted to deputy director at her organization. To Blanca, it felt as if everyone there was running the eternal sprint, working sixty to seventy hours a week and traveling three hundred days out of the year. Staff often complained that they had too much on their plates and were moving too quickly all of the time. Blanca saw stepping into this new position as an opportunity to shift the culture to have a more sustainable pace. But to do that, she knew she needed to find new tools to bring to the organization.

One day, a friend mentioned an upcoming mindfulness retreat for social change activists. Blanca was intrigued because it was led by two women of color, one of whom also came from the climate change movement. She was excited to learn new practices that she could use to help the organization.

We met a few days after her retreat ended, and I was happy to hear about her rich experience and aha moments. Her realizations particularly struck me because of the nature of the issue; many activists in the climate change movement are understandably driven by fear of what will come with out-of-control global warming. Being able to stop and deeply reflect during the retreat helped Blanca see how challenging it is to be in fight or flight mode all of the time as activists carry this collective trauma. After spending a week meditating and slowing down, Blanca realized how rare it was for her to be present in the moment at work. She realized that she could regulate her emotions more effectively when she moved with mindfulness. She began to understand how much her work was driven by anxiety and fear. This anxiety and fear was also negatively affecting her sleep, her ability to think expansively, and her interactions with her team and her kids. After the retreat, her focus improved dramatically. Instead of feeling pulled in fifty directions and having her attention divided over email, text, and phone, she experienced much more capacity to reflect deeply and gain new insights on the key problems she had been facing over the last few months; she knew she would not have achieved this without slowing down.

Together, we worked on creating a growth path for Blanca so she could further integrate these mindfulness practices into her daily work life. She started doing a twenty-minute meditation every morning and scheduled forty-five minutes every other day to eat lunch in the park by her office. She also set designated times to check her email and phone instead of compulsively checking them throughout the day. In addition, she and a few other activists from the retreat agreed to meet regularly to support each other and decided to attend a similar retreat together. As the months went by, Blanca began to notice that her sleep was getting better, and she was less tired. Slowing down allowed her to be driven less by fear and threat and more by her core values. She limited her work time during the weekends and spent more time with her kids, which made her whole family happier. When Mondays came around, Blanca returned to work with more energy and creativity than if she had worked through the weekend.

Once confident in her practice, Blanca set up quarterly half-day retreats with the teams she led. Each retreat started and ended with a brief mindfulness meditation, a team-building activity, and time to reflect and strategize together. Over time, her teams appreciated these sessions so much that they made them full-day quarterly retreats. They found them especially useful in taking a step back every quarter, reflecting on the impact and progress of the work, and making adjustments as needed. Doing this made their strategies much sharper and their impact greater as they could adapt to their changing environment much more quickly than if they waited until the end of the year, which they had traditionally done.

Kelly Overcomes the Self-Doubt Spiral

Kelly is a two-spirit Diné single parent raised in the Navaho Nation. Growing up, Kelly faced a lot of challenging conditions. Their grandfather physically abused them while their mother, the primary breadwinner, worked long hours; Kelly was left alone a lot. Many of Kelly's friends didn't graduate high school, but Kelly was determined to get their degree and be the first in their family to attend college. With the support of their aunt and a teacher, Kelly graduated at the top of their class and received a full scholarship to the state college.

After college, Kelly was hired at a local community clinic, where they answered the phones and made patient appointments. But they had their sights set on other positions. They soon applied for a program assistant position at a local nonprofit that provided services to the nearby immigrant and Indigenous communities. Kelly was a hard worker and volunteered for everything they could, and in a year and a half, they were promoted to take over the program manager position. Then, they were hired as a program director at another organization. Over the next decade, Kelly applied for graduate school and received a master's in public health.

I started working with Kelly when they were first hired to direct a program at the county hospital to help unhoused young people get services and mental healthcare. Very few people of color were employed at their level within the hospital, and none of them were Indigenous. Kelly came to me for help navigating imposter syndrome. Even with their impressive track record and credentials, Kelly was plagued with self-doubt. They second-guessed themselves when making decisions, managing staff, and speaking up at director-level meetings.

We had one of our sessions after Kelly accidentally miscalculated an expense, pushing their allotted budget into the red. Kelly's supervisor was not pleased and told them they had to manage their budget more carefully. I asked them to write down all the messages they were telling themselves about this mistake. After looking at all twenty-four messages they wrote down, they realized how harsh their negative self-talk was, including referring to themselves as a horrible person who was greedy and irresponsible. Kelly called this familiar process their "self-doubt death spiral," which would often take them into days of feeling down or even depressed. Kelly was struck with the vitriol these messages carried in response to an accounting error. They also realized that some of these were the same messages they received from their grandfather and other adults as a child. This was an aha moment for Kelly, and they asked me to help them work on this habit of self-doubt because it was causing them a great deal of internal suffering.

Self-doubt can have roots in childhood, as Kelly had realized. Fortunately, Kelly was just beginning to work with a therapist who could help them explore the impact of their childhood trauma and adverse experiences on their self-confidence and self-esteem. On a parallel track, Kelly and I started creating a growth plan for their leadership at work. I was impressed with Kelly's determination to tackle this issue in therapy and in our coaching sessions.

I asked Kelly to make a list of their internal resources. They jotted down bullet points that included their core values, their strengths, accomplishments, and lessons learned that have positively contributed to their leadership. Kelly created four pages of bullet points, which I asked them to tape to the wall next to their computer for easy reference.

I then invited Kelly to take a few minutes at the end of their workday to reflect on any moments of self-doubt they experienced. After doing this for a couple of weeks, Kelly was surprised to see that messages of self-doubt were creeping in during the day quite frequently and that they were often unaware that these messages were in their head.

After doing this for another couple of weeks, Kelly was more able to catch themselves when they were starting a self-doubt spiral. During those moments, we agreed that Kelly would step away from their desk and sit in a predetermined comfortable chair where they could take a few minutes to breathe deeply, focusing on the exact points when they switched from an inhale to an exhale and vice versa. After they could feel their heart and breathing rates slow down, they would refer to the four-page document of bullet points they created, continuing to breathe deeply. Kelly reported that after doing this for a few weeks, they could see results. The deep breathing helped to interrupt their process of going down into the death spiral, and looking at the document helped remind them about all the assets they had brought to their leadership.

In doing this repeatedly, Kelly could see that they have the inner resources to deal with their worst fears should they happen, and if they made a mistake, they would be able to grow from it. For example, after Kelly made the accounting mistake, they developed a practice of reviewing any big-ticket items with the finance director to double-check their arithmetic and ensure they were not over their budget. However, the bigger lesson Kelly learned was to be more self-compassionate after making mistakes. This growth enabled Kelly to recover from mistakes or failures more quickly. Instead of defaulting to a shower of negative self-criticism, they worked to be gentler and more compassionate with themselves.

Like many of us plagued with self-doubt, Kelly's work continues today. But the benefits from their commitment to addressing it for over three years now have been palpable. The frequency of them feeling like an imposter has gone down dramatically. They can catch themselves much more quickly before they go too far down the self-doubt death spiral, preventing a lot of self-induced suffering. They can see the contributions and benefits they are bringing through their leadership with greater clarity and appreciation.

POWERING UP MY LEADERSHIP
A CASE STUDY

The components we've been discussing—your dashboard of needs, set of internal resources, and superpower of self-growth—are rewarding when you use them separately. But now, let's look at how much more powerful they can be when you use them together. Here, I give you a snapshot of my process for creating a big project. I include a part of my overall purpose and then show how I use the Powering Up components together to create synergy. When using the Courageous Operating System, you don't have to use the components in the order I have presented them in this book. Feel free to find the order that works best for your current situation. For this example, I start with purpose and then move immediately to my superpower of self-growth as I created Stepping Into Power, which, as I have mentioned before, was a nine-month experiential movement-building fellowship for leaders.

Purpose

One of my core purposes for this program was to create an environment where participants could engage with the Courageous Operating System using their whole selves and build a community in which they felt a deep sense of belonging.

Superpower of Self-Growth

Whenever I create or facilitate a program, it is an opportunity to deepen or expand my capacities. I was eager to use

Stepping Into Power to explore how I could incorporate different methodologies to complement the mind-body practice I was utilizing so that participants could engage even more fully with the material and with each other while bringing their full selves. Music, art, and storytelling deeply touch me. Because I know how movements around the world have used these modalities to create powerful change, I was excited to learn how to integrate them into my work with leaders.

Assessing My Leadership Dashboard of Needs

When I assessed my dashboard of needs, one of the first things I focused on was Gauge 3—Thought Partnership and Guidance. I knew that I needed to enlist my colleague, Amy Wu, to the team. Not only would the program benefit from her incredible graphic design talents, but she would also serve as a critical thought partner as I designed the fellowship.

Because leading people in song and storytelling were not two of my strengths, I needed to find people who would partner with me. I was thrilled when Melanie DeMore, a grammy-nominated singer-songwriter and self-identified "vocal activist," and Michael Balaoing, who had taught communications and storytelling to tens of thousands of people worldwide, decided to join my team.

I was also thankful for my team at Forward Together, who offered a variety of essential support, including facilitation, administrative and logistical assistance, event planning, and, of course, ensuring we had delicious food. I was confident that this team would provide outstanding care for the participants and foster a welcoming atmosphere for these leaders.

Calling Forth My Values

Although I was clear about the fellowship's purpose, I used my values to guide the experiences I wanted the participants to go through as they engaged with the material. These were the values I focused on:

- Promoting a sense of belonging
- Meeting the diverse learning needs of participants
- Acknowledging that every one of the participants has something to teach and to learn from each other

Using My Strengths

I used many of my strengths to create this fellowship. One of them was my ability to create conditions that help people, who may initially be strangers, connect over time and build a deep community of trust and collaboration. The first thing I did was set up an interview with each participant two months before the program started. I talked with them about their learning style. I got a good sense of the talents and strengths they could bring to the collective work we would be doing together. They also informed me about questions they were grappling with in their leadership. Later on, after the program started, participants shared how these conversations helped them feel welcomed, seen, and valued as they came to their first session, enhancing their ability to dive into our work together.

I leveraged my ability to design intricate curricula that seamlessly integrated multiple learning methodologies into a cohesive experience. Each day included movement and breathwork, multiple engagements with Melanie to experiment with music and rhythm, and opportunities to tell their stories of leadership with the support of Michael. Additionally, I incorporated a variety of learning environments to accommodate the diverse needs of participants, including large group discussions, small group peer consultations, and individual or paired reflections. These different formats were designed to address various learning styles, promote inclusivity and relationship-building, and foster strategic collaboration within the group.

Fruits of My Labor

After months of planning, the first day of Stepping Into Power arrived. The stakes were high. I had spent so much care and time building out this fellowship, and now was the moment of truth. As I walked into the building with butterflies in my stomach, I didn't know what to expect. Participants came from all over, and few knew each other. This was the first time I had done something like this. Fears, in the shape of questions, swirled around in my head. Would this group gel? Would they find the material and methodology engaging? At the end of the session, would they walk away with what they needed?

But as I entered the room, I walked into a space buzzing with positive energy. Even though this was my first time meeting the attendees in person, all of the preparatory work my team had done with each participant had already created a culture of community.

Leaders laughed and got to know each other over breakfast, their first of many meals together. Because I had previously had virtual introductory meetings with the participants, we greeted each other with great warmth, as if we were already friends.

As I started facilitating, I began to see all of the parts I had worked so hard to create unfold as each connected with another and with the participants in the room. Amy's incredible art canvases lined the room, making the components of the Courageous Operating System come alive. I was nervous about whether the participants would be willing to sing together. But leaning into the positive vibes at breakfast, everyone brought an open spirit and answered Melanie's call to create rhythms and music together as we moved from the cafeteria to the meeting space. As we clapped our hands and sang in call and response, I could see the bonds between participants strengthen. This generated a joyful energy in the room and extended a wonderful invitation for us to embrace ourselves, each other, and our leadership in a positive and affirmative way.

This was the perfect segue into the Courageous Operating System. I invited participants to share a personal story of a courageous moment in their leadership when they faced great odds and stood up for what they believed in for themselves and their communities. As they shared their stories, I felt the level of collective respect, compassion, and inspiration building. Some told their stories for the first time and witnessing them own their leadership in this new way was truly powerful.

As we moved our way through the day, participants were filled with their experiences from that morning, which connected them to their courage, to each other, and to the impact of their leadership. This created a seamless bridge enabling them to share their leadership visions with each other. Michael asked them to convey their leadership vision while adding dynamic range to their voices and using gestures, posture, and movement to bring their vision alive to the audience. In just one hour, we saw a dramatic improvement in their public speaking. Seeing them take command of the front of the room with confidence, humor, and grace was breathtaking.

The last day of the fellowship came all too soon. Participants shared that being in this program helped them feel more prepared to tackle challenges and complexity. It was the shot in the arm they needed to return to their leadership's front lines, bolstered by their discoveries and the new community they were now a part of.

After the fellowship ended, many participants worked on joint projects together. Some were promoted to positions of greater responsibility and influence. Together, we went on a journey that brought us individual and collective joy, meaning, purpose, community, and growth. I felt like a composer who powered up each individual's leadership to create a marvelous symphony.

Your Turn

Get into a State of Readiness

You can use the relaxation activity outlined at the beginning of the Your Turn section in chapter 1 or select one that works for you.

Creating Your Dashboard of Leadership Needs

To create your dashboard of needs, you can start with the gauges I outlined earlier and add your own.

Baseline of Support: Do you have enough support from your key stakeholders to perform your role? Do you have solid relationships with people on your team who support your leadership? Does your work culture support your leadership and the leadership of those around you?

Meaning: Do you have opportunities and space to connect to your purpose and vision? What meaningful difference are you making in your leadership? Are there pieces of your work that you are especially excited about?

Thought Partnership and Guidance: Do you have a circle of people to turn to for support, guidance, and problem-solving? Do you have people who will challenge you compassionately to be your best? Who do you need to bring in to create this circle?

Professional Development: Do you have opportunities to gain the skills you need and continue to grow your leadership? Did you build in time for development in our ongoing workplan?

Spaciousness: Do you have time to focus on strategy, think innovatively, grapple with big dilemmas, and find inspiration? How can you block off the time you need?

Restoration: Are you taking time to restore yourself during the day and throughout the year so that you can replenish your reserves and continue over the long term?

Celebration: Do you often celebrate and honor the victories you have gained?

Which of these gauges, including any you added, need your attention? And of the ones that need your attention, which are the ones that, if addressed, would make a significant difference in your leadership moving forward?

Assessing Your Set of Internal Resources

Your internal resources will continue to grow over time. It is a good idea to periodically assess these assets so you can readily leverage them when needed.

Creating Your Moral Compass

A. Think about a current or upcoming project or effort you are embarking on.

B. Write down the core values you want to embody, keeping in mind

- How you want to show up as a leader
- How you want to make big decisions
- How you want to treat those around you, especially in difficult times

Keep this set of values readily accessible so you can refer to them during moments of confusion, when charting your path toward purpose, or whenever you need grounding for your action.

Auditing Your Strengths

Use this activity, developed by Rich Snowdon and Michelle Gislason, to help you identify your strengths:

A. Find a person or two to do this activity with.

B. Each of you should think about a time when you were in your leadership flow—when you were making the kind of impact you were excited about, or perhaps when you were having a greater impact than you ever imagined.

C. Take turns telling each other your leadership story. As the listener(s), write down each strength on an index card or Post-it for every strength you hear in the story.

D. When the storyteller is done, the listener(s) enumerates each strength and then gives the stack of strengths to the storyteller.

E. When everyone is done telling their story, each of you can lay out all of your strengths in front of you. Group them according to themes. Note any surprises. Note if any core strengths are missing and add them.

F. During the week following, notice when you use your strengths and if there are any that you missed.

CHARTING YOUR SELF-GROWTH PATH

A. Think about a current or upcoming project or effort you are embarking on.

B. Answer the following questions about keeping your project in mind:

- What new mindsets will you need to develop?
- What skills will you need to deepen or acquire?
- Are there behaviors you will need to change or shift?
- Who are the people you can enlist to help you?
- What knowledge, analysis, and information will you need?
- What new practices will facilitate success?

C. For each answer you wrote down, develop a way for you to grow in that manner. For example, if you write down "learning how to give and take feedback," jot down a few notes about how you will do this. This might include coaching or training, or finding opportunities to practice giving and receiving feedback.

D. Once you have a pathway for growth, you need to make room for it in your calendar and workplan.

7

TAKING CARE OF YOURSELF, TAKING CARE OF THE WORLD

Our healing is within us. When we acknowledge our pain and take the time to care for ourselves, we are honoring our ancestors and paving the way for future generations.

—SHIRLEY CHEECHOO

Caring for myself is not self-indulgence. It is self-preservation, and that is an act of political warfare.

—AUDRE LORDE

Caring for Ourselves

Once, I asked a group of thirty leaders if creating conditions for their communities to live healthy and vibrant lives was one of their top priorities.

Without hesitation, they all nodded yes. Next, I asked if one of their top daily priorities was to take care of themselves, so that they, as leaders, could live healthful, vibrant lives. This time, very few people responded with a yes. Wanting to explore this more, I asked the group to call out what came to mind when they thought about "caring for themselves." Here are the words that spilled out:

- Self-indulgent
- A luxury
- Something I don't have time to do
- Gets in the way of the "real work"
- Inconvenient
- On my wish list
- Something only people with money can do

Why do we consider the health and well-being of our communities as critical, while putting our own needs at the bottom of our priorities? What happens when we isolate the care of our emotional, physical, and spiritual health from our social change work? What are the implications of putting our well-being last?

To help answer some of these questions, I invited the leaders to recall a time in their lives when they were at their most depleted, running on fumes, or on the verge of burnout. Once they each had a moment in mind, I asked them to talk about the consequences of being in this state for themselves and then for others—their family, their community, and coworkers. Here are some of their responses:

- "I lost my temper easily and constantly yelled at my kids."
- "I felt like I was on a hamster wheel—not accomplishing anything, going around in circles, but unable to get off."
- "It took me three times as long to do things—I was very inefficient."
- "My colleagues started avoiding me because I was bringing them down."

- "I woke up with dread because I knew I couldn't accomplish everything on my day's to-do list."
- "My family and coworkers became concerned about me and I felt like I was taking away from them rather than giving back to them."

I could feel the energy seep out of the room as they commiserated with each other with these all-too-familiar sets of feelings and experiences. Next, I asked the group to physically or emotionally shake off that moment while taking some deep breaths together to generate fresh energy in their bodies. "Now," I told them, "I want you to visualize a time when you were in your flow and functioning at your best. Think of a time when you felt well rested, energized, connected to your work, family, and community—a time you were doing what you loved and using your strengths." Once they each had a moment in mind, I asked the group to talk about how their state of being affected them and those around them. This time, their responses were very different:

- "I woke up excited and ready to go every morning because I had the energy to get things done."
- "People around me were inspired by the creativity that I brought to my work and they created more."
- "Even though I wasn't working long hours, I got twice as much done as I usually did."
- "I spent less time procrastinating and more time *doing*."
- "My joy spread to others around me—my kids were happier."
- "I felt more grounded and balanced so that when something unexpected happened, I handled it better."
- "Because I was exercising regularly, I had an outlet to release my stress and move forward with much less anxiety."
- "My best decision-making happened not at my desk, but when I was taking some down-time."
- "I was well rested."
- "I experienced joy more often."

- "I felt more alive and was physically and emotionally healthier."
- "I felt more connected to my family and community."
- "I was able to have the space to relax and rejuvenate."

Caring for ourselves. This concept is critical to our well-being as leaders, but unfortunately the notion of self-care has been co-opted and deployed by policy makers and consumer culture to erode the social safety net and the responsibilities of the state for the health and well-being of its citizens. A cornerstone of democracy is that the government has a responsibility and role for the care and welfare of all its citizens. When the onus is on individuals to tend to their well-being based only on the resources accessible to them, low-income and otherwise marginalized communities are disproportionately burdened by the harmful economic, social, and political structural forces they face. As healing and disability justice activists have argued so powerfully, we cannot separate the health and well-being of the individual from the oppressive conditions and responsibility of larger societal institutions. And, within this context, it is still vital for us to attend to our own care and healing.

Journeys of Self-Discovery

As leaders, we work every day to address urgent societal conditions so our communities can get vital needs met, like clean water, accessible transportation, and freedom from violence. It can be challenging to prioritize caring for ourselves. But our physical, emotional, mental, and spiritual well-being strengthens us as human beings and as leaders. Many personal care strategies depend on access to resources and employment opportunities that unfortunately aren't available to everyone. Examples include visiting a doctor, going to the gym, or taking sick and vacation time off. However, I am aware of many leaders who, despite having access to these resources, still do not take advantage of the care they need.

We can take care of ourselves in many ways; some of them I briefly mention in chapter 2 when I discuss the courage to nourish ourselves.

In chapter 6, I focused on creating conditions for leaders to address their professional leadership needs. In this chapter, I explore the inner work we, as leaders, can undertake to connect with our personal needs, no matter how messy or uncomfortable they may be. I discuss how we can tend to these needs over time, leading to positive and profound changes that help us evolve as individuals and leaders.

If we are running on fumes, we become role models for burnout. If we are not aware of the ways oppression has shaped and hurt us, we can internalize harmful narratives about ourselves that keep us thinking and acting in small ways. If we don't make the time to process the trauma we've experienced, healing may not happen. I have found that when I carve out time to take care of my core personal needs, the journey can take me on a path of self-discovery that is transformative for myself and my leadership.

Untangling My Rope of Vigilance

My stress has manifested itself in my sleep. When I was young, I often had nightmares of being chased by people or monsters. Afterward, I would wake up out of breath. I can't remember a time when I didn't struggle with insomnia. In early elementary school, exasperated after lying awake for what seemed to be hours, I would get my dad, and he would lie on the floor next to my bed until I fell asleep.

My insomnia continued into my early career. But what kept me awake was no longer fear, but excitement. It was invigorating to take on leadership for big projects. My mind was in perpetual problem-solving and planning mode, so a good night's sleep was elusive, and I was frequently tired. My allergies grew worse. I developed the beginnings of chronic digestive issues. I wanted to manage my stress because it was starting to affect my quality of life.

First, I looked for a tool to slow my racing mind when I went to sleep. At the suggestion of a friend, I started meditating for forty-five minutes before I went to bed. The meditation did help me calm my mind and sometimes, not always, I was able to fall asleep with slightly more ease.

During this time, I also started reading books by Thich Nhat Hanh and attending his dharma talks when he came to the Bay Area. I learned the importance of slowing down, not just right before bed, but during parts of the day. I started taking mindfulness walks to work. I tried to eat mindfully. I began to see the benefits of living a less frenetic life. I had more clarity. I was able to get through the day with more energy. I found joy and awe in the small things, like the magnificent magnolia trees in my neighborhood, with thousands of vibrant purple and white flowers that exploded like fireworks onto their branches.

Eventually, my partner Jen and I decided to have kids, and once we did, my meditation and slower daily life actions paused. I had no time or energy to sit in stillness or eat mindful meals because we were so busy taking care of these two amazing little beings who had become the center of our lives.

Being fatigued became a regular part of my life again as a new parent with nightly and early morning waking further exacerbating my ability to sleep long and deeply. I was also in the early stages of running an organization so a lot was on my plate. I knew that I needed to prioritize finding a way to rest and be energized. As I continued looking for solutions, my doctor suggested a sleep study and I was subsequently diagnosed with moderate sleep apnea. The puzzle of why I was waking up out of breath at night was finally solved.

Although wearing the god-awful mask that comes with a CPAP machine did help me feel more rested after sleep, it didn't stop my insomnia. So, I tried adding exercise to my daily regimen. I started taking walks around the neighborhood. To my surprise, I soon found these walks were not only beneficial physically but also helpful psychologically. Back then, the way that I dealt with challenges or difficulties was to push aside any big feelings that came up in response to what I was facing so that I could move to problem solving or intervention. During my walks, the emotions that I had previously buried or compartmentalized had space to bubble up to the surface. Finding it easier to work with them while I was in motion,

I was able to stay with them and process them rather than run away from them. Over time, I noticed that doing this regularly enabled my sleep to get better.

By the time Trump was elected the first time, I was getting up early to walk every morning. I desperately needed this time to calm my nervous system. As I mentioned in chapter 2, in 2019, within a period of six months, my parents both had strokes and my mom's Alzheimer's grew much more severe. I dealt with one medical crisis after another. And then COVID hit. As I was facing all of the challenges that the pandemic brought to my work, I also had to help my family navigate everything that we were experiencing. I needed to manage my stress and work on keeping myself grounded like never before. I wanted to move through this chaos with as much clarity as possible and keep my wits about me. I found a therapist to help me carry what I felt was too much to hold on my own.

Not surprisingly, my sleep was affected. It was very frustrating because just when I was about to nod off, I would jolt myself awake. I grew angry at myself. Why would I sabotage my sleep in this way? Why would I want to keep myself from falling asleep?

My therapist encouraged me to take a deep dive into exploring the vigilance that I had identified that was keeping me up. Doing this deeper psychological exploration was akin to looking at a rope from a different perspective. When you look at the rope from far away, you view it as a single entity. But when you come closer, you can see the different strands that create the whole. I knew that my hypervigilance was a barrier to sleeping, but I had never taken the time to really examine it. When I started looking more closely, I saw that many strands were woven together to form this rope of vigilance.

One of the strands I first explored was connected to the racism I experienced as a child. As I explained in the chapter 1, when I was five, my world was rocked when Billy started taunting and teasing me for being Chinese. I learned from that experience that it was never safe to let down my guard. Every time I got targeted with racist taunts, this strand grew stronger.

Another strand in this rope of vigilance focused on my fear of mortality. My father was a worrier. He went through the world looking for signs of perpetual danger. When I was growing up, he would tell us stories of having to run from Japanese soldiers when he was a child in China. It was only when I was in my forties that I made the connection between my nightmares of being chased incessantly and my parents' experiences of immigration, displacement, and loss. My parents taught me that staying vigilant kept us safe as a family.

The third strand was my need for control. It gave me comfort to think that in any situation, I could do something to make things better. I had to come to terms with the fact that I had very little or no influence over the political climate and my parents' deteriorating health. It felt like falling off a cliff because I had nothing to hang on to. This was how I had coped with danger and crisis throughout my life. I put my armor up. I mustered up the courage I needed to move forward. I fixed things. I solved problems. I was a planner and made sure everyone had what they needed. But I was starting to see that this habit was actually contributing to my suffering and negatively impacting my physical and mental health because it was all based on an illusion.

I identified another strand that emerged when I became an executive director. I experienced pretty early on that when women of color step into positions of power, many of us face intense scrutiny and criticism. Sometimes, the feedback was important for me to hear, to learn from, and to be accountable for. And at other times, I became a lightning rod for misplaced anger or frustration due to misunderstandings. My commitment to take responsibility for any adverse consequences caused by my actions and my desire to be prepared for lightening-rod moments increased my motivation to scan my environment constantly.

The final strand of hypervigilance came from the part of me that used fear and intense pressure to keep myself motivated. If I had an upcoming deadline, these fears and pressure I put on myself would keep me awake with concerns that I wasn't going to finish in time. If I had a significant training coming up, my overactive mind would tell me that I still had time to prepare and to make sure that I didn't forget anything. If I had a big project with high stakes, it would remind me about all of the people who were counting on me to succeed, and it would show me how many would be disappointed if I didn't do my best.

Holding the rope in this way was excruciatingly difficult at times. I learned I had to feel into the hard emotions that came with each strand. I had to find courage to sit with all the internalized shame that came from my experiences with Billy and the hurtful messages I gave myself about my worthiness and value. I had to surrender to the reality that some of life challenges are far beyond my control. I did not previously regard myself as being a fearful person. I still don't. In my daily life, I carry myself with confidence and welcome trying new things. However, this process made me see the various fears I had suppressed that were lying just underneath the surface. Fear of not meeting expectations. Fear of being judged. Fear of being isolated. Fear of being incompetent. Fear of loss. Fear of dying. I started to see how these strands were building up over time and, when woven together, they created this very strong rope of vigilance that was diluting my power, shrinking my sense of self, and keeping me from letting down my guard, even in sleep.

With the support of therapy, I found the courage to turn toward these big feelings instead of stuffing them deep inside. I learned not only to acknowledge them, but to embrace them as parts of myself that were trying to protect me the best way they could. Instead of being frustrated or angry with these parts within that kept me awake, I worked to develop compassion for them. Seeing the individual strands gave me the ability to work with each of them as they were calling for different things from me. Turning toward my shame, instead of banishing it, helped me release it and start to heal from that self-hatred cultivated by racism.

Stepping through one of my greatest fears—losing my parents—created space for me to be in stillness with them. When I was growing up, I was so scared of my parents' death that I doubted my ability to be there for them during their final days. But, as I worked with this strand, I found that I was more able to be still with them, sitting in immense gratitude for all that they have given me and my brother, and I was able to accompany them on their last chapter, including my father's passing. Now I am able to catch myself when I start excessively worrying or feeling responsible for situations beyond my control, I can lean into my growing self-trust. I trust that I will be able to handle what comes my way as a leader, as a parent, and as a human being.

Being on this journey has helped me become a much stronger leader because I can help others go on their journeys of self-discovery by attending to their needs. I have a bigger bandwidth to hold complexity and have used what I've learned in my work with diverse leaders in the movement, leaders in philanthropy, and leaders in the mental health field. In my work with them, I can help them find their own rope that has been a persistent presence in their lives.

These ropes come in different shapes and sizes. Some leaders have a rope that causes them to shut down in challenging situations. This rope can also be made up of many strands, including previous experience with violence or abuse, fear of failing, or being conditioned to avoid conflict. Other leaders I have worked with have a rope that makes it hard for them to ask for what they need. This rope can be made up of strands that include traumatic experiences from childhood, socialization and gender norms, and fear of rejection or judgement.

We, as leaders, can care for ourselves in countless ways. This inner work is very personal and, as a result, we don't hear enough examples of how this happens. The following are three stories from leaders who are dear to my heart and who exemplify the courage and commitment it takes to do the kind of work that benefits them and those around them and that inspires the change that needs to happen in our world.

Malkia Transforms Grief

Malkia Devich-Cyril is an award-winning activist, writer, and public speaker on issues of digital rights, narrative power, Black liberation, and collective grief. They are the founding and former executive director of

MediaJustice, and since 2019, have served as the organization's senior fellow. I have known Malkia for over two decades. We both started as brand-new executive directors a few years apart, simultaneously growing our respective organizations. We both led small local efforts focused on young people that, over the course of two decades, would expand to national organizations with staff across the country. Malkia is a champion for Black liberation and a future where we are all "connected, represented and free," and has led successful campaigns to keep powerful institutions from silencing and exploiting the nation's most vulnerable voices. I have been inspired by Malkia's unyielding commitment to disrupting capitalism, patriarchy, and white supremacy. And, over the years, I have learned from Malkia a different way to hold grief.

Traumatic loss has been an ongoing companion in Malkia's life. Growing up in Brooklyn in the 1980s, they experienced the loss of many loved ones and community members from sickness and violence caused or exacerbated by patriarchy, state-sanctioned violence, structural inequality, and anti-Black oppression. In 2001, the same year the project that would become the MediaJustice organization launched, Malkia learned that their beloved mother, Janet Cyril, a leader in the Harlem chapter of the Black Panther Party, would soon die from sickle cell anemia. For the next four years, Malkia flew across the country one week out of every month to help relieve their sister of caregiving duties. Their mother was a key shaper of Malkia's politics, principles, and practice, and her passing had a profound impact. When she died, what Malkia needed most was to take time from work, but that was not to be.

After Janet passed, Malkia's organization was still a nascent, fiscally sponsored project with a budget of less than $200,000. They didn't have any long-term bereavement leave or disability policies, which were generally absent from nonprofits back then. Malkia couldn't walk away from their work, even if they wanted to, because they had no access to a salary or health insurance. In addition, at that time, grassroots nonprofits didn't have built-in administrative, HR, or operations support, so a lot of those functions fell on the executive directors. Malkia was concerned that taking time off could threaten the stability of the organization. So while Malkia grieved the death of their mother, they also carried the life of a new and necessary organization on their shoulders.

To make it even more challenging, Malkia worked at the intersection of strategic communications and digital rights and power where very few people of color were in leadership positions. In fact, the media justice sector as we now know it did not exist. Instead, it was led primarily by white male attorneys, technologists, and policy wonks based in Washington, DC. In the words of Malkia, "At the time, Black male leadership in these fields was rare and primarily rooted in large civil rights organizations. Black women leaders in these arenas were even less recognized, and Black studs like me were relatively invisible. If they were in those sectors, I didn't know about it. To the best of my knowledge, I was the only one for a very long time." The pressure Malkia faced to succeed was tremendous.

When we talked, Malkia shared that at the time of their mother's death, they didn't have the skills or support to fully process the loss; it felt all-encompassing and too overwhelming. As a result, they threw themselves into their job—working through the night and traveling all of the time. In doing so, Malkia ensured the organization's survival. They led successful national campaigns and helped to build the new media justice and digital rights social justice sector. But, as Malkia reflects back now, these wins came at extraordinary personal costs that affected others around them as Malkia suffered burnout and poor health.

Eight years later, Alana entered Malkia's life. She and Malkia connected as former college classmates. They become good friends, then best friends, and then soulmates. The combination of the two created a brightness that was exponentially expansive and full of joy. Tragically, just one year after their marriage in 2015, Alana was diagnosed with incurable end-stage gastroesophageal cancer. Malkia dove into becoming a full-time caregiver with the support of their large community. The journey was excruciatingly painful, including twelve rounds of forty-eight-hour chemotherapy infusions, brain surgery, and frequent emergency hospitalizations. Alana courageously fought the cancer with everything she had, even creating an award-winning documentary short, "My Life, Interrupted," which has since screened in various places around the country. As Malkia says, "Cancer could never beat Alana. Alana won. Alana's life remains a breathless act of intention and inspiration, a grace the world has never seen before and may never see again."

When Alana died, almost fifteen years after Malkia's mom's passing, Malkia was less alone with their grief. They were already part of a caregiving support group. Over four hundred people came to Alana's service, some of whom were involved in helping with Alana's care. This time, Malkia was able to lean into their grief because they and their material conditions were different. Malkia was now a seasoned leader and a more grounded and centered human being. They "surrendered to the reality that they were going to be a mess" and they made plans to leave the organization. Their organization was at a mature state, with a budget of $3 million, and they had multiple staff overseeing finance, operations, and administration, which enabled Malkia to take some time off for bereavement leave. But Malkia knew they needed even more space to move through this momentous loss. They worked with the board to create a succession plan, bolstering the organization by raising additional funding and staff, and they stayed to effectively transition the organization to its new leader.

Then the pandemic started and with it came a disproportionate number of deaths within Indigenous, Black, and Brown communities. Malkia faced another round of acute grief. Isolated and alone in quarantine, they found it utterly devastating. Like many of us during that time, Malkia had a deep need to connect and to take care of their physical and emotional well-being. So, they addressed these needs in a number of creative ways, centered in community care. What started as a small gathering of family and close friends coming together for song, meditation, a brief sermon, and fellowship, swelled into a group of between sixty and one hundred and fifty people. Malkia's Pandemic Joy, a Zoom event on Sundays, became a powerful way to build community in an ongoing way within the horrible conditions of COVID. When restrictions started lifting, Malkia brought people together to engage in other ways. Malkia needed physical exercise to manage their diabetes and found it easier to do this with company. They started organizing community walks with ten to twenty people at a time. They rented out swimming pools for the day to invite people to join and called it the Pool Sharks Swim Team. They rented entire restaurants and movie theaters, hosting dinners and movie nights, trusting that those who came would not only provide good company but help cover the costs. They took the initiative to move through this process by placing grief where it belonged—inside community. Malkia knew that they would need not just space but time to focus on and process their grief for a number of years.

Coming out of this period, grief has become central to Malkia's movement work at the individual, community, and structural levels. They are in the process of starting a grief lab to experiment with how modern freedom movements lead through this era of loss, and they are developing strategies for healing and sustainable work for social justice organizers in California in partnership with the new Movement Innovation Collaborative. They have visited incarcerated people in hospice to help them process their grief and talk about the legacy they want to leave. They have worked with School Crisis Recovery and Renewal to create a grief bill of rights with educators and families in the aftermath of destructive wildfires and the COVID pandemic. They seek to develop support for organizers, strategists, and changemakers who are in their mid-to-late careers to focus on financial and end-of-life planning, creating wills, and determining power of attorney for themselves and their loved ones. Across all of these emergent projects, Malkia is calling for the social justice movements to learn what it takes to navigate through disaster, mass loss, and crisis.

They have emerged from this decades-old journey of being present with, processing, and honoring the role grief has played in their lives to encourage us all, as leaders, as a community, and as a society, to walk into our individual and collective grief in its various layers and use it to catalyze the change we need.

Shiree Champions Love

Shiree Teng's work in the social sector started over thirty years ago when she was a community organizer for farmworkers. I have had the great fortune of working with her in different capacities over the course of my career. Shiree is boldly authentic, asks questions that strike to the heart of the matter, exudes generosity and warmth, and is a fierce advocate for those who dedicate their lives to social change. Two common threads that have been present throughout all my interactions with Shiree is her commitment to speak her truth unapologetically and to move with deep integrity.

Growing up under British colonial rule in Hong Kong, Shiree knew that she and her family didn't have power and would never attain it. When she immigrated to the United States, she experienced additional layers of oppression as she struggled to learn English as a second language and faced anti-Asian racism. Surrounded by racial, sexual, and economic prejudice from both of these countries, Shiree was inundated with harmful and hurtful messages, some of which she unavoidably internalized.

But Shiree is a fighter. Driven by her commitment for social change, Shiree continued to find opportunities to create better conditions for grassroot communities that faced disenfranchisement because of capitalism, patriarchy, and colonization. Ten years ago she began working as an evaluator for nonprofits. Shiree was frustrated with the limitations of traditional forms of evaluation that were supported by research and academic institutions. These methodologies focused on objectivity, being evidenced-based, and being measurable, which were not conducive to measuring issues and dynamics such as courage, culture change, or leadership transformation. As she grappled with this tension, Shiree started consulting with a nonprofit organization that was working to reduce recidivism rates among formerly incarcerated men of color by "delivering programs rooted in love, hope and healing." At one point an executive director she was working closely with, Sammy Nunez, asked her, "Shiree, how do you measure love?" This stopped Shiree in her tracks because no one had ever asked her that before. Love is seemingly so amorphous. It's a feeling. Its subjective. It is individual. It is immeasurable. Or is it? Sammy's question stayed with Shiree for five years. And in response, an inner dialogue emerged from deep within her, "If we are not full of love in this work, why are we here? Making change does not result in a high paycheck or prestige. We do it out of love. Love for our families, our communities, and for a better world. And yet, we don't talk about love enough in our social change work." Shiree set out to learn how to measure love.

She invited Sammy to coauthor a brown paper, "Measuring Love in the Journey for Justice," and enlisted the support of Audrey Jordan and Kate Morales.[1] Together, they sought to provoke discussion on how love shows up in social change work, raising questions such as "How much am I loving?" "How am I wielding power fused with love?" and "Are we loving bravely enough?" One of the paper's central tenants was that learning to love is a radical and conscious act of resistance in the face of injustice, colonization, and imperialism. They bring out various dimensions of love as it shows up in leaders, in community, in the movement, and in larger society. The paper identifies ways to measure love that are both visible and invisible through our behaviors, actions, and feelings; it is a call to action to highlight the importance and power of love in making social change. Inherent in the practice of justice are the qualities of truth, reconciliation, forgiveness, and reparations. And, according to the authors of this paper, you can't have any of those qualities without love. "No love, no justice." The paper articulates twelve dimensions of love on the individual, group, community, and societal levels.

A few weeks before they were going to publicly release the paper, a news story erupted about Sammy. He had been arrested on allegations of child sexual abuse of a family member. Shiree was beyond devastated. She went through a period of shock and disbelief and felt the sky had dropped on her. Questions swirled through her mind. How could this have happened?

Who was the real Sammy? How could she have held Sammy so close to her heart? As a survivor herself and advocate in the sexual assault field, how could she have missed this? How was she going to get through this?

Shiree went into a period of deep reflection that included wading through anger, betrayal, sadness, and grief, which brought her to the core of what it meant to be human. As she processed this previously unimaginable turn of events, she asked herself, "What is the worst thing *I* have ever done? Have I done what I needed to do to repair the people whom I have harmed? Is Sammy's life not to be considered sacred because of his worst actions? Is my life not to be considered sacred because of my worst actions?" She recognized that the harm she had caused was not close to the magnitude caused by sexual abuse and she was in no way excusing his actions. But she also realized that as human beings, we all have the capacity to hurt others to various degrees. So how do we hold ourselves and those around us accountable with compassion?

Shiree believed in practicing what she preaches. She looked at one of the core principles from the paper, which invited readers to align their behaviors with their core values. For Shiree, this meant shining a light on what she identified as her *shadow self*. We all have shadow selves that are made up of past behaviors that we are ashamed of, mistakes we have made that have hurt others, or personality traits and emotions that are difficult to acknowledge. Those of us who have done it know that it is not easy to address these shadows as they often are not aligned with the core values we carry as leaders moving against the current. It takes great courage, and for Shiree, this process was, in her words, "hard as hell." She wrote in her journal the names of people who she wished she had treated differently and with whom she felt she might need relational repair. She knew these conversations were not going to be easy. Some of the breaks she had experienced with these people had occurred thirty years prior. She knew it was possible that doors might be slammed in her face. But her commitment to be in integrity with herself and her truth drove her to persevere. According to Shiree, "in a society that is constantly gaslighting us, including how this country was 'created,' dishonesty is the norm. Asking for honesty in this context takes so much courage and I realized it has to start with me."

Through this period of deep inner work that included a combination of processing past events and letting go, Shiree worked to repair and restore relationships. She learned that by having the strength to look at those hard things and heal from them, she could handle anything. Her heart and spirit grew. Along with that, she increased her capacity for self-forgiveness. She discovered that a lot of the shame and negative messages she had held about herself came directly from oppression and discrimination and she was able to release them. She trusted herself in ways that she had never experienced before and with that came joy—a type of joy that she now knows will catch her during the challenging moments. She was breaking free of the self-hatred that was imposed on her growing up and was learning to love herself more and more.

Shiree and her team (Audrey, Kate, and Rosa Gonzalez) wrote a follow-up paper, based on this experience, called "Healing Love: Into Balance," which includes what they learned from processing their experience with Sammy.[2] This paper focuses on how to use love to bring our world back into balance. In a world that is broken, we may also feel broken at times. How do we avoid further contributing to the existing damage and how can we act in ways that don't result in breaking other people around us? As the authors posit, "We are all capable of giving and denying life. We are at once all of our best and worst qualities." By loving with courage, telling the truth as we heal, and being truly authentic in our relationships, we can be in better balance within ourselves, with others, and in our work for community change.

Transformed from this experience, Shiree is helping others live into measuring and experiencing love. For example, Shiree has been working with C. Nathan Harris, the Director of Community Philanthropy at the Oregon Food Bank. Nathan wanted to move from a charity framework in which rich people donate to the poor and the hungry to one that authentically reflected how capitalism and systemic oppression create hunger in our society. Nathan wanted to pivot to using love as the measure of the organization's success. Shiree worked with them to devise a survey for their team, the staff of the organization, and their donors that included the twelve dimensions of love outlined in "Healing Love: Into Balance." She also facilitated a number of discussions and exercises with the team to help them practice loving themselves and infusing love into their team and with their donors. These efforts along with Nathan's leadership resulted in impressive outcomes. They have raised more money, obtained more small donors, and partnered with more donors of color than ever before.

The average job length for a fundraiser is just sixteen months, according to one study.[3] Fundraisers leave for a variety of reasons including burnout and low salaries. In addition, the power dynamics within philanthropy creates situations in which fundraising staff are vulnerable to sexual harassment and abuse. In fact, nonprofit scholars have found that three out of four fundraisers have experienced sexual harassment, often from donors.[4] When Nathan created an environment where team members felt valued, seen, well-compensated, and respected, employee turnover rates decreased significantly. More donors than ever now regard the Oregon Food Bank as their political home.

Shiree continues to live her life with deep integrity. This isn't a passive process. It takes a lot of effort. She has a daily practice of deeply reflecting on her actions, experiences, behaviors, and feelings. Figuring out what needs to be digested. What needs to be purged. What needs to die. She then harvests the remaining nutrients and lessons. And when you meet Shiree, you can see the fruits of her labor. Joy, love, and authenticity flow freely from her as she welcomes you with her expansive smile and all-embracing hugs.

Ezak and Community Care

Ezak Amaviska Perez is a two-spirit, Hopi Native American, a Xicanx leader, co-founding member of Indigenous Pride LA, and a nationally recognized trans leader. I met Ezak when they joined Stepping Into Power, a fellowship I created for leaders. One of the first things I was struck by was Ezak's kind and gentle spirit and their deep love and care for the community. For Ezak, caring for themselves and caring for their communities are inseparable.

Ezak and their two siblings were raised by their mother, Yvette Amaviska Perez. Growing up, there were times when they didn't have access to many resources, leaving them unhoused. But Yvette did everything she could to care for her kids. She surrounded them with love, something that Ezak knew growing up was unfortunately not a given for every kid. Yvette's mandate for her children was that even though they didn't have much money, they could move in the world with dignity and know they belonged. In turn, she was relentless in finding ways to provide for their needs. At times, she couldn't afford to buy new clothing, so she made their clothes. Somehow, she figured out how to get them into summer camps with free scholarships. She did her best to move them to places where they would be safe. Ezak learned about the power of kindness as their mom sometimes cared for kids from other families who needed attention. Yvette was also fierce in her care for her friends. One friend, with whom they were staying at the time, was in an abusive relationship with a police officer. Yvette organized community support for her through letter writing and phone calls that resulted in the department firing the abuser.

Growing up, Ezak longed to be in community. In high school, house parties and raves were where it was at for Ezak. They and their friends would gather at someone's house and dress up in their queer attire, which allowed them to express their gender identities in flamboyant ways that were not welcomed at school. As they moved from apartment to apartment, sometimes they didn't know where they would be when the sun rose the next day. But in a world that was otherwise very unsafe, they created this space to be fully themselves with each other, and that made all the difference.

As Ezak grew older, they started going to places to get food, vouchers, and stipends. They came to get the essential items they needed and for community. Wherever there was community care, they knew they would find queer and trans people providing services. Wanting to give back, they began to volunteer at these places. They were contributing to the strong tradition of mutual aid in the queer/trans community from the times of the Stonewall Uprising, to the AIDS crisis to the pandemic.[5] LGBTQ+ individuals who face discrimination and are often denied support by the medical system and other societal structures have relied on network and community support for care. As they entered these spaces, Ezak felt they could breathe easier, see themselves reflected in others, and tap into a bigger community aligned with their core values.

Ezak learned from their mom as well as from their ancestors that resistance, love, and kindness get you through the most challenging times. When Ezak started working at Gender Justice LA (GJLA), they wanted to continue building community and deepen their understanding of what care could look like for nonbinary and trans communities. One of the very first community events they hosted was a pool party. Ezak loves swimming and has been doing it ever since they were a baby. One of their fondest memories growing up was swimming with their cousin for hours upon end. It was one of the few places where Ezak felt truly free; being in the water was pure joy. But as they grew into their queer and trans identities, swimming became much less accessible for Ezak. During the few times they would venture to the public pool, they always made a safety plan with their partner in case any pool staff or customers perpetrated any transphobic harassment or violence.

One warm day, Ezak and a GJLA volunteer were brainstorming ideas for bringing community together. They asked themselves, "What would be fun? What does our community need? And what do we want to do right now?" The idea of a pool party was born. They had very little funding, so they had to be creative in pulling this off. They made a flyer with a cartoon illustration of a pair of feet and hairy legs at the edge of a swimming pool and posted it on Facebook and at other LGBTQ+ organizations. Someone they knew had a connection with the city of West Hollywood and could reserve a public pool for a few hours. They brought snacks and nonalcoholic drinks and then waited, hoping some people would show up.

And the community responded. People started pouring into the pool. One of the first things Ezak noticed was how relieved people felt when they realized they could choose to go into either of the locker rooms and be completely free to dress or undress as they wished. At first, people seemed shy about getting into the pool, but gradually, one person got in and then another. And soon, after seeing the fun people were having, more and more people jumped in. Some were fully clothed. Others had their shirts off, maybe for the first time ever in a public pool. People spontaneously started playing Marco Polo and other games. At one point, Ezak looked around in amazement at the intoxicating joy that the community was experiencing. Unfortunately, being fully themselves at a public pool was a very rare experience. As word got around, people continued showing up with their kids, and bringing pizza to share for the group, which grew to one hundred people. Ezak saw that community, relationships, and love interests were forming right in front of their eyes.

Over the years, Ezak has continued their commitment to community care, coupling it with other strategies to evoke systemic change that benefits the health and well-being of trans communities of color. For example, during the pandemic, Ezak prioritized caring for themselves and their communities during this challenging time. They established TGIFridays (TGI stands for transgender, gender expansive, intersex in this case) at the GJLA Center, offering free acupuncture, massage, reiki, and workshops focused on healing and wellness. For some people who came, it was the first time they felt comfortable getting these services because they hadn't had access to nonbinary and trans healers and wellness practitioners before. It was a space to relax, enjoy each other's company and have fun. But the center was also a place where people could come to make memorial candles and grieve the deaths of those in their communities from COVID or gender-based violence. Ezak and their staff felt the need to be prepared for any emergency. They started organizing workshops where participants could 1) do pod mapping, as first described by disability justice activist Mia Mingus, 2) assemble emergency supply backpacks with blankets, masks, COVID tests, charging stations, and first aid kits, and 3) include an extra supply of estrogen or testosterone as needed.[6]

Providing spaces for community care was necessary for Ezak and GJLA. Still, they knew that it was also critical to address institutional changes that document and provide healthcare to nonbinary and trans communities in Los Angeles. In 2021, they published the largest participatory health study on transmasculine people in that county.[7] The report called attention to the serious health disparities facing this community and put forth an agenda for health and research justice. This participatory action research involved members of the trans community who played key roles in the process, including defining the research questions, collecting the data, creating the illustrations, and analyzing the results.

This report is one of the few research models for and by trans people. Most public funding for research related to transgender health is initiated and implemented by people without lived experience.[8] There have been instances of researchers harming trans community members who volunteered as subjects for their studies. One such research project, which claimed to help trans folks, used unethical methodology which caused mental health distress in its participants. Ezak and other leaders put out a warning to trans, gender nonconforming, and intersex community members about this harmful effort and successfully demanded that the project be halted immediately.[9] They have since put out a guide to help trans people avoid exploitation as they participate in future research studies.

Since then, Ezak and other trans activists, scholars, and advocates were invited to be part of a research collaborative network housed at UCLA, which was formed to recognize the harm that academic and other institutions have enacted on TGI people. The goal of this effort was to "increase access to university research resources for transgender, two-spirit, gender-expansive and intersex communities and to align these resources with the needs of these communities."[10]

GJLA, under Ezak's leadership, has not only survived the pandemic but has doubled in size and budget. Their model of community care continues to have a significant impact. In 2022 alone, Ezak and GJLA served over twenty-four thousand community members through in-person and virtual outreach and community-building activities, mutual aid efforts, policy campaigns, programs, and participatory research initiatives. In February of 2023, they opened a beautiful new community center to expand their services and build out their art, healing, wellness, and research justice services. Ezak is a shining example of how caring for oneself as a leader is inherently connected to caring for community. By caring this way, we transform ourselves, our community, and the world.

Elements and Outcomes of Self-Discovery and Transformation

To transform the world, we need to heal and transform ourselves. Malkia, Shiree, and Ezak's inspiring examples demonstrate the powerful results that can happen when we embark on these journeys of self-discovery, healing, and transformation. While no template works for everyone, these examples show that common elements and outcomes arise from each of our stories.

ELEMENT 1: THE COURAGE TO EXPLORE DIFFICULT EMOTIONS

Each of these leaders was courageous in exploring difficult emotions. Feelings of shame, self-hatred, grief, isolation, yearning, and loss were present in each of their experiences and were part of the driving force that allowed each of them to begin their journeys. They were open to looking at places in themselves that were raw, messy, and tender. They sat with the unknown and embraced their discomfort and pain as they interrogated what was wrong or hurting inside them. Marshall Rosenberg, founder of Nonviolent Communication, relates how emotions tell us a lot about our needs. He writes, "There are no positive or negative emotions, just emotions we feel when our needs are met and emotions we feel when our needs are not met."[11] He created a list of feelings that are associated with unmet needs.

ELEMENT 2: CONNECTING WITH COMMUNITY

In their journey to care for themselves, these leaders were deeply connected to community. They used their vulnerabilities and strengths to help themselves and those around them. Enlisting community support and giving back to community were elements interwoven throughout their processes. They took what they learned about themselves and regifted it back in spades to help those around them build their capacity to care for themselves.

ELEMENT 3: COMMITTING TO PERSONAL GROWTH AND PRACTICE

They used this opportunity to address their core needs: to grow, heal, and transform themselves. Theirs was not a one-time effort. They went on their journey for years, prioritizing this inner work and continuing to delve deeper on an ongoing basis so they could get to the root of what they needed for healing and understand how they could resist and fight against oppression that negatively impacted them. They are different people than they were when they started their journey.

ELEMENT 4: CONTEXTUALIZING EXPERIENCES

Each contextualized their experiences within the societal forces that impacted them. The roots of their suffering were connected to the oppression they faced, whether it was sanctioned state violence, colonialism, transphobia, patriarchy, or capitalism. They each recognized that their healing included continuing to work for systemic changes as well as their individual efforts for growth and transformation. Furthermore, they found the courage to value themselves and prioritize their well-being within a society whose values and practices contributed to their pain and suffering.

These elements were not easy to integrate into their lives, but the results that they experienced from their efforts were transformational.

OUTCOME 1: MORE JOY

Each leader told me that joy is one of the primary outcomes of their journeys. Not only do each of them experience joy more, but they can inspire others to find their joy through this profound work.

OUTCOME 2: INCREASED CAPACITY

Their processes also helped them gain an increased capacity to handle the challenges that come their way and to help others do the same. By turning toward and honoring their vulnerability, pain, and loss, they grew their courage, learned how to give themselves what they needed to heal, and gained new insights and tools that they could use to help those around them.

OUTCOME 3: TRANSFORMATION

Each of these leaders is different from when they started their journeys; the changes they made were significant and immutable. They will never go back to how they were before. They will continue to leverage this transformation for current and future growth in their leadership, benefiting themselves and their communities.

Your Turn

Get into a State of Readiness

You can use the relaxation activity outlined at the beginning of the Your Turn section in chapter 1 or select one that works for you.

Identifying Unmet Needs

As mentioned earlier, Marshal Rosenberg believes that certain feelings point to unmet needs. Here are some examples of feelings from his inventory:[12]

• Fear	• Anger	• Tension
• Aversion	• Pain	• Vulnerability
• Annoyance	• Embarrassment	• Yearning
• Confusion	• Sadness	• Shame
• Agitation	• Fatigue	• Grief
	• Disconnection	• Self-hatred

The following questions will help you uncover your unmet needs by focusing on your feelings.

- Do any of the feelings in the list above resonate for you right now? Are there any that call for your attention?
- What unmet needs do these feelings point to for you?
- What would it take for you to start addressing these needs? What kind of support would help you? How can you make time in your life to attend to them? What might change for you if you prioritized meeting this need?
- After looking at this list, did you notice that any of these feelings have been a persistent presence in or have had a negative impact on your life in multiple ways? If so, explore whether this could be your rope (see the analogy discussed in detail earlier in this chapter) and see if it's helpful to identify the multiple strands that affect its strength.

Identifying Ways to Take Care of Yourself

Here is an activity to help you explore different ways to care for yourself.

A. Think about a time when you were well rested, had the energy you needed, and were functioning at your best (however you define it).

Perhaps this was also when you felt connected to your work, family, and community.

B. Write down your answers to the following prompts:

- What kind of support did you have?
- What external conditions existed that enabled you to be in that state?
- What personal behaviors or habits helped you during this time?
- How does being in this kind of state benefit you as a leader?

C. Reflect on your answers and identify supports, conditions, behaviors, or habits you want to implement or strengthen.

Identifying Next Steps to Care for Yourself

This activity can help you come up with a self-care plan.

A. Take a few minutes to brainstorm answers to each of the following areas of self-care:

- What activities feed my spirit, bring joy, and connect me to gratitude?
- How can I receive support and connect more with my friends, family, and community?
- Who do I need to convene in my circle of support? (This can be trusted colleagues, dear friends, therapists, and other trusted people in our network).
- What practices help me process and digest my emotions?
- What activities and habits can I integrate that support my physical, emotional, and spiritual well-being?

B. Looking at your answers to the preceding questions; circle the ones that are the low-hanging fruit—ones that you are ready to implement immediately.

C. Look at your answers again. Star the ones that would be a game-changer if you started doing it. In other words, identify any answers on your list that would have a significant impact if you were to implement them.

D. Is there something you have learned in your healing that you can use to supercharge your ability to help others? For me, it was my rope of vigilance; for Malkia, it was their grief; for Shiree, it was self-love; and for Ezak, it was care. What is it for you?

8

CREATING MOMENTUM

We should learn to accept that change is truly the only thing that's going on always, and learn to ride with it and enjoy it.

—ALICE WALKER

You cannot value dreams according to the odds of their coming true. Their real value is in stirring within us the will to aspire. That will, wherever it finally leads, does at least move you forward.

—SONIA SOTOMAYOR

Ways to Generate Momentum

As leaders moving against the current, we fight a never-ending upstream battle. In addition to our adversaries having many more resources than we do, we are struggling against systemic oppression. We must find ways to broadcast our vision, narratives, and values of justice and liberation in a world that is increasingly powered by dominant forces seeking the exact opposite for our communities. To do so, we must leverage any of the support we can to win this David and Goliath battle. This is where momentum comes in.

The *Merriam-Webster Dictionary* defines momentum as "a strength or force gained by motion or by a series of events." I have learned that when working with other leaders from a wide range of movements, the more we work together, the better we can create momentum. We can do so by looking for opportunities in our external environment, by leveraging our collective resources, and by bringing together our efforts to create a tipping point. Using momentum in these ways can help magnify our efforts, propel our work forward, and attract increased attention and engagement from our key stakeholders. Here are four strategies for creating momentum:

- Build a springboard.
- Leverage strengths and values.
- Harness a wave generated by external factors.
- Build critical mass.

Generating Momentum by Creating a Springboard

In 2013, Albuquerque, New Mexico, was the site of Republican-led efforts at the municipal level to restrict abortion access through a ballot measure in the upcoming election. This ballot measure, if passed, would have ended the practice of later second and all third-term abortions in any circumstances other than a direct threat to a pregnant woman's life. This would not only affect New Mexican residents because patients from neighboring states with restrictions on abortion traveled, sometimes hundreds of miles, to these clinics to access reproductive healthcare. In addition, a victory for the opposition would encourage Republicans to set their sights on other cities nationwide.

This measure made it onto the ballot less than twelve weeks before the election. Early polling showed that the popular vote *favored* the ban by a wide margin. In September 2013, two months before the vote, the *Albuquerque Journal* reported that 54 percent of all voters approved the ban, and 39 percent opposed it. The support for the ban was even higher among Latinos, with 57 percent supporting the ban (33 percent opposed) including registered Democrats.[1] Moving enough voters to defeat the initiative in this purple state was daunting, given the wave of successful state-wide restrictions on abortion access across the country—most recently in Texas and Ohio. Coming out with a victory by over ten points was unimaginable. But the Respect ABQ (Albuquerque) Women campaign, cocreated and co-led by a local steering committee, did just that.

Seven organizations[2] came together as the executive committee to make this campaign a success. But it was the foundational work they did years before the campaign that enabled them to move so quickly and effectively to defeat the ballot measure.

Three years prior, Adriann Barboa, the founding director of Bold Futures (previously Young Women United), asked Forward Together to facilitate sessions with organizations working for reproductive rights, health, and justice. Up until then, there was conflict and division between women-of-color-led organizations and the larger white-led groups over the differential of power and resources. These sessions aimed to create a collaborative effort with a shared long-term policy agenda in New Mexico on the local and state levels.[3] Each organization identified the strengths they could contribute and the group planned how to use them to work in concert with each other collectively. Through this facilitated process, white leaders from the larger organizations acknowledged the higher degree of privilege and power they held compared to the women-of-color leaders of smaller organizations. The discussions culminated in a memorandum of understanding of how the group would communicate, make decisions, share resources, and navigate through conflict to mitigate power differences along the lines of race and organizational size and resources. Because of their foundational work and agreements, the groups could win legislative victories they couldn't have won working alone. Adriann was the first woman of color to be elected the chair of the New Mexico Coalition for Choice, cementing this new era of collaboration.

Through these experiences, relationships strengthened, and trust among the organizations deepened as they established a track record of collaboration. By the time the Respect ABQ Women campaign was launched, this set of groups had been working together for a year, collaborating successfully to defeat harmful bills and pass policies that positively impacted New Mexican families across the state. Their ability to work productively in the trenches gave them a springboard to launch their campaign efforts quickly and provided a roadmap for moving through tension and tough decisions.

Creating Momentum by Leveraging Collective Strengths and Values

LEVERAGING STRENGTHS

Momentum was further generated in the Respect ABQ Women campaign as each steering committee organization led with its respective strengths. Planned Parenthood and the ACLU of New Mexico brought significant funding and their established base of active, mostly white volunteers, donors, and supporters. The reproductive justice organizations Forward Together and Bold Futures contributed their approaches to organizing and building with communities of color. This was critical because New Mexico has the highest percentage (47.7 percent) of Latinx communities of any state.

Another set of strengths proved critical to the campaign's ability to reach voters of color. The campaign relied on the resources and expertise of the larger organization to conduct polling for the campaign. One of the most significant decisions during any campaign is how key messages will be shaped to target voters. Historically, national campaigns on abortion have focused on the "right to choose" or "right to privacy." The majority of the polling research done to create these messages has focused only on white, older women. Planned Parenthood and the ACLU, both part of this steering committee, favored adopting these traditional messages.

Adriann and Micaela Lara Cadena, the two reproductive justice leaders of color on the steering committee, come from New Mexican families with some members who have been there for many generations. From their expertise as seasoned abortion activists, they knew which messages would best resonate with their communities. They knew that traditional pro-choice messages would not only fail to speak to such communities but would drive away potential voters who personally supported abortion but felt disconnected or excluded from the larger white-led reproductive rights movement. Adriann and Micaela used their negotiation skills and commitment to what they knew to be strategically best for the campaign to stand up to the pressure from others who wanted to rely on traditional messages. They convinced the campaign to connect with the values of "respect" and "family," both deeply held by communities of color in New Mexico. These messages, coupled with messengers of color, were key to the campaign reaching a much broader audience.

Bold Futures and Forward Together recruited nearly 40 percent of Respect ABQ Women's volunteer base. They also used this as an opportunity to train young people and people of color to speak about reproductive justice and the need to defeat abortion restriction measures and to build their capacity to mobilize their communities for change. Of the volunteers they engaged, nearly half were people of color, over half were young people, 20 percent were men, many were young men of color, and 30 percent were LGBTQ+.

ATTRACTING KINDRED SPIRITS THROUGH SHARED VALUES

Forward Together's Strong Families Network in New Mexico invited new organizations that had never worked on abortion before to join them. These leaders and organizations came together in this network because of a shared core value of family. Together, they worked to ensure that all families, no matter how they are formed, have access to the dignity and resources they need to thrive. They saw a strong family as one in which each member, whether they were queer, trans, single, immigrant, incarcerated, young, or undocumented, had the opportunity to thrive.

One of the new organizations to join was Equality New Mexico, the state-based LGBTQ+ organization. During the campaign, Equality New Mexico engaged its membership for the first time in defining the issue of abortion as an LGBTQ+ issue. Similarly, organizations working with immigrant rights, Native communities, and rural communities spoke out on protecting abortion access for the first time.

SUCCESS THAT HAD RIPPLING EFFECTS INTO THE FUTURE

Because of their foundational work, the campaign could move into action quickly, broaden its base significantly, recruit many committed volunteers, and bring in new organizations. They had developed a springboard that served them well. They defeated this initiative by over ten points, shocking all the pundits. And this springboard continued to serve them in other future wins, including the 2021 repeal of an antiquated abortion ban that could have criminalized abortion when *Roe v. Wade* was overturned. They also developed a new clinic in Doña Ana County, serving rural and border communities and providing a complete integrated spectrum of reproductive healthcare, including gender-affirming care.

Creating Momentum by Harnessing the Waves Generated from External Factors

Aligning our efforts with external events that amplify our visibility, urgency, or collective energy can generate momentum for our efforts. Tying our actions to significant moments such as notable current events, cultural celebrations, or national trends allows us to leverage existing public attention. Additionally, connecting to the waves of public enthusiasm, dissatisfaction, or outcry can boost support for our efforts.

One of the first joint campaigns our Strong Families Network launched was on Mother's Day, 2010. According to the National Retail Federation, for Mother's Day 2019, people in the US spent a record $25 billion. We wanted to take advantage of this high level of engagement to create a megaphone for our issues. Until then, Mother's Day had primarily been the day you called your mom and spent some money on gifts. In addition, most depictions of mothers in the media often reinforce traditional ideas of family and motherhood that narrowly define one way to be a family, excluding mothers based on their race, immigration status, sexual orientation, and more.

Our Mama's Day campaign was designed to celebrate all the mamas who don't get represented on a Hallmark card: queer, single, trans, undocumented, nonbinary, incarcerated, and domestic caregivers. The campaign aimed to use Mother's Day to promote the narrative that mamas need more than a bouquet or a brunch once a year.[4] They need a living wage, clean drinking water, paid family leave, and access to complete healthcare.

In our second year of the campaign, we created Mamas Day ecards designed by artists to highlight a range of mamas in our communities. We called it Mama's Day Our Way. We made a website for people to download the cards and a customizable message they could send to the mamas in their lives. Initially, we imagined working with three to four artists to create at most ten cards. However, so many artists wanted to participate that the project grew to nine artists and eighteen cards. We encouraged our networks to download the cards a few days before Mother's Day and post them on social media.

We were able to generate momentum for this campaign by connecting our efforts to other factors happening in the environment. The first factor was the amount of national attention and popularity of celebrating Mother's Day. The second factor was the amount of dissatisfaction from marginalized communities with their lack of representation on mainstream cards and media for Mother's Day. And the third factor was the serendipitous endorsement from President Obama of same-sex marriage, which came the day after we released our e-card site. We jumped on the news of his announcement and made a custom card, which got tremendous traction on Facebook and beyond. Altogether, the cards got several million views and were downloaded by people in nineteen countries worldwide, allowing us to reach a scale of visibility that would have been unimaginable the year before. Over the years, this campaign has partnered with organizations working with young mamas, mamas in detention, Muslim and refugee mamas, and Black mamas, creating a gravitational force that engages people to get involved and support these communities.

Creating Momentum by Consolidating a Critical Mass of Support

We will likely face resistance when we work for change, whether small or big. Change is difficult for many people, whether it's an unwillingness to let go and share power or resources, discomfort with being asked to do something differently, or fear of the unknown. As a result, we will likely face people who put up roadblocks inadvertently or consciously.

In my coaching sessions with other leaders, I remind them to put their organizing hat on and figure out, "Who are your ABCs? The As are your advocates. Advocates are people who are already with you. They are your champions. Bs are the bystanders." These people should be with you if only they could hear your message and understand why your effort matters to them. And Cs are the challengers—people putting up roadblocks in your quest to achieve your purpose. So, the most effective strategy is to focus on getting your As to join you in taking action, turning your Bs into As, and not wasting time trying to convince the Cs to join you. By focusing on the As and Bs together, you can generate momentum and move the group in the direction you need to go.

I recently coached Lisa, who came to me exasperated about her board. Her relatively new organization was maturing into a new stage of development. For the last few years, board members had been very much engaged in day-to-day operations. However, with increased resources, they hired Lisa as the executive director.

When we first started meeting, she was in the middle of implementing a strategic plan initiated by her board the year before. As part of this plan, the board agreed to transition out of their direct engagement in programmatic work and become more of a governing board. They would focus more on the organization's larger legal and fiduciary matters, becoming a thought partner to Lisa and helping her raise money.

This is a typical scenario of board development when organizations reach a stage in their growth and can hire staff to implement programmatic work. However, while it is common, it can be a difficult transition for board members because they have to use different skills than they have before. They have to let go of the programmatic work, which may be much more exciting than looking at financial statements.

Lisa was frustrated because, a year after adopting the strategic plan, she was still frequently asked questions by some board members about her programmatic decisions and the organization's day-to-day functioning. She spent more time dealing with the board than recruiting and hiring the new staff that the organization desperately needed. She worried about meeting grant deliverables when the organization was not fully operational. Lisa felt distraught, undermined, and unsupported by the board.

We used her coaching sessions to look more closely at her situation to see where to focus her efforts strategically to get the board's support. I asked her to identify her board's ABCs (advocates, bystanders, and challengers). Out of the twelve board members, she identified five advocates or As. When I asked her to look more closely at the As and rate their level of advocacy, she identified two people, including the board chair, who actively supported her in board meetings and would always follow through with the tasks they committed to. The other three advocates were individuals she could rely on as thought partners outside of board meetings to help her with finances, development, and strategic thinking. All of the As were invested in the organization and the strategic plan and were committed to helping her to move forward.

We then moved on to the Bs, the bystanders, of which she identified five. These Bs didn't voice their opinions at board meetings and weren't active between meetings. I asked her to tell me more about what she knew about each in terms of their commitment to the organization, her leadership, and the strategic plan. She identified that two of them were committed to the overall direction and her leadership and chalked up their silence at board meetings to their reserved nature rather than their lack of interest. The other 3 Bs had been on the board for a while and hadn't attended meetings as frequently. We noted that Lisa needed more information from these folks to assess where they stood more accurately.

So that left two challengers, the Cs. Let me add a note about Cs. When discussing challengers, I am speaking about the people who use their influence to intimidate or manipulate others to move their agenda forward, which is often not aligned with the group's agenda. I am not speaking about people who raise productive critical questions or give constructive feedback to help inform the group process. We need people who are willing to challenge the group and promote a diversity of opinions. In fact, that is an excellent role for some of your As to play, as it will help strengthen your strategy and effort. The Cs I'm talking about often don't listen well to others, have big egos, and get threatened easily. They may dominate the conversation, become easily defensive, and primarily think from their own individual or organizational perspective. Sometimes, they can be bullies who use intimidation and threats to get what they want or to halt positive group processes.

I asked Lisa to tell me more about how these two board members were putting up roadblocks. The first person, Chris, was the most vocal on the board. As Lisa thought more about it, she realized that he was the main person who derailed the discussions at board meetings and most frequently questioned Lisa's decisions in front of other board members. Chris also contacted staff members and tried to give them "advice." He had been part of founding the organization five years earlier and had a sense of owner-ship. The other C, Robin, often sided with Chris as they were good friends. While Robin didn't initiate any conversation with other staff or wasn't as vocal at the board meetings as Chris, she often sat at the board meetings with her arms crossed and rolled her eyes at times, which naturally made Lisa feel disrespected.

After doing this ABC mapping, Lisa immediately realized that it didn't make sense for her to continue to regard the board as a monolithic entity moving in lockstep. In reality, only two people on a board of twelve were obstacles. While a few other members' commitment wasn't readily appar-ent, the majority of the board actually supported her leadership and the direction the organization was taking.

For the past year, Lisa's stress had been so wrapped up in the Cs that she hadn't paid attention to the As and Bs. After our talk, Lisa implemented a plan we created together to turn things around based on her ABC map. Following this plan, she focused on the As and Bs. She first met with her two strongest As and shared what happened over the last year. Until then, she hadn't engaged anyone on the board to help her deal with her frustra-tions. In that meeting, she and those board members agreed to initiate a process at the next board meeting, with the help of a consultant they had just hired, to create a work plan for the board to transition from a working board to a governing board in the next year. In that meeting, the two As came up with the idea to get the other three As to commit to taking lead-ership at board meetings to bring the Bs along.

Now, it was time to focus on the Bs. Before the board meeting, Lisa identified an A to meet with her and each of the Bs. In those meetings, Lisa and her A would work with the B to assess 1) their interest in staying on the board, 2) their investment in moving the board in this new direction, 3) their willingness to take on more active roles in helping the board achieve its goals. After these meetings with the Bs, Lisa and the As discovered that three of the Bs were very invested in helping the organization achieve its vision. They also found out that one of the Bs had a family illness she was dealing with and was feeling overwhelmed by having a job, taking care of her sick relative, and being on the board. The other B revealed that they were not excited about being on a governing board because they did not have the financial or fundraising skills they needed and they were not showing up to meetings because they didn't think they could contribute much. These conversations enabled Lisa and the As to introduce the idea of a graceful exit for these two Bs, which turned out to be a relief for them.

This left the Cs. I suggested that Lisa talk with the board chair, one of the most active As, and ask her to meet with the other two Cs. The board chair, Deb, had separate conversations with Robin and Chris. With help from Lisa, Deb laid out the board support (which now included all of the As and the initially labeled Bs who were now As) for the strategic plan and identified behaviors that Robin and Chris were exhibiting that might point to a potential discomfort or disagreement with the plan or with Lisa's leadership.

At the end of their conversation, Chris revealed that he had contributed a tremendous amount as a founder and wanted to be recognized for his leadership and work. Now that the board was moving away from the programmatic work and Lisa's leadership was growing, Chris felt that his contribution to the organization was being minimized and overlooked.

This gave Deb more insight into what motivated Chris's behavior. Deb suggested to Lisa and the other As that the organization recognize and honor Chris and the other founders at the next big event. Chris appreciated the gesture and, in subsequent meetings, began to soften his tone and critiques of Lisa and the organization. Nine months later, Chris and Robin both willingly rolled off the board.

This initial mapping process effectively gave Lisa a more accurate and nuanced picture of who was on her board. Once she categorized the members into As, Bs, and Cs, she could develop a strategy to understand their underlying motivations and interests and get the members more involved, give them appropriate roles, or have conversations that could lead to greater alignment, even if it meant that some people had to leave. Lisa was overjoyed that once we initiated this process, she would spend most of her time with the people who supported the organization and her leadership.

Whenever you work with a group of people with mixed levels of support or resistance, you can use this ABC process to help you diagnose how to focus your efforts to build a critical mass of support. Understanding the group's dynamics ensures that your efforts are more focused, efficient, and effective, ultimately leading to more substantial collective support and successful outcomes.

Your Turn

Get into a State of Readiness

You can use the relaxation activity outlined at the beginning of the Your Turn section in chapter 1 or select one that works for you.

Identifying Places Where You Can Build Momentum

Think about a purpose you are working on or will be working on in the future. Now, with that purpose in mind, you can go through the following exercises to help you identify ways to build momentum.

Building a Springboard

Here are some questions to help you identify ways that you can build a springboard:

If you are working with a coalition or network, what group agreements can you set now to provide a foundation to propel future collaboration?

- How will you make hard decisions?
- How will you share resources equitably?
- How will you mitigate power differences?
- How can you build lasting relationships over time?

Creating Momentum Using Your Internal Resources

Here are some questions you can use to create momentum by combining your assets from your internal resources:

- What strengths can you combine to amplify your efforts?
- What are the core values you are bringing to the work? Can you operationalize and broadcast these values to attract kindred spirits to your cause?
- How can you use this purpose to catapult the growth your efforts need?

Creating Momentum by Harnessing Waves Generated by Factors In Your External Environment

Here are some questions you can use to create momentum by connecting to surrounding conditions:

- What upcoming external events (holidays, elections, supreme court rulings, national media attention) are happening that you can utilize to capture a larger audience to support your cause?
- Can you focus your efforts in one direction to create synergy together and catapult your organization further?

Creating Momentum Through Building Critical Mass

Think about a situation or project where you are experiencing or anticipating difficulty moving the group forward. Here are some questions you can use to create a critical mass of support for your efforts:

- Take out a sheet of paper and draw three circles. In the first circle, name your As (people who are your advocates and ready to move with you). In the second circle, put down your Bs (bystanders who should be with you). In the third circle, name your Cs (challengers who are actively putting up roadblocks).

- How can you focus your time and effort on the As and Bs to help create momentum forward together?
- How can you create a gravitational force by bringing a critical mass of people or organizations to your effort?
- What resources, people, conditions, and strategies can you combine to create synergy and advance your work?

9

SOARING WITH THE COURAGEOUS OPERATING SYSTEM

If you want to fly, you have to give up the things that weigh you down.

—TONI MORRISON

There are opportunities even in the most difficult moments.

—WANGARI MAATHAI, *UNBOWED*

NOW THAT YOU HAVE seen the potential gifts each component of the Courageous Operating System can give you, it's time for some fun. When you start combining them, you'll experience the multiplier effect, which will help you sail through turbulent waters. The Courageous Operating System is not a set formula. You can creatively navigate this system using the order and combination of components that best fit each situation.

Throughout the book, I have provided numerous examples of how I and other leaders have used each component of the system. In chapter 6,

I showed how I combined several elements of this system to develop a national movement-building fellowship.

In this chapter, I share two in-depth case studies that illustrate how leaders can use different combinations of the parts of the entire system together, depending on their particular circumstances. Note that in Renata's story, I used the elements in a slightly different order than what has been presented so far in this book. When you become more familiar with the system, you can adapt it in ways that make the most sense for you alone or when you are working with others. Roxanne's story demonstrates how leaders can use the Courageous Operating System simultaneously with themselves, with others, and with a team. I hope you will find ways to use it that bring significant transformations in your life and leadership.

Renata Makes a Key Discovery When Grappling with a Big Dilemma

Renata Moreira is a queer single mama of Indigenous Xucuru-Kariri and Portuguese ancestry who has provided leadership in the LGBTQ+ movement for fifteen years. I have known Renata for eight years and worked with her closely when she enrolled in Stepping Into Power. As executive director at Our Family Coalition, Renata faced many challenges, which she worked valiantly to overcome to stabilize and grow her organization. However, after receiving a serious health diagnosis and dealing with the death of her sister, Renata left the position to take care of herself and her family.

While on that path of healing and grief, Renata found herself following her deep commitment and connection to spirit through the land, nature, community, and family. Renata, a leader with cross-cutting talents, has since merged her multisector leadership and coaching experiences into the healing justice field as a trauma-informed clinical hypnotherapist, Reiki master teacher, and wellness consultant. She continues to provide executive coaching, strategy development, and capacity-building consulting services to progressive organizations nationwide.

I met with Renata one day recently as she was about to launch a new office for her clinical services. Knowing how stressful these situations can be, I was eager to see how she was doing. I got my answer as soon as I saw her. Her nonverbal expressions relayed everything. Her breathing was high in her chest, her face looked weary, and her shoulders were tight. She told me that the stress she felt came from having second thoughts about opening this site and that she was unsure if this was the right decision. She was anxious about the sustainability of paying for this space and the overhead of running a brick-and-mortar business while simultaneously building out a pipeline for her services. This is a challenge that most self-employed people must grapple with: How much financial investment can we expend to garner adequate potential income? "What would you do in this situation?" she implored. I knew the answer to this dilemma resided within her if she could only give herself some space to hear it.

Finding the Right Purpose

With her permission, I led Renata through an activity that helped slow her breathing and come back into her body. I could see she was lost in the fearful future and not grounded in the present moment. When we are in moments of stress, our bodies become rigid, which affects our ability to see expansively. I could see that she felt constrained and trapped by the lack of choices she saw in front of her. I invited her to use her breath to create space throughout her body and let go of any tension she didn't need. We then talked about her fears, which revolved around her financial stability. I asked her where courage was coming up for her at that moment. After taking a few deep breaths, she told me she needed the courage to step back from the urgency of deciding about this office space to gain the perspective she needed to think about the big picture.

I then asked Renata to reconnect to her purpose from her heart. I knew she had a big, loving heart full of care for everyone around her. After a few moments, she smiled. She told me that the purpose she had been working with over the last few months was to open an office because it would give her clinical work credibility. She was laughing at the fact that her wise self knew this was not the right direction and was attempting to let her know in various ways. For example, a week prior, she had been working on the page of her website that described the services she would provide in her new office, including helping people with anxiety and those moving through deep burnout, grief, and loss. But she had struggled with the language because it didn't feel true to her justice and spiritual health framework. A week before we met, she was finally able to create a description of her pricing and services. She also added her testimonials and demonstration videos. Then, she somehow "accidentally" deleted everything. It was all gone.

Our discussion helped Renata understand that her hesitancy about the lease on the new office space was not only for financial reasons. She realized that she didn't want her primary focus to be on patients' individual clinical needs. Although she certainly could help people deal with burnout and grief, what she really wanted to do was work with leaders who have a big vision of change and who need support to achieve that impact. Moreover, if she worked with leaders in this way, she wouldn't need this office space since the organizations she worked with had their own offices that she could utilize. Setting up an office was not necessary for the work she was called to do. Her new purpose was to let go of the office and develop a pipeline for finding clients with whom she was passionate about working and who were committed to social change. She had successfully gotten herself out of the pitfall of staying with a purpose that didn't take her in the direction she wanted to go. Instead, she was using her moral compass of values, as discussed in chapter 6, to guide her toward the right purpose.

Calling on Courage

Renata demonstrated profound courage in pivoting her purpose quickly, especially when she was set to open her space up that very day. We all understand how difficult it is to let others know we have changed our minds. She knew that informing the colleagues with whom she was planning to share the office would be difficult in the short term, but it was much better to be upfront now than to back out later. Our session helped Renata call on her courage to jump off of one path and course correct to a path that connected directly to her purpose and her passions.

Cultivating Success

As Renata landed on the purpose of working with leaders, I asked her to reflect on what success would look like for her five years from now. She immediately described her practice as evolving to collaborate with other global majority practitioners who would give and receive multidimensional support for the heart, body, and mind. She envisioned creating circles of leaders within the broader movement, coming together in a welcoming and warm space to do individual and collective healing and transformative work with each other. Renata had gained profound wisdom and healing through her work with plant medicine, and she felt inspired to incorporate this approach into her leadership coaching. Instead of clinic rooms, Renata saw herself traveling into the communities calling for her medicine and convening sessions in retreat spaces in which leaders would gather, connect, and deepen with their hearts, purpose, and one another.

This was the first time Renata verbalized this powerful vision of success. Defining success in this way differed from how she had thought about her purpose before, which involved providing direct services to clients. She could feel her creativity open up and generate even more possibilities. Reflecting on success brought forth her love for collaborating with kindred spirits, addressed her need to be in community, and made her commitment to working with families and children even more visible. She saw how she could integrate her mindfulness, plant medicine, and healing justice experiences with movement leaders who had a deep spiritual lens—something she had not previously connected.

Transforming Failure

I asked Renata to think about what failure would look like as she moved toward this new purpose. She told me that failure would be living through other people's fears and not returning to her own heart and purpose. The friends who were empathetic to Renata's financial concerns and saw how experienced and skilled she was encouraged her to find a job at a nonprofit, perhaps even become an executive director again. However, Renata knew that becoming an ED was not the correct container for who she was and what she wanted to do. It was too limiting for her vision of success and purpose now.

She also defined failure as betraying her own recovery journey from her self-defined "addiction to speed and production." She operated in "go" mode for years, doing multiple things simultaneously to be as productive as possible. This way of being led to health problems and burnout. She no longer wanted to operate at speed. She understood that slowing down meant she would be more able to tap into her creativity and experience deep abundance and joy.

Powering Up Her Leadership

Dashboard of Needs

We looked at Renata's renewed purpose and explored her dashboard of needs. This purpose would help with Gauge 2: prioritizing the work that gave her deep meaning. It would also help her with Gauge 4: meeting the needs of continuing her professional development. What she needed more at that moment was thought partnership and guidance to help her figure out what opportunities were available to her and how she could make them happen.

Set of Internal Resources

As I mentioned, Renata used her values as a compass to guide her toward this renewed purpose. With this newer purpose in mind, Renata could see clearly how many of her strengths would come into play. She identified her extensive facilitation and training skills, her keen ability to help leaders deal with challenging organizational dynamics and innovative fund-development strategies, and her talents in assisting organizations to move from crisis to growth. In addition, she had so many cultural strengths to contribute, including the holistic ways she could bring her mind, body, and spirit to work to support struggling leaders.

Taking Care of Herself

Renata was realistic about the financial challenges that she still faced. As a single parent, even though she was committed to focusing on this purpose, she also had to be pragmatic. She would continue to grow her practice of working with leaders. In the meantime, until it became financially feasible for her to focus solely on this, she would look for job openings that aligned with her values, strengths, and passion but that would also be flexible enough to allow her to build her practice.

Creating Momentum

Because Renata was familiar with the Courageous Operating System, she immediately brainstormed ways to generate momentum. Previously, she had focused on trying to "chase" clients, a common strategy that can be very labor-intensive. Chasing clients in this way can create pressure and anxiety as you try to adapt what you offer to fit the needs of a broad range of clients. Renata realized she could instead focus on being clear about her offerings and attracting potential clients who shared her values.

Thinking about creating momentum in this way helped Renata remember a conversation she had a few years ago with an acquaintance from a local foundation who was excited about her work and encouraged her to submit a proposal when she was ready. Renata was ready now.

As we ended our meeting, Renata looked like a different person. Her huge smile lit up the room and her eyes were shining. She decided she was going to spend time with her plants outside. Her energy was bright and calm and her spirit was vibrant once again.

The day after our meeting, Renata contacted someone she knew at a national nonprofit that works with girls and young women. This person was delighted to reconnect with Renata, and they set up a meeting to talk. The conversation went so well that it led to a job offer for a development and partnerships director position where Renata will supervise and oversee a primarily BIPOC senior leadership team. There, she will help expand the young leaders program for young girls and gender-expansive youth who are finding their voice as future climate and social change leaders. She will also raise resources for mental and emotional health programming for young women and girls in low-income communities and communities of color. This job will allow her to develop an extensive network of people working in foundations and state and federal government who support holistic healing models in the community. This network will be invaluable to her as she builds out her healing work with leaders over the next ten years.

In addition, shortly after she released the attachment to running an entire "healing the healers pathway" program by herself, she received a two-year grant she had applied for in collaboration with a former mentor to work with fourteen nonprofits developing similar programs. This funding will support Renata and a collaborative of mental health practitioners to help nonprofit leaders build systems and infrastructure to create healing practices within their organization and to create healing-oriented programs that they can implement among their leadership and the populations they serve. Renata is well on her way to fulfilling her new purpose and helping countless leaders along the way.

Roxanne Helps Her Team Move from Crisis to Success

The Courageous Operating System

Roxanne, a young mixed-race Japanese Black leader, was energetic and passionate about her organization, which focused on mental health issues impacting children. A number of years ago, Roxanne joined the organization as a youth leader, was hired as a program coordinator, and continued getting promoted until she became the deputy director.

Joanne, the long-time executive director, had been grooming Roxanne for the last two years to become the leader of the organization when Joanne retired. I had been working with Joanne, Roxanne, and the team of directors over the last year to support this leadership transition. Joanne was supposed to stay until the end of the year; however, six months before her tenure was slated to end, Joanne announced to Roxanne and the rest of the directors' team that she was suffering from a health crisis and would have to leave immediately.

At that time, the organization had several big balls in the air. The program and communication teams were starting a publicity campaign to announce a new program they were running in partnership with a local clinic. Because the organization had received an influx of funding, the recently completed strategic plan included efforts to double in size in two years. The HR staff planned to hire four new employees, and the operations and finance staff were researching new systems for accounting and payroll.

Joanne's premature departure meant Roxanne had to manage the transition while facing an organization that was moving in multiple directions. Roxanne contacted me for additional support for herself and her leadership team of directors as they navigated this challenging situation. She and I decided to use the Courageous Operating System both in our coaching sessions and in my work with the team.

Working with Roxanne to Take Care of Herself

Roxanne told me that when she first heard of Joanne's sudden departure, she froze in panic. She called me to schedule an immediate session. The next day, we met, and while I could see a part of her was moving into problem-solving mode, she was still feeling flooded with anxiety. Before moving to other parts of the Courageous Operating System, we both decided it best to start grounding her nervous system. I knew that talking about the situation might escalate her stress levels even more, so we started with a mindful exercise to help her focus on the present moment and slow down her breathing.

After she was in a calmer state, she was more able to identify the emotions she was feeling. She shared that she was deeply disappointed not to have her mentor around those last few months to support her as she stepped into the new position. She mentioned that while she understood why Joanne had to leave, a part of her felt abandoned. As Roxanne kept talking, she mentioned this feeling of abandonment a couple more times. I stopped her and asked her to describe the ways Joanne abandoned her. After a minute of thinking, Roxanne replied, "Joanne didn't abandon me. She has supported my leadership since I first got here and has never turned away when I needed help." And yet, Roxanne's feeling of abandonment persisted. We then talked about how her fear of abandonment was showing up right now in her work. She told me that she felt alone and isolated. Joanne was the person she turned to for support, and she was worried that now she would have no one.

To counter her worry, we did a quick reality check. I asked her to identify members of her staff with whom she had worked closely over the last year and the kinds of support they had given her. She named almost everyone on the director's team, the executive assistant she shared with Joanne, and the program team. She realized that instead of leaning on Joanne for support, she could call on others around her to partner with her. I could see some tension leave her face and shoulders after she realized that she was indeed not alone.

As we talked more, Roxanne realized that this situation was triggering past experiences she'd had with her parents when she was younger. According to therapist Deb Dana, our nervous systems are primed to respond to external factors before our minds can. She states, "We think that our brains are running the show, but in reality, our experience begins with our nervous system." Because Joanne's unexpected leaving brought up past situations of abandonment, Roxanne's nervous system was responding with shock because of cues of perceived danger, and she went into survival mode and froze in fear.

Fortunately, Roxanne had previously processed this dynamic with her therapist, so she decided to revisit it at her next therapy session to help her distinguish between the current situation and her past with her family.

I then checked in with Roxanne about ways she could navigate the stress of this transition but also feed feelings of connection that could counter some of her fears of abandonment. We focused on three areas of self-care: focusing on her physical/mental health, receiving support, and finding ways to pause, rest, and relax. Our conversation reminded Roxanne that she could throw a couple of weekly classes into her gym routine, which would also help her reconnect with people she enjoyed seeing.

When I asked Roxanne to identify people in her personal network whom she would love to see more regularly during this time, she grew excited about reconnecting with people like a fellow book club member and a former yoga instructor. She came up with a list of eight people she was looking forward to connecting with over coffee or a meal.

Before she knew that Joanne would be leaving a few months early, Roxanne had scheduled a much-needed upcoming two-week vacation. Her first instinct was to cancel it, given the new circumstances. While I agreed that taking a vacation of that length soon might not be the best idea, I encouraged her to look at her schedule and her organizational calendar for the next six months and see if she could move it to the second half of the year. She saw she could choose a different two-week time spot when the organizational activities were at a lull. I encouraged her to find some time between now and that vacation to take a few long weekends off with friends and extended family so that she could have some scheduled shorter breaks.

As we ended this session, Roxanne was visibly calmer and feeling good about having a plan to bolster her sense of connection and support over the next few months. She was then much more able and ready to move her focus to ensure that she and her staff had what they needed to move through the transition successfully.

Working on Purpose with Roxanne

Roxanne and I were ready to dive into purpose at her next coaching session. Roxanne listed ten purposes right off the bat. We then started sorting them into those that fit into various time horizons: 1) three years from now, 2) four to six months out, and 3) next month. I invited Roxanne to identify one purpose to prioritize in each category. She came up with the following:

1. To identify her leadership goals over the next three years based on the strategic direction of the organization.

2. To come up with high-level goals for the following year.

3. To work with the staff around adapting to the transition of Joanne leaving and Roxanne taking on the new position in the next two weeks.

We proceeded to work through the Courageous Operating System for each of these purposes. For the sake of brevity, I will focus on her near-term purpose for the next two weeks.

Working On Courage with the Leadership Team

IDENTIFYING THE FEARS FIRST

It takes courage to go through a leadership transition. Roxanne was not the only person with feelings resulting from this surprise departure. I began working with the rest of the leadership team using an activity in which I invited each of the directors to write down any fears or concerns that they or their team members had expressed about the transition. Here are a few of their responses:

- My team members are confused about how to move forward.
- I am concerned about Joanne. Is she going to be okay?
- How can we support Roxanne? Does she feel ready and prepared to start in her new position?
- What should we tell our organizational partners, colleagues, and donors? Will they understand? Will we lose funding?
- How will the board respond?
- We planned to have six more months before the transition; I'm concerned about how this will impact my workplan. What do we do about the new projects we have on deck?
- Are we going to get through this okay?

As we worked through the entire list, which was three times longer than this one, everyone spoke rapidly, and I could see both the individual and collective stress levels of the team rising. I asked them to pause, take some deep breaths, and center their awareness within their bodies and in the present moment.

CONNECTING TO COURAGE

I then asked the leadership team to recall a moment when they were using their courage and pair up to share that memory with the person sitting closest to them. They shared stories that included harrowing journeys of immigration to the United States, healing from childhood trauma, making the difficult decision to leave a job, facing a health crisis, setting limits with a coworker, and leading a new project for the first time. The energy shifted immediately. Their speech patterns and breathing were slower and more deliberate. The act of listening and paying attention to each other helped to ground the conversations. Participants shared stories of courage, including everyday acts. When I ended the activity, participants rejoined the circle inspired by their partner's story and connected to their own moment of courage.

IDENTIFYING WAYS TO CALL ON COURAGE

Now that the directors were in touch with their courage, I asked them to identify how they could call on their courage to meet the unexpected transition. They took turns naming how they could call on their courage to:

- Walk into the unknown until they had a plan in place.
- Stay calm and wait to find out if there are ways to support Joanne and Roxanne.
- Move forward without having all the answers right now.
- Sit with their fears and the fears of their team and have faith that they will be able to handle challenges that arise.
- Focus on how they could contribute positively to the situation rather than ruminate on the worst-case scenarios.
- Help them be flexible and encourage their team to be agile, too.
- Be willing to make necessary changes in their work plans.

Participating in this set of activities around courage helped the team move from their fears toward focusing on where/how they could use their strengths in the situation. Talking about acts of courage reminded them of their own strengths and assets and how they had used them in the past to overcome challenging situations. The group ended in a place of initiative and agency. Focusing on courage together enabled them to see that they could hold each other's vulnerabilities and also leverage their teammates' contributions during this transition.

Working with the Leadership Team to Identify Their Purpose

After we worked together on courage, we moved to purpose. Roxanne wanted to work with the leadership team to develop a six-week transition plan for the entire organization. Given the time constraints involved in this transition, she presented this proposed purpose to the leadership team and asked for feedback.

In response, the leadership team discussed the importance of getting feedback from their teams and came up with additional language to reflect their concerns. The final proposal that they created was

> *To come up with a transition plan the directors would implement throughout the organization as soon as possible that would include the needs of each team.*

Working with the Team and the Rest of the Staff on Defining Success

Identifying Different Metrics of Success

One of the benefits of redefining success with groups is that doing so illuminates the diverse ways each team member may be thinking about success. After Roxanne's team finalized their purpose, I asked them to use the flipcharts I had placed around the room to write down what success would be like for them if they implemented this plan. Here is a sampling of the metrics of success that they identified:

- I will have a clear sense of how my work will flow for the next two months.
- I will have a way to answer questions the people whom I supervise ask.
- As a director's team, we will communicate effectively throughout the process and handle challenges as they arise.
- The board will believe in the staff's ability to run the organization.
- Roxanne will have the support she needs to step into her new position.
- We will have a plan that aligns our efforts.
- We will inform all stakeholders about the transition and be able to answer any questions they may have.

- The donors will continue to support the organization and might increase their contributions during this time.
- Staff members will have a place to express their concerns.
- We will be able to deal with challenges as they come up.

I asked each team member to review the statements and categorize them into overarching themes. From that process, they came up with the following themes that included each of their metrics of success:

- The organization will function effectively and be able to address challenges that come up.
- The organization will have a plan to communicate with external stakeholders.
- Team members will be able to express their responses about the transition and offer support to Joanne and Roxanne.

From these themes, Roxanne and her team could see that the dimensions of success that they collectively identified involved different levels of the organization, from the individual staff and board level to external stakeholders. Participants expressed how doing this together helped illuminate the multiple layers of success that they needed to pay attention to when moving through this transition. On their own, they believed they would only have come up with a fraction of the metrics of success that they discovered together.

Integrating the Feedback from the Rest of the Staff

When we ended this first meeting, I asked each member to return to their teams (which would include the rest of the staff) and present the purpose, and these themes. I also asked the directors to inform their teams of a core value of the organizational culture that they wanted to keep in mind as they moved toward success during this transition.

A week later, the directors returned with feedback, noting that their staff were eager to share their thoughts and appreciated the opportunity Roxanne and the leadership team had given them to voice their opinions.

It is critical that staff are part of the process, especially during a significant leadership transition. Joanne and Roxanne had initially planned to involve the staff more deeply in the transition process. However, given the new circumstances, the staff were eager for a plan to be put in place and understood that the leadership team needed to act swiftly.

Aligning Values and Success Themes

Here is the final list of core values the staff wanted the organization to embody as they achieved each theme:

Success Theme 1: The organization will function effectively and be able to address challenges that come up:

> **Value 1:** Ensure that each part of the organization and each team member will have adequate support to move their work forward.
>
> **Value 2:** Cultivate an environment where questions are welcome and we can ask for help.
>
> **Value 3:** Agility is better than rigidity. We need to be ready to go with the flow because challenges will come up, and changes will need to be made.
>
> **Value 4:** Be solutions-oriented. Do your best to see problems before they become big. Do your best to come up with possible solutions.
>
> **Value 5:** We need to give each other the benefit of the doubt. Ask out of curiosity instead of blame.

Success Theme 2: The organization will effectively communicate internally to staff and externally to stakeholders (donors, vendors, organizational partners):

> **Value 1:** The leadership team communicates frequently with staff about the latest developments/changes regarding the transition.
>
> **Value 2:** When communication challenges pop up, we will give each other grace and work toward clarity, understanding that some answers may need more time to emerge.

Value 3: Our relationships with external stakeholders are important to our organization and should be treated with care. Different stakeholders need different kinds of information. Some stakeholders will need to be told before others.

Success Theme 3: The organization will provide ongoing opportunities for team members to ask for and offer support from/to each other:

Value 1: The organization will create a space where everyone can share their authentic responses to the transition.

Value 2: We will support each other through this.

Value 3: We will support Roxanne as she moves into her new leadership position.

Value 4: We will hold Joanne's spirit in the work and send her well wishes.

The staff now had the building blocks to create an effective transition plan. Based on this list, the leadership team created a work plan for the next six weeks under each theme and shared it with team members for feedback. Roxanne was thrilled when these work plans were finalized within three weeks of Joanne's premature departure.

Creating Momentum

At this point in the process, Roxanne and her leadership team wanted to build momentum for this plan. As they paddled upstream, they needed to jumpstart their efforts by figuring out how to move together. If they were to proceed without making any changes to their current work before Joanne had to leave, various parts of the staff would be moving in different directions. One-third of the organization would focus on the publicity campaign for their new project, another group would work on replacing a critical component of their financial system, and a third group would be tasked with recruiting and hiring four new team members.

Roxanne and the directors realized that for this transition to be successful, all teams needed to row in the same direction. They spoke to each group to determine how to reprioritize their work. The staff overseeing the hiring processes were more than happy to postpone their efforts until the beginning of the year as long as they could hire temporary help to fill some pressing gaps. Given their growth, the finance team was a little more reluctant because they desperately needed a new payroll system. The compromise they reached was to continue the research, but at a much slower pace, dedicating only a few hours each week. The rest of the time would be spent focusing on other priorities.

The program and communications teams had the biggest challenge in refocusing their efforts. The hospital was relying on the publicity campaign to introduce the community to the new program, which was launching in a month. This was a complex and exciting program for their organization, and Roxanne and her team didn't want to do anything to jeopardize the success of its launch. In trying to come up with a solution, one of the directors creatively found a way to use the launch to continue building momentum for Roxanne's leadership transition. She proposed that they start the publicity campaign with an event hosted by the hospital, where Roxanne, in her new leadership position, could announce the new program. If they got the hospital to agree to postpone their campaign launch for a few weeks and host the event, the program and communications staff could focus the bulk of their efforts on the transition until then. Also, the event would be a public platform for Roxanne to introduce herself to the community.

Those changes made all the difference in building momentum, allowing the entire staff to feel invested in the plan without feeling stretched in multiple directions. Everyone was aligned for the next six weeks and knew their particular role in helping the organization move forward.

Powering Up Their Collective Leadership

CONDUCTING A TEAM AUDIT OF RELEVANT STRENGTHS AND EXPERIENCES

Having a roadmap is not the same as being ready to execute it. Armed with these new plans, some directors felt confident about leading their teams through the transition. Other directors were more unsure of themselves as they had never led an organization through a leadership transition. Still, others questioned their ability to do things the "right way." Everyone, including Roxanne, felt trepidation because they had previously relied on Joanne to lead the way. They relied on her confidence and decisiveness, which had developed from decades of leading organizations. Now, they were all challenged by her leaving to do things in a different way. As the directors were working with their teams to operationalize the plans, Roxanne and I thought it would be helpful for the leadership team to map the strengths and past experiences *they* could bring to this transition.

We started by having them reflect on a time when they successfully helped lead a group through a major transition. As each member shared their story, a diverse set of transitions unfolded before us. We heard about the kind of leadership needed to help a volunteer group of LGBTQ+ youth activists become a nonprofit, the challenges that were overcome to allow an immigrant rights organization to move through a financial crisis, and the rapid growth of an antiviolence project that moved from a state-wide focus to national in scope.

As I wrote up these transitions on a big piece of flipchart paper, the group noticed that while only one of the stories they shared involved a leadership transition, each contained at least one component applicable to the situation they were now facing. This part of the exercise helped them be more aware of the increased capacity and skills they received from past transitions that would greatly benefit their current situation. This included bringing people together, helping others manage adversity, and working with the team to develop a shared vision and path forward.

I then asked the group to identify any strengths they heard in the stories. They came up with a list of twenty-four strengths:

- Think well under pressure.
- Stay calm in the midst of crisis.
- Figure out the right people to pull in for help.

- Listen to what staff needed.
- Be calm in the face of the storm.
- Bring a sense of humor to give people perspective.
- Bring people together and move in one direction.
- Act with agility at a moment's notice.
- Respond to team members who are having a difficult time without judgment and with kindness and empathy.
- Be open to multiple possible outcomes.
- Identify potential solutions quickly.
- Sense when disruption is occurring and help to de-escalate the situation.
- Mediate conflict.
- Engage people in problem-solving.
- Ask for help as many times as needed.
- See two steps ahead and around the corner.
- Act without ego or agenda.
- Focus on what is best for the group.
- Help people name what they are feeling and work with them.
- Help others through crisis.
- Think creatively into the unknown.
- Learn quickly.
- Bring out the best in others.
- Help others see their role and contribution.

As the group looked at this large and diverse list, I could see many of them relax into the realization that they had so many strengths at their collective disposal. We then organized each of them into the following categories: engaging with the team, embodying effective leadership qualities, and dealing with change.

To complete this activity, I asked each team member to put their name in the category of strengths that best fit their leadership style when helping groups through transitions. The directors appreciated knowing to whom they could turn for guidance or support among themselves for each of these categories. As we ended the activity, many directors commented on how this process made visible the expertise, wisdom, and strengths held by their colleagues. It also served as a reminder to themselves about the resources they each brought to the table.

Working with Roxanne on Her Dashboard of Leadership Needs

I continued working with Roxanne and her directors to support them for the first few months of the transition. At this point in our coaching sessions, Roxanne and I went back to look at *her* leadership needs dashboard to ensure she had the support she needed to oversee the transition. She decided to focus on four of the gauges on the dashboard identified in chapter 6.

Gauge 1: Baseline of Support

By this time, Roxanne felt quite confident and appreciative of the support she was receiving from the leadership team and the rest of the staff. Fortunately, Joanne had facilitated a process of bringing Roxanne to board meetings regularly over the past year, so Roxanne felt comfortable with most of the board. As soon as Joanne left, the board chair reached out to schedule monthly meetings with Roxanne to support her. We discussed Roxanne's need to develop a plan to deepen her relationships with each board member over the next year.

Gauge 3: Thought Partnership and Guidance

While Roxanne felt a high level of support, she was less sure about whom to turn to for thought partnership. Joanne had been Roxanne's main thought partner up until this point. We looked at her contact list to see if anyone popped up as someone she could turn to for help and guidance. To her surprise, Roxanne identified a few people, some of whom she spoke to regularly and others she trusted, but only talked to occasionally. This included a close friend of hers, the human resource director of a small company to whom Roxanne would turn for advice on hiring, retaining, and letting staff go. Over the last year, she had also started having regular coffee dates with a colleague who had recently become an executive director. I asked her if she thought the board chair could be part of her trusted circle of advisors, and Roxanne agreed, even though the thought hadn't occurred to her before. Roxanne was off to a good start with three potential people who could serve as thought partners. I asked her to identify areas of support missing from the people in this circle. She named fundraising since that was one of Joanne's superpowers. So, we brainstormed a list of people Roxanne could approach to see if they would be willing to support her in this area.

Gauge 5: Spaciousness

This was an area that Roxanne knew she needed to address. Because the transition happened earlier than expected, she was carrying her workload as the deputy director and Joanne's workload as the incoming executive director. This was untenable. So, we got to work on getting enough space in her schedule and workload to sustain her pace.

The desire to work at a sustainable pace is something almost every leader I have worked with wants. Unfortunately, too few find the will or the strategies to do so. We often have more control over our pacing than we realize. Too often, leaders throw their hands up in the air at the prospect of having a work schedule that allows for breaks and meals that give them time to think and plan and enables them to have the time to go to the gym, make dinner, or be with their family. Setting a desired pace is key to getting the space that leaders need.

I asked Roxanne to create a list of her key work priorities for the next three months, including her role in the work plans developed with the director team and staff for the leadership transition. A few months prior, I had worked with Roxanne to develop three core purposes she wanted to adopt when she stepped into the role of executive director based on her passions, strengths, and the organization's needs. They included overseeing the leadership transition, building and deepening relationships with key stake-holders, and identifying the hiring timeline and plan for the following year. We took her list of seventeen priorities and grouped them under these purposes; twelve of them fit in her core purposes, and five were outside of them.

We then went through a process of figuring out what she could let go of and created a new work plan that would give her enough space to succeed at her core purposes while also meeting the needs of the organization. We started with the low-hanging fruit and put aside anything that could be **dropped** altogether. These included activities outside of her core purposes, such as participating in upcoming meetings where she didn't have a particular role, or filling in for Joanne, who had planned to speak at an upcoming conference in a few months. While these things were urgent, they were not important. We then looked at anything that could be **postponed** to the second part of the year. She identified two new projects that could be moved to the beginning of the next fiscal year, which freed up significant space for the upcoming year. I then asked her to identify work that could be **delegated**. This included delegating the supervision of several staff members, planning the next staff retreat, and hiring a new administrative assistant.

This process reduced her list by more than half, leaving her with a manageable eight priorities. Roxanne visibly relaxed as she saw the list shrink. Next, we reviewed the current list of directors, and she identified potential team members who could take on the tasks she planned to delegate. She would then apply a similar approach with them, helping to identify anything they could drop, delegate, or postpone to ensure they, too, had manageable work plans.

Finally, we reviewed Roxanne's calendar for the next three months and scheduled time for her to complete these eight activities so she could be confident that she had enough time. In addition, we also scheduled blocks of time (up to half a day every six weeks) reserved for Roxanne to use at her discretion for anything from strategic thinking to problem-solving to relationship building that she didn't otherwise have time for.

Gauge 4: Professional Development

Roxanne was keen to focus on development and growth as this was her first time as an executive director. Fortunately, the board's executive committee was very supportive of the organization, providing Roxanne with resources for leadership coaching and ongoing professional development. They paid for her to attend various leadership trainings to learn new skills and connect with other leaders across the country in her field. Roxanne knew that she needed support around fundraising, so in addition to the leadership coaching that I was providing, she worked with another coach for some time to help her specifically build a professional development plan for raising resources. The board chair happened to be a seasoned executive director, and she volunteered to spend part of their monthly meetings providing mentorship to Roxanne on specific challenges she was facing. We created a plan within our coaching sessions for Roxanne to continue identifying growth opportunities and ways to get support for her journey.

Creating a space where Roxanne could focus on herself by honoring her initial feelings and responses was critical to her ability to take the next step with the leadership team. Working with both the leadership team and Roxanne to process their fears and concerns enabled them to connect to their courage, fueling their planning process with the rest of the staff. Moving through the Courageous Operating System enabled Roxanne and the leadership team to engage with the rest of the staff to build ways to move through this critical moment with a shared purpose and collective clarity on what success looked like and how they were going to achieve it.

It was so gratifying to see what emerged from this process. Roxanne and the other directors integrated practices to bolster their individual and team efforts, which included the following:

- Spontaneous "courage huddles" that any leadership team member could call to boost their courage at critical times by reminding each other of their collective strengths and assets

- A growth plan for each team member, including resources from the organization to help them gain the skills they needed to perform new tasks that were added to their work plans
- A designated portion of their weekly team check-ins to identify things that didn't go as planned and time to brainstorm ways to deal with them
- A culture of appreciating everyone's contribution to the effort
- Ongoing celebrations within staff meetings whenever they hit key metrics of success

Together, Roxanne and her staff made it through the transition by hitting all of their success metrics and created practices of team culture and collaboration that provided a firm foundation for their future growth.

Going Upstream Together with More Power and Ease

Whether you are using it to help you through an urgent dilemma, like Renata; you are trying to launch a big project; or you are moving through a crisis, like Roxanne, the Courageous Operating System provides a way for you to fuel your efforts so that you can make the journey upstream with more ease and success.

Roxanne and Renata used the Courageous Operating System in a way that suited their situations, starting with the components that spoke to them the most at that time and then moving on from there. Roxanne and her team used the system interactively, enabling the staff to move deftly out of the crisis together.

As a result, Renata and Roxanne experienced fundamental changes that helped them come into their own power. They will continue building off these changes and leveraging them as they move forward.

I encourage you to explore this system by first working through each component and applying it to your situation. Sometimes, it might be helpful to deepen your understanding and practice with one of the components. For example, I have spent much time working with failure—revisiting those moments, understanding when I'm being set up, and failing forward when I make mistakes.

Sometimes, you may want to take a few components and work with them, as I demonstrated in my Stepping Into Power case study in chapter 6. This system is designed to adapt to whatever challenge you are facing, big or small, urgent or long-term, alone or with others. I look forward to seeing how you make this your own and, in doing so, continue to evolve it even further.

Closing Thoughts

IF YOU HAVE MADE it this far, thank you for including me on your journey. I want to express my immense gratitude for you and your leadership. It is difficult to lead against the current. The growing attacks on our communities mean that we, as leaders, must act in the face of escalating risk. During this moment of disruption and upheaval, your courageous leadership is precisely what is needed.

Yours are the voices leading the charge for change, bravely amplifying the stories and struggles of those who have been invisible, marginalized, or pushed to the side. Your commitment to equity and justice creates ripples of hope and transformation in communities everywhere.

Thank you for your relentless pursuit of justice, for challenging the venom of oppression, and for your unwavering belief in a better future.

You have my deepest respect and appreciation. Knowing you are out there makes traveling through these rough waters easier.

Notes

Introduction

1 Now known as Forward Together.

Chapter 1: Leadership Operating Systems

1 Elephant Voices, "Elephants Are Socially Complex."
2 Ogden, "Pachyderm Politics."
3 Bhanoo, "Older Elephant Matriarchs."

Chapter 2: Building Your Well of Courage

1 Ransby, *Baker and Black Freedom Movement*, 4.
2 Ransby, *Baker and Black Freedom Movement*, 182.
3 Ransby, *Baker and Black Freedom Movement*, 189.
4 Ransby, *Baker and Black Freedom Movement*, 4, 180.
5 The nine organizations included Forward Together, then known as Asian Communities for Reproductive Justice; California Latinas for Reproductive Justice; Young Women's Freedom Center, then known as Center for Young Women's Development; Unite for Reproductive and Gender Equity, then known as CHOICE USA; Movement Strategy Center; National Asian Pacific American Women's Forum; National Latina Institute for Reproductive Justice, then known as National Latina Institute for Reproductive Health; Western States Center; and Political Research Associates.

6 Abichandani, *New Era of Philanthropy*.

7 Cavanagh and Moberg, "The Virtue of Courage within the Organization."

Chapter 5: Transforming Failure

1 Adamovic and Leibbrandt, "Ethnic Minorities and Leadership Glass Cliff," 1–15.

2 Lawrence, "Harvard's Claudine Gay Ousted."

3 Gay, "What Just Happened at Harvard."

4 Adapted from an activity that Norma Wong created when working with our staff.

5 Chen, "How Accurate Are Memories of 9/11?"

Chapter 6: Powering Up Your Leadership

1 Teng and Nuñez, "Measuring Love in the Journey."

2 A. Jordan et al., "Healing Love."

3 Rizkallah, "Shutting the Revolving Door."

4 Beaton and LePere-Schloop, "3 in 4 Fundraisers Have Experienced."

5 Méndez, "How Mutual Aid Helps LGBTQ+ Communities."

6 Mingus, "Pods and Pod Mapping."

7 Louie, "How Trans People Are Making."

8 S. Jordan et al., "Research as a Practice of Collective Care."

9 Perez and Cesena, "Advocacy for TGI Research Participants."

10 Brown et al., "Trans Futures."

11 Rosenberg, *Nonviolent Communication*.

12 Rosenberg, "Feelings and Needs Inventory."

Chapter 8: Creating Momentum

1 James Monteleone, "More voters support abortion ban," *Albuquerque Journal*, September 9, 2013.

2 The ACLU of New Mexico; Planned Parenthood; Forward Together + Strong Families New Mexico; Bold Futures, formerly known as Young Women United; Faith Roots Reproductive Action, formerly known as New Mexico Religious Coalition for Reproductive Choice; Progress Now New Mexico; and the Southwest Women's Law Center.

3 Led by Moira Bowman.

4 Designed and implemented by Shanelle Williams, Micah Bizant, and Lisa Russ.

Index

Bibliography

Abichandani, Dimple. *A New Era of Philanthropy: Ten Practices to Transform Wealth into a More Just and Sustainable Future.* North Atlantic Books, 2005.

Adamovic, Mladen, and Andreas Leibbrandt. "Ethnic Minorities and the Leadership Glass Cliff: Insights into a Field Experiment." *Industrial Relations: A Journal of Economy and Society*, September 19, 2024. https://doi.org/10.1111/irel.12378.

Angelou, Maya. "Interview with Dr. Maya Angelou," by Unknown, *USA Today*, March 5, 1988.

Anzaldúa, Gloria, and AnaLouise Keating. *Light in the Dark/ Luz en lo Oscuro: Rewriting Identity, Spirituality, Reality.* Durham, NC: Duke University Press, 2015.

Beaton, Erynn, and Megan LePere-Schloop. "3 in 4 Fundraisers Have Experienced Sexual Harassment on the Job—Often Because of Inappropriate Behavior from Donors." *The Conversation*, May 26, 2022. https://theconversation.com/3-in-4-fundraisers-have-experienced-sexual-harassment-on-the-job-often-because-of-inappropriate-behavior-from-donors-183332.

Bekoff, Marc. "In Elephant Society, Matriarchs Lead (Op Ed)." *Live Science*, January 14, 2014. Accessed November 3, 2024, https://www.livescience.com/42576-elephant-matriarchs-guide-society.html.

Bhanoo, Sindya N. "Older Elephant Matriarchs Keep the Lions at Bay." *New York Times*, March 16, 2011. https://www.nytimes.com/2011/03/22/science/22obelephant.html.

Brown, Cydney, Dannie Ceseña, Mel Y. Chen, Chris Hanssmann, Grace Kyungwon Hong, Sid Jordan, Ezak Perez, and Vanessa Warri. "Just Research? Trans Futures in Health and Scientific Knowledge." Center for the Study of Women, July 18, 2023. https://csw.ucla.edu/research/trans-futures-in-health-and-scientific-knowledge/.

Cavanagh, Gerald F., and Dennis J. Moberg. "The Virtue of Courage within the Organization." In *Business Ethics and Social Responsibility: Essential Works of Fr. Gerald F. Cavanagh S.J.*, eds. Joseph G. Eisenhauer and Lawrenc E. Zeff. Ethics International Press, 2023.

Chang, Justin. "Film Review: 'American Revolutionary: The Evolution of Grace Lee Boggs.'" *Variety*, June 25, 2013. https://variety.com/2013/film/markets-festivals/film-review-american-revolutionary-the-evolution-of-grace-lee-boggs-1200501618/.

Cheechoo, Shirley. *Path with No Moccasins: A Play*. n.p., 1993.

Chen, Ingfei. "How Accurate Are Memories of 9/11?" *Scientific American*, September 6, 2011. https://www.scientificamerican.com/article/911-memory-accuracy/.

ElephantVoices. "Elephants Are Socially Complex." Elephant Sense & Sociality. Accessed November 3, 2024, https://www.elephantvoices.org/elephant-sense-a-sociality-4/elephants-are-socially-complex.html.

Erdrich, Louise. *The Painted Drum*. Harper Perennial, 2019.

Estés, Clarissa Pinkola. *Women Who Run with the Wolves: Myths and Stories of the Wild Woman Archetype*. Ballantine Books, 1997.

Gay, Claudine. "Claudine Gay: What Just Happened at Harvard Is Bigger Than Me." *New York Times*, January 3, 2024. https://www.nytimes.com/2024/01/03/opinion/claudine-gay-harvard-president.html.

Hill, Anita. "The Smearing of Kamala Harris." *New York Times*, October 28, 2024. https://www.nytimes.com/2024/10/28/opinion/kamala-harris-dignity.html.

Jordan, Audrey, Kate Morales, Rosa Gonzalez, and Shiree Teng. "Healing Love: Into Balance." Shireeteng.org, October 2022. https://shireeteng.org/s/ST_Healing-Love-IntoBalance_October2022.pdf

Jordan, Sid, Cydney Brown, Ezak Perez, Gia Ryan Olaes Miramontes, Héctor Planscencia, Jaden Fields, Luckie Alexander, and Lylliam Posadas. "Research as a Practice of Collective Care and Resistance: A Roundtable Conversation with Transmasculine Health Justice: Los Angeles." *QED: A Journal in GLBTQ Worldmaking* 9, no. 3 (Fall 2022). https:// muse.jhu.edu/article/885051/figure/fig01.

LaDuke, Winona. *All Our Relations: Native Struggles for Land and Life.* Haymarket Books, 2015.

Lawrence, Andrew. "Harvard's Claudine Gay Was Ousted for 'Plagiarism.' How Serious Was It Really?" *The Guardian*, January 6, 2024. https:// www.theguardian.com/education/2024/jan/06/harvard-claudine -gay-plagiarism?trk=public_post_comment-text.

Lin, Maya, and Michael Brenson. *Maya Lin: American Academy in Rome, 10 dicembre 1998–21 febbraio 1999.* Milano, Rome, Italy: Electa; American Academy in Rome, 1998.

Lorde, Audre. *Sister Outsider: Essays and Speeches.* Crossing Press, 2015.

Lorde, Audre. *A Burst of Light and Other Essays.* Ixia Press, a division of Dover Publications, 2017.

Louie, Candex Seokyi. "How Trans People Are Making Healthcare Better for Us All." *Rewire News Group*, March 31, 2021. https://rewirenews group.com/2021/03/31/moving-beyond-visibilty-to-improve -transmasculine-health-outcomes/.

Maathai, Wangarĩ. *Unbowed: A Memoir.* Random House US, 2008.

Madeson, Melissa. "Embodiment Practices: How to Heal Through Movement." PositivePsychology.com, August 14, 2024. https://positive psychology.com/embodiment-philosophy-practices/.

Méndez, Victoria. "How Mutual Aid Helps LGBTQ+ Communities Care for Each Other Through Crises." GlobalGiving, June 2023. https:// www.globalgiving.org/learn/lgbtq-mutual-aid/.

Mingus, Mia. "Pods and Pod Mapping Worksheet." Bay Area Transformative Justice Collective, June 2016. https://batjc.wordpress.com /resources/pods-and-pod-mapping-worksheet/.

Mock, Janet. *Redefining Realness: My Path to Womanhood, Identity, Love and So Much More.* Simon and Schuster, 2014.

Morrison, Toni. *Song of Solomon.* Vintage International, 2019.

Ogden, Lesley Evans. "Pachyderm Politics and the Powerful Female." *New Scientist*, December 31, 2013. https://www.newscientist.com/article/mg22129500-900-pachyderm-politics-and-the-powerful-female/#.Us8ahf22Q4M.

Perez, Ezak, and Dannie Ceseña. "Advocacy for TGI Research Participants." California LGBTQ Health and Human Services Network, January 2021. https://californialgbtqhealth.org/advocacy-for-tgi-research-participants/.

Ramón Pelinski, "Embodiment and Musical Experience," ResearchGate, January 1, 2005, https://www.researchgate.net/publication/242627979_Embodiment_and_Musical_Experience.

Ransby, Barbara, *Ella Baker and the Black Freedom Movement*, University of North Carolina Press, 2003.

Rizkallah, Nicole. "Shutting the Revolving Door of Development Turnover." *Philanthropy Daily*, February 3, 2020. https://philanthropydaily.com/shutting-door-development-turnover/.

Rosenberg, Marshall. "Feelings and Needs Inventory." Center for Nonviolent Communication. Accessed November 3, 2024. https://www.cnvc.org/store/feelings-and-needs-inventory.

Rosenberg, Marshall B. *Nonviolent Communication: A Language of Life.* 3rd ed. PuddleDancer Press, 2015.

Ryan, Michelle K., and S. Alexander Haslam. "The Glass Cliff: Exploring the Dynamics Surrounding the Appointment of Women to Precarious Leadership Positions." *Academy of Management Review* 32, no. 2 (April 2007): 549–72. https://doi.org/10.5465/amr.2007.24351856.

Sotomayor, Sonia, and Rita Moreno. *My Beloved World.* Vintage Books, 2014.

Strehlke, Sade. "How August Cover Star Simone Biles Blazes Through Expectations." *Teen Vogue*, June 30, 2016. https://www.teenvogue.com/story/simone-biles-summer-olympics-cover-august-2016.

Teng, Shiree, and Sammy Nuñez. "Measuring Love in the Journey for Justice: A Brown Paper," Shiree Teng, July 2019. https://static1.squarespace.com/static/558dac6fe4b0f42cdd435abd/t/634e1201ba433209dd70ceb3/1666060815439/MeasuringLove2019.pdf.

Acknowledgments

I WOULD LIKE TO start by thanking Jen, my partner in life. Who knew that co-leading a self-esteem support group in college would lead to this incredible journey we are making together?

Thank you to my parents, Clare and Hsieh-Wen for everything you did for me and Tony. Because of you, I have an incredible capacity for love, curiosity, and problem-solving. Thank you, Dad, for passing on your great love of water to me. Thank you, Tony, for being the best brother and partner in caretaking that anyone could ask for. Thank you to my daughters, Jessica and Rose, who continue to inspire me with their brilliance and courage. Thank you to my beloved community, especially the Wachters and the Luna-Sparks families, for being such anchors over the years.

Thank you to all of the staff and board members of Forward Together with whom I had the privilege and honor of working for over two decades. There are too many people to thank individually, but know that I think of all of you often. A special shout out to Moira Bowman, for our amazing ten years of partnership, and to Lisa Ikemoto, Kay Fernandez Smith, and Rosie Abriam, for all of your support as board chairs.

Thank you to all of the people who have generously shared their wisdom and guidance with me over the years, especially Rich Snowdon, Norma Wong, and Shiree Teng.

Thank you to the dream team of Amy Wu, Melanie DeMore, Michael Balaoing, and Tjasa Rihar.

Thank you to my friends and family, who were editors and readers of different versions of this book: Latonya Slack, Michelle Gislason, John

Luna Sparks, Jeff Luna Sparks, Jen Wachter, and Rose Shen-Wachter. Special thanks to Jane Anne Staw who supported me for nearly a decade and believed I could write this book. Thank you to Janet Papale, who first taught me that writing can be part of a process of deep discovery and growth. Thanks to Taj James who has provided key support over the years, including helping in the proposal/publishing stages of this book. Thank you to the leaders who generously shared their stories for this book: Lio Sandy Saeteurn, Adriann Barboa, Wendy Chun-Hoon, Angie DeLille, Tamieka Atkins, Hillary Brooks, Daroneshia Duncan-Boyd, Kalpana Krishnamurthy, Corrine Oqua Pi Povi Sanchez, Malkia Devich-Cyril, Shiree Teng, Ezak Amaviska Perez, Dimple Abichandani, and Renata Moreira. And thank you to all of the leaders whom I have coached, or with whom I have partnered and co-conspired, whose spirits and wisdom are found in these pages. Much gratitude to the following people who provided support and resources during the journey of this book: Brook Kelly-Green, Bia Vieira, Laura Katzive, Joanna Lauen, Sarita Gupta, Rajasvini Bhansali, Akaya Windwood, Dimple Abichandani, Staci Haines, and Aspen Baker. I am grateful to Tim McKee and the team at North Atlantic Books for all of the generosity and expertise you provided. A special thank you to Gillian Hamel for your patience, care, and understanding throughout this process!

Thank you to my circle of healers, John, Bowbay, and Kimberly, who have held me during the rough patches and supported my continued growth and evolution as a human being. Sending you love Michelle Nicholas, RIP.

About the Author

EVELINE SHEN cultivates individual and collective leadership transformation. A key leader in growing the national Reproductive Justice movement from 2000 to 2022, Eveline also directed Forward Together, a national, multi-issue, women-of-color-led organization, for two decades. Under her leadership, Forward Together launched many initiatives for BIPOC leaders, including the Strong Families Initiative, engaging more than two hundred organizations nationwide, and Stepping Into Power, a movement-wide fellowship bringing hundreds of leaders together to find and hone their courageous leadership.

Eveline is currently the principal at Leading Courageously, where she teaches her Courageous Operating System to help leaders of color face any challenging situation with courage, confidence, and strength. An award-winning leader herself, Eveline has coached and trained hundreds of leaders from all over the country in the gender, reproductive, and social justice fields and the philanthropic sector. She integrates creative mind-body practices to help leaders connect to their whole selves and step more fully into their power.

Eveline's leadership has earned national recognition throughout her career. Her *New Visions* white paper became the clarion call for reproductive justice and has been used as a teaching resource for feminist courses in universities and colleges across the country. In 2020, the University of California, Berkeley, School of Public Health named her one of sixteen women who changed public health.

About North Atlantic Books

North Atlantic Books (NAB) is an independent, nonprofit publisher committed to a bold exploration of the relationships between mind, body, spirit, and nature. Founded in 1974, NAB aims to nurture a holistic view of the arts, sciences, humanities, and healing. To make a donation or to learn more about our books, authors, events, and newsletter, please visit www.northatlanticbooks.com.